155 BA

The Tyndale Old Testament Commentaries

General Editor:
PROFESSOR D. J. WISEMAN, O.B.E., M.A., D.LIT., F.B.A., F.S.A.

DANIEL

D1428659

TO MY PARENTS
whose ready co-operation enabled me
to find time to write this book

224.5
B181d

DANIEL

AN INTRODUCTION AND COMMENTARY

by

JOYCE G. BALDWIN, B.A., B.D.

Dean of Women, Trinity College, Bristol

INTER-VARSITY PRESS

INTER-VARSITY PRESS
38 De Montfort Street, Leicester LE1 7GP, England
© Joyce G. Baldwin 1978

All rights reserved. No part of this publication may be reproduced, stored in a retrieval system, or transmitted, in any form or by any means, electronic, mechanical, photocopying, recording or otherwise, without the prior permission of Inter-Varsity Press.

First Edition 1978
HARDBACK EDITION 0 85111 631 0
PAPERBACK EDITION 0 85111 832 1
USA ISBN 0 87784 961 7

Printed and bound in England by
Staples Printers Rochester Limited
at The Stanhope Press.

Inter-Varsity Press is the publishing division of the Universities and Colleges Christian Fellowship (formerly the Inter-Varsity Fellowship), a student movement linking Christian Unions in universities and colleges throughout the British Isles, and a member movement of the International Fellowship of Evangelical Students. For information about local and national activities in Great Britain write to UCCF, 38 De Montfort Street, Leicester LE1 7GP.

CONTENTS

GENERAL PREFACE

THE aim of this series of *Tyndale Old Testament Commentaries,* as it was in the companion volumes on the New Testament, is to provide the student of the Bible with a handy, up-to-date commentary on each book, with the primary emphasis on exegesis. Major critical questions are discussed in the introductions and additional notes, while undue technicalities have been avoided.

In this series individual authors are, of course, free to make their own distinct contributions and express their own point of view on all controversial issues. Within the necessary limits of space they frequently draw attention to interpretations which they themselves do not hold but which represent the stated conclusions of sincere fellow Christians. The book of Daniel more than most is the subject of diverse debates and interpretations, some of which seriously obscure the meaning and message for the church today or tend to lessen the impact of the book in a welter of critical detail. The author here aims to set out her own sincerely held and closely argued views on many aspects of the prophecy which, although it may remain a 'mystery' until that Final Day, demands further study now to show its relevance for our own troubled times.

In the Old Testament in particular no single English translation is adequate to reflect the original text. The authors of these commentaries freely quote various versions, therefore, or give their own translation, in the endeavour to make the more difficult passages or words meaningful today. Where necessary, words from the Hebrew (and Aramaic) Text underlying their studies are transliterated. This will help the reader who may be unfamiliar with the Semitic languages to identify the word under discussion and thus to follow the argument. It is assumed throughout that the reader will have ready access to one, or more, reliable rendering of the Bible in English.

Interest in the meaning and message of the Old Testament continues undiminished and it is hoped that this series will thus further the systematic study of the revelation of God and His will and ways as seen in these records. It is the prayer of the editor and publisher, as of the authors, that these books will help many to understand, and to respond to, the Word of God today.

D. J. WISEMAN

AUTHOR'S PREFACE

W RITING a commentary on the book of Daniel at the present time is like being deep in the crest of a swelling wave. There is surging movement; learned articles appear in spate, and radical thinking is calling in question the long-established maps by which scholars of the past have charted their course. There is bewilderment, a feeling of being 'at sea', not knowing for sure the direction in which one is being carried, and of having too little specialist knowledge to be able adequately to assess one's bearings. Nevertheless it is an exciting situation to be in, if only one can keep afloat. Too often, I fear, I have been submerged under a mass of ideas and have had to surface again and start afresh.

My dependence on many scholarly books and commentaries will be apparent to all. I have tried to acknowledge in footnotes the source of ideas and information whenever I have been conscious of them, but there could be unconscious debts which I have not acknowledged. My thanks are particularly due to Mr A. R. Millard, Rankin Senior Lecturer in Hebrew and Ancient Semitic Languages in the University of Liverpool, and to Dr L. C. Allen, Lecturer in Old Testament Language and Exegesis at London Bible College, who read the manuscript and brought their learning to bear on it. I am extremely grateful for their suggestions, most of which have been incorporated into the text. I also want to thank Professor D. J. Wiseman, Editor of the *Tyndale Old Testament Commentaries,* for inviting me to contribute another volume, and for putting at my disposal his wisdom and specialist learning.

I am conscious that this book is going out before it is ready, but at some point a halt has to be called, or, to revert to the sea metaphor, one has to burn one's boats and face what comes. If Christians are encouraged to work at the book of Daniel afresh, so that together we come nearer to feeling its heartbeat, then any effort of mine will have been worth while.

September 1977   JOYCE BALDWIN

CHIEF ABBREVIATIONS

ANEP	*The Ancient Near East in Pictures*[2] edited by J. B. Pritchard, 1969.
ANET	*Ancient Near Eastern Texts Relating to the Old Testament*[2] edited by J. B. Pritchard, 1955 ([3] 1969).
Aram.	Aramaic.
AV	English Authorized Version (King James), 1611.
BA	*The Bible Archaeologist.*
BASOR	*Bulletin of the American Schools of Oriental Research.*
CB	*Cambridge Bible: The Book of Daniel* by S. R. Driver, 1900.
CBQ	*Catholic Biblical Quarterly.*
Delcor	*Le Livre de Daniel* by M. Delcor, 1971.
DNTT	*The New International Dictionary of New Testament Theology* edited by Colin Brown. Vol. 1, 1975. Vol. 2, 1976.
DOTT	*Documents from Old Testament Times* edited by D. Winton Thomas, 1958.
EQ	*Evangelical Quarterly.*
ET	*Expository Times.*
ET	English translation.
EVV	English Versions.
FSAC	*From the Stone Age to Christianity*[2] by W. F. Albright, 1957.
HDB	*Dictionary of the Bible* edited by J. Hastings. 5 vols, 1911.
Heb.	Hebrew.
IB	*The Interpreter's Bible* VI, 1956.
ICC	*International Critical Commentary: The Book of Daniel* by J. A. Montgomery, 1927.
IDB	*The Interpreter's Dictionary of the Bible.* 4 vols, 1962.
IEJ	*Israel Exploration Journal.*
IOT	*Introduction to the Old Testament* by R. K. Harrison, 1970.
JB	*The Jerusalem Bible,* Standard Edition, 1966.

JBL	*Journal of Biblical Literature.*
JCS	*Journal of Cuneiform Studies.*
JNES	*Journal of Near Eastern Studies.*
JSJ	*Journal for the Study of Judaism.*
JSS	*Journal of Semitic Studies.*
JTC	*Journal for Theology and the Church.*
JTS	*Journal of Theological Studies.*
KB	*Lexicon in Veteris Testamenti Libros* by L. Koehler and W. Baumgartner, 1958.
Lacocque	*Le Livre de Daniel* by A. Lacocque, 1976.
LOT	*Introduction to the Literature of the Old Testament* by S. R. Driver, 1909.
LXX	The Septuagint (pre-Christian Greek version of the Old Testament).
mg.	margin.
MT	Massoretic Text.
NBD	*The New Bible Dictionary* edited by J. D. Douglas, 1962.
NEB	The New English Bible : Old Testament, 1970.
NIV	The New International Version of Daniel, 1976.
NPOT	*New Perspectives on the Old Testament* edited by J. Barton Payne, 1970.
NTS	*New Testament Studies.*
PCB²	*Peake's Commentary on the Bible* (Revised Edition) edited by M. Black and H. H. Rowley, 1962.
Porteous	*Daniel. A Commentary* by N. W. Porteous, 1965.
POTT	*Peoples of Old Testament Times* edited by D. J. Wiseman, 1973.
1Qp Hab	*Commentary on Habakkuk* from Qumran.
1Q M	*The Rule of the War* from Qumran.
RB	*Revue Biblique.*
RQ	*Revue de Qumran.*
RSV	American Revised Standard Version, 1952.
RV	English Revised Version, 1881.
TBC	*Torch Bible Commentary: Daniel* by E. W. Heaton, 1956.
TDNT	*Theological Dictionary of the New Testament* edited by R. Kittel. 10 vols, 1964–77.
TOTC	*Tyndale Old Testament Commentaries.*

VT	*Vetus Testamentum.*
Vulg.	The Vulgate (Jerome's Latin version of the Bible).
ZAW	*Zeitschrift für die Alttestamentliche Wissenschaft.*

INTRODUCTION

THE book of Daniel stands apart from the rest of the books which make up the Old Testament. This is apparent even to the reader without theological expertise. Though it is found in our English Bibles among the prophets, it does not contain proclamations in the name of the Lord after the manner of the prophets; nor is it historical in the sense that the books of Kings are historical, though it begins from a point in history and is clearly concerned with history. By the use of dreams and visions, signs, symbols and numbers it appears to be declaring the course of history, and to be drawing attention to the significance of history, by mapping out its course as it proceeds towards its end. In technical language the book is therefore eschatological (Gk. *eschaton,* end). Like the early chapters of Genesis it is universal in its scope, and in addition it takes a comprehensive view of historical time. This is made possible by a series of special visions which reveal to Daniel God's purpose for the world. Such an unveiling of history from a divine standpoint is a salient feature of apocalyptic (Gk. *apokalypsis,* revelation), a type of literature to which Daniel is usually assigned, and to which it will be necessary to return for further consideration in the light of recent studies.

Different the book may be in its concepts and methods, but there is theological continuity with the law and the prophets, especially with their presupposition that the God who initiated human life controls history and will bring it to its appointed goal. Only in Israel of all the nations was such an understanding of history possible, because only to Israel had God made Himself known. Not that Israel's history was in some way a super-history; on the contrary it was quite ordinary history, verifiable with reference to that of the nations round her, but her knowledge of God, which accounted for her existence as a nation, and in particular her heritage of God's promises, gave her historical perspective and a means of interpreting events. 'The tension between promise and fulfilment makes history. The development of the Israelitic writing of history is distinguished by the fact that the horizon of this history becomes ever wider, the length of time spanned by promise and fulfilment ever more extensive.'[1] Thus the book of Daniel extends the course of history to its conclusion. Prophecy had looked towards a goal, but it was usually limited to the fulfilment within history of the promises to Israel. Daniel's wider perspective applied the promise-fulfilment theme to all nations, as indeed the writer of Genesis 12 : 3 had done, and looked on to the end-time and the completion of God's purpose for the world He created.

Sensing that this is so, it is not surprising that young Christians, and especially those who are aware of their minority in a hostile society, are particularly drawn to this book. 'Please finish the notes on Daniel first and then go on with Genesis,' wrote Lisu tribes people in Thailand to one who was preparing literature in their language.[2] It was part of Israel's heritage to know for certain that God's purpose could not be thwarted, whatever the threat to her national life, and it is the Christian's privilege to know that the gates of hell will not in the end prevail against God's church. To be deprived of this knowledge is to be deprived indeed, as the Marxist government well knows when it forbids the preaching of the last things in church sermons. There is indeed a more subtle reason for cutting out reference to books such as Daniel, for they undermine confidence in human governments generally and in those which depend on the proud tyrant in particular. Would that the church took as seriously as the Communist the positive teaching of this book, and so benefited from the incentive it gives to courageous, confident service.

In fact the book of Daniel has been under eclipse in the world of academic theology for over a century. The reason is not far to seek, for 'the heritage of nineteenth-century biblical scholarship has burdened us with a mortgage in the apocalyptic sphere'.[3] The literary criticism school of Wellhausen and Duhm had laid down criteria of acceptability which ruled out the apocalyptic books and relegated post-exilic prophecy in general to a place of minor importance. Thus, in order to be approved, an Old Testament book had to be seen to speak in historical terms to a recognizable historical situation. The

---

[1] W. Pannenberg, *Basic Questions in Theology*, I (SCM Press, 1970), p. 19.
[2] Article in *East Asia Millions*, bulletin of the Overseas Missionary Fellowship, December 1973.
[3] K. Koch, *The Rediscovery of Apocalyptic* (SCM Press, 1972), p. 36.

eighth-century prophets, for example, could be seen to be addressing the political, economic and religious practice of their day, and to the extent that they did so their message was accepted as authentic. When they appeared to deviate, as for example when they looked ahead to an era of prosperity and blessing, such passages were judged inauthentic, the additions of a later editor. By this canon much prophetic literature came to be undervalued, especially any that could not be dated with certainty because historical allusions were used as literary devices to convey the prophet's spiritual insights. This was the case with Zechariah 9–14, a much-neglected part of the prophetic literature, and sections of Isaiah, such as chapters 24–27, which did not seem to fit into the historical world of the eighth century BC. Between the exile and the New Testament it even became customary to postulate a great hiatus, all the prophecy that came between being regarded as of inferior status, lacking in originality and largely an imitation of earlier and better works. Apocalyptic fared even worse, being regarded as a desperate attempt to revive hope when all was lost; it was reckoned to be the result of human speculation, written 'to satisfy human curiosity, without any interest in salvation'.[1]

Despite this blighting influence from the Continent there were scholars in Britain who devoted themselves to apocalyptic literature, notably R. H. Charles, whose *Apocrypha and Pseudepigrapha of the Old Testament* (1913) made available the text of books which would otherwise have been inaccessible, together with a commentary, so providing a vast background for his commentary on Daniel. H. H. Rowley's *The Relevance of Apocalyptic* (1944), S. B. Frost's *Old Testament Apocalyptic* (1952) and D. S. Russell's *The Method and Message of Jewish Apocalyptic* (1964) have continued to keep the subject to the fore, but without restoring confidence in the intrinsic value of biblical apocalyptic. Any such change would have to arise in the ranks of those who established the literary-criticism school in the first place, namely the theologians of the German universities.

Since the end of the Second World War such a change has been taking place, and evidence of it has been reaching the English-speaking world through translations of the writings of

[1] O. Cullmann, *Salvation in History* (SCM Press, 1967), p. 80. Cullmann dissociates himself from this view, and is arguing for a neutral as opposed to a derogatory use of the term apocalyptic.

Wolfhart Pannenberg of Mainz University. It is at least true to say that the old entrenched position has been effectively challenged. In the opinion of Klaus Koch, 'With Wolfhart Pannenberg the renaissance of apocalyptic in post-war theology begins' . . . 'It leads to an express acceptance, not only of apocalyptic ideas but of the total apocalyptic picture.'[1] The reason for such a complete about-turn is that Pannenberg has challenged the various presuppositions regarding history which underpinned the old view. These include the 'critical-historical investigation as the scientific verification of events' which did not seem to leave any room for redemptive events; existential theology which dissolves history into the 'historicity of existence' and the idea that the real content of faith is supra-historical.[2] He contends that history as reality is accessible through the biblical revelation and that history needs a universal horizon if individual events are to be appreciated in their full significance. 'Without world history there is no meaning of history.' 'Only a world-historical viewpoint can provide an adequate basis for the division of the course of history into periods.'[3] Though Pannenberg is referring not to such divisions of time as occur in Daniel but to the more general divisions that create the sections of a history book, what he is saying has an important bearing on all the literature in the Bible that we call apocalyptic. Thus, on his understanding of history, Daniel, far from being relegated to a minor role, is seen to stand at the intersection between the Testaments, and at the crossroads of history. It is part of the considerable literature that bridges the gulf between the Old Testament and the New, and so provides a necessary preparation for an understanding of the ministry of Jesus.

It remains to be seen whether the movement centred round Pannenberg will so shift theological thinking in Germany that the prejudices of more than a century are replaced by a positive appreciation of the apocalyptic literature of the Bible. Klaus Koch is optimistic : 'Through the attempts to grasp anew the obscure power of apocalyptic, a new movement has unmistakably entered theology, a movement which can be

---

[1] K. Koch, *op. cit.*, p. 101.
[2] For a full outworking of this thesis see W. Pannenberg, *op. cit.*, pp. 69ff.
[3] *Ibid.*, p. 69.

salutary if it brings a careful working out and evaluation of the material in its train.'[1] The return to a study of Daniel is therefore timely, but not only on account of current thinking in the scholarly world. The whole church needs the kind of reassurance that a study of this book can bring, not least in view of Marxist claims to hold the key to history and to be able by human strategy to introduce a utopian world government. No wonder the church becomes defeatist if it sets on one side an important part of the Bible's understanding of history. Moreover its evangelism becomes ineffective without the message of the apocalyptic books. When the church lets part of its message go by default people look elsewhere for a substitute. The church has only itself to blame if, in the minds of many, faith in an impersonal dialectic has superseded faith in the Mighty God as the controller of history. Secularism denies the supernatural. All the more reason, then, why the church needs to be counting on the certainties proclaimed in Daniel, namely that God is constantly overruling and judging in the affairs of men, putting down the mighty from their seats, overthrowing unjust regimes and effectively bringing in His kingdom, which is to embrace all nations. Full, confident proclamation of God's purpose for the whole of history needs to be heard without delay.

To assert so much, however, is to appear naïve, as though it were an easy thing to expound a book which has, at least in certain key passages, defeated the most skilled expositors. Opinions are divided on almost every issue. The way ahead must therefore be to take account of these differences of opinion, to state them as objectively as possible, together with the reasons underlying them, and to indicate what seems to me to be the straight furrow that exposes the truth.

I. A PRELIMINARY LOOK AT THE BOOK

According to the dates given in the text the twelve chapters of Daniel span the exile. The book opens with information which translates into the year 605 BC, when Nebuchadrezzar was first setting foot in Syria-Palestine after defeating and pursuing the Egyptian army, and the last date mentioned is the third year of King Cyrus, 537 BC (10:1), just after the

[1] K. Koch, *The Rediscovery of Apocalyptic*, p. 131.

first company of exiles had returned to Judah to rebuild the ruins. The book divides into two equal parts : chapters 1–6, relating incidents which happened to Daniel and his friends, and chapters 7–12, which overlap chronologically and recount four visions which came to Daniel in his old age.

Another way of dividing the book is to take note of the use of two different languages, for though the book opens in Hebrew (1 : 1 – 2 : 4a), it then continues in Aramaic as far as the end of chapter 7, and finally reverts to Hebrew. The Aramaic 'core' of the book thus links the two halves and suggests its unity.[1]

With the contents dated in the sixth century it would be natural to look for a sixth-century background as the historical setting of the book, but here the student finds that most commentaries direct otherwise, for almost without exception it is taken for granted that the book was written in response to a religious and political threat upon Judea in the second century BC. The writer, using legendary material well known to his fellow Jews, and adding the visions to bridge the course of history between the exile and his own day, was encouraging opposition to the foreign oppressor and rallying the faithful to the fight. So firmly is this viewpoint maintained that many commentators do not explain the reasons for their statements asserting a second-century date. The task was well performed by S. R. Driver early in the century[2] and the reader cannot do better than to look at the arguments through his eyes, keeping in mind, however, that, while he considered it *probable* that the book was written in 168 or 167 BC, he was convinced that internal evidence showed that it must have been written not earlier than *c.* 300 BC, and in Palestine. His reasons come under three headings, historical, linguistic and theological. Increased knowledge of the ancient languages has necessitated modification of the linguistic argument, and Aage Bentzen takes account of this,[3] but there has been little change in the standard presentation of the historical argument since Driver, despite the lapse of time and the growing volume of documents with a bearing on the period which have come to light.

[1] For a discussion of the unity of the book see below, pp.35–46.
[2] *LOT*, pp. 497–515; *CB*, pp. xlvii–lxxvi.
[3] A. Bentzen, *Introduction to the Old Testament*, II (Copenhagen, 1957), pp. 199–200.

It is a fact that the book of Daniel refers to people and events not otherwise known, either from the biblical books or from secular history. This could be because the writer had particular reason to mention them whereas others overlooked them as irrelevant to their purpose; it could be that the writer of Daniel had his own sources of information which have not yet, and maybe never will, come to light; or it could be that the writer lived so long after the events to which he referred that he had only a hazy knowledge of the relevant historical data and so made mistakes. The majority of scholars have assumed that the last is the most likely explanation, even though the author could have avoided some of the alleged errors by referring to the historical books of the Old Testament and the prophets, which must have been accessible in Jerusalem by the second century BC.

a. The siege of Jerusalem in the third year of Jehoiakim
   (Dn. 1 : 1)
With his characteristically scholarly accuracy S. R. Driver admits that the statement in the opening verse 'cannot, strictly speaking, be disproved' but is 'highly improbable : not only is the Book of Kings silent, but Jeremiah, in the following year (c. 25, &c. . .), speaks of the Chaldeans in a manner which appears distinctly to imply that their arms had not yet been seen in Judah'.[1]

It is true that there is no mention of a siege of Jerusalem at this time in 2 Kings, though it does say that in the days of Jehoiakim 'Nebuchadnezzar king of Babylon came up, and Jehoiakim became his servant three years' (2 Ki. 24 : 1), and Chronicles adds, 'Against him came up Nebuchadnezzar king of Babylon, and bound him in fetters to take him to Babylon' (2 Ch. 36 : 6). The presence of Nebuchadrezzar in Jerusalem is thus doubly attested prior to the siege of 597 BC, which was in Nebuchadrezzar's seventh year, just after the death of Jehoiakim in his eleventh year (2 Ki. 24 : 6–10).

The publication of the Babylonian Chronicles in the British Museum[2] made available an independent source of precise

---

[1] *LOT*, p. 498.
[2] D. J. Wiseman, *Chronicles of Chaldean Kings (626–556 BC)* (London, 1956). *Cf.* A. K. Grayson, *Assyrian and Babylonian Chronicles, Texts from Cuneiform Sources,* V (New York, 1975).

information relating to the events of Nebuchadrezzar's accession. The following table sets out the details as they can be reconstructed from the Babylonian data for 605 BC :

January/February	Army returned from a campaign to Babylon.
April/August (probably May/ June)	Battle of Carchemish, after which Nebuchadrezzar pursued the Egyptians south and conquered the whole of Hatti-land (*i.e.* Syria-Palestine).
August 15	Death of Nabopolassar, father of Nebuchadrezzar.
September 7	Accession of Nebuchadrezzar.

In the light of this information the biblical statements begin to look probable. Jehoiakim had been put on the throne by the Egyptian Pharaoh Neco (2 Ki. 23 :34) and therefore Nebuchadrezzar, in taking all that belonged to the king of Egypt (2 Ki. 24 :7), would need to include the king of Judah. This would be the occasion when Jehoiakim became his servant and was bound in fetters to be taken to Babylon. Whether he actually made the journey or not we cannot know. The Bible is consistent in asserting that Nebuchadrezzar put pressure on Jerusalem and its king; the Babylonian evidence allows time for him to do so. It is also clear why the outcome is left vague. The death of his father made the return of the crown prince imperative (he had been called king proleptically, as in Je. 46 :2); he would need to leave the army in the command of his generals and travel light with all speed back to Babylon, as Berossus recounted.[1]

The second, though much smaller, difficulty in Daniel 1 : 1 arises out of the biblical evidence, for whereas Daniel dates the intervention of Nebuchadrezzar in the third year of Jehoiakim, Jeremiah 46 :2 gives the fourth year of Jehoiakim as the date of the battle of Carchemish (*cf.* Je. 25 :1, where the fourth year of Jehoiakim is said to be the first year of Nebuchadrezzar's reign). It is now well known that two methods of reckoning the years of a reign were in use in the Ancient Near East : the one most usual in the history books of the Old

---

[1] In Josephus, *Contra Apionem* i. 19. See also D. J. Wiseman, *Chronicles of Chaldean Kings*, pp. 25–27; and 'Some Historical Problems in the Book of Daniel' in *Notes on Some Problems in the Book of Daniel* (Tyndale Press, 1965), pp. 16–18.

Testament counts the months between the king's accession and the new year as a complete year, whereas the method most usual in Babylon called those months the accession year and began to count the years of the king's reign from the first new year. The date in Daniel would appear to have come from a source compiled in Babylon and those in Jeremiah from a Palestinian source, but rightly understood there is no discrepancy.[1]

Whether or not the invasion of Nebuchadrezzar could be described as taking place in the third year of Jehoiakim depends on the period of the year when the New Year was celebrated, and on the time of year when Jehoiakim came to the throne. 'On the accession year system and with an autumnal New Year, his first year would run from September 608 to September 607, his second 607–606, his third September 606–October 605. This last would just accommodate the statement of Daniel 1:1 in chronological terms.'[2] The statement, while not without its uncertainties, can nevertheless be envisaged as a possibility, and while that is so it should not be dismissed as inaccurate.

b. King Belshazzar

Three chapters of Daniel are dated by reference to this ruler, and yet, as any king-list of Babylon shows, there was no king of this name in the Neo-Babylonian period. Bēl-šar-uṣur, as his name transliterates from cuneiform, was the eldest son of the last king of Babylon, Nabonidus, and is frequently named on the contract tablets because as crown prince he acted as regent in the absence of his father.[3] Since Nabonidus was campaigning in Arabia for as long as ten years, and did not return until after the fall of Babylon, Belshazzar was in effect king there for more than half of the seventeen-year reign. Moreover his father 'entrusted the kingship to him'[4] and Bel-

---

[1] Application of so-called 'post-dating' and 'accession year' systems to the date of Jehoiachin's release, and therefore quite unbiased with regard to Daniel 1:1, is to be found in R. H. Sack, *Amēl-Marduk 562–560 BC (Alter Orient und Altes Testament,* 4, 1972), p. 28.

[2] A. R. Millard, 'Daniel 1–6 and History', *EQ,* XLIX, 2, 1977, p. 69.

[3] See, for example, Yale Babylonian Collection, No. 39, published by A. T. Clay (1915) and quoted in *ANET,* pp. 309, 310, n.5.

[4] R. P. Dougherty, *Nabonidus and Belshazzar* (Yale Oriental Series, XV, 1929), pp. 105–111; Sidney Smith, *Babylonian Historical Texts* (London, 1924), pp. 84, 88.

shazzar's name appears associated with that of the king in the oath formulae of that reign.[1] Since this happened to no other king's son in all Babylonian history, Belshazzar is shown to have been king in all but name. There is evidence that he received royal dues and exercised kingly prerogatives, but he could not bear the title king in the official records because, while his father lived, he could not perform the New Year Festival rite of 'taking the hands of Bel', an act carried out only by the king.

Since Belshazzar was to all intents and purposes king, it is pedantic to accuse the writer of the book of Daniel of inaccuracy in calling him 'Belshazzar the king'. This is especially out of place in the light of Daniel 5 :7, 16, 29, where the reward for reading the mysterious writing was to be made third ruler in the kingdom. Evidently the writer knew that Belshazzar was second to his father Nabonidus.[2]

A second objection which is raised in connection with the historicity of Belshazzar is his lineage. Five times in chapter 5 Nebuchadrezzar is referred to as his father, and Belshazzar is called his son (5 :22). The assumption has often been made that the author's knowledge of the period was so defective that he thought Belshazzar was literally son of Nebuchadrezzar, whereas we know that his father was Nabonidus, son of a Babylonian nobleman, Nabû-balaṭsu-iqbi. It needs to be borne in mind that the terms 'father' and 'son' are used figuratively in the Old Testament. Elisha called Elijah 'my father' (2 Ki. 2 :12); 'sons of the prophets' were their disciples, and there is some evidence that outstanding kings gave their name to successors who were not of their dynasty.[3] There is in 1 Esdras 3 :7; 4 :42 an interesting example of a king bestowing as a

[1] Dougherty, op. cit., pp. 96–97.
[2] J. V. Kinnier Wilson (The Nimrud Wine Lists [London, 1972], p. 7) has produced evidence for a kind of triumvirate in the Assyrian capitals and certain provincial capitals. There is, for example, a text from Assur which refers to hazannus (mayors) of the Ashur Gate, the Shamash Gate and the Tigris Gate, so making three. Another speaks of the second and third hazannu. Though this information may have a bearing on the text of Daniel 5, its application to Babylon must remain tentative.
[3] E.g. Shalmaneser's Black Obelisk, engraved c. 830 BC, calls the revolutionary Jehu 'son of Omri'. It is most unlikely that Shalmaneser III, who conducted many campaigns in Syria-Palestine between 859 and 841, did not know that Jehu slaughtered the descendants of Omri in 841 BC.

prize the honour of being called his kinsman, or cousin. Nevertheless the constant repetition of the father-son theme in Daniel 5 appears to imply more, as though the legitimacy of the king might have been under attack.

The possibility that Nabonidus married a daughter of Nebuchadrezzar and that Belshazzar was grandson of the great king was explored by R. P. Dougherty.[1] It now seems that it was Neriglissar who married Kaššā, daughter of Nebuchadrezzar, and that Neriglissar himself was born of a line with royal connections. The son of the union was Labashi-Marduk, who was deposed in favour of Nabonidus, whose powerful and dominant mother was Adad-Guppi, but whose paternity is unknown. The insistence of the text of Daniel on 'King Nebuchadnezzar, your father' (grandfather) may be the literal truth.[2]

In short the chapter contains circumstantial details. Considering that within a few decades of Babylon's fall Belshazzar was practically forgotten to history, there is important evidence here for a contemporary witness.[3]

c. Darius the Mede

After the assassination of Belshazzar which marked the end of the Babylonian empire, the author says that Darius the Mede received the kingdom (5 :30), and 6 :28 appears to imply that this Darius preceded Cyrus. Considering that Cyrus was well known from the biblical books as the liberator of the Jews from Babylon, this was an extraordinary mistake to make (2 Ch. 36 :22–23; Ezr. 1 :1–8; 3 :7; 4 :5; 5 :13 – 6 :14; Is. 45 :1). Since there was a Darius on the Persian throne from 522 to 486, Darius I Hystaspes, it has commonly been assumed that the writer so confused the history that he thought this Darius preceded Cyrus (king in Babylon 539–530 BC). It is claimed that he was writing 'consoling history from what you can remember', after the manner of *1066 And All That*.[4]

At this point it will be useful to review what is said about

---

[1] *Nabonidus and Belshazzar,* pp. 63–80.
[2] A. R. Millard, 'Daniel 1–6 and History', *EQ*, XLIX, 2, 1977, p. 72.
[3] *Cf.* R. P. Dougherty, *op. cit.,* pp. 199f.
[4] *TBC*, p. 56. The Dean of Durham is surely less than generous, however, to suggest that 'In our day its author will certainly have been a Doctor of Divinity and would, in all probability, have occupied a professorial Chair of Biblical Exegesis' (p. 19)!

Darius in the book of Daniel. First of all he is called Darius the Mede (5:31), perhaps to distinguish him from Darius Hystaspes, and his age is given, 'about sixty-two years old'. To judge by the length of his reign (36 years) Darius Hystaspes is not likely to have been sixty-two years old when he ascended the throne. He 'received the kingdom', an expression which H. H. Rowley has shown to mean no more than that he succeeded to the throne.[1] In chapter 6 Darius is called king twenty-eight times, and, at the instigation of the satraps he had appointed, he passed a decree which he was powerless to repeal. The chapter ends with the statement that Daniel 'prospered during the reign of Darius and the reign of Cyrus the Persian', which could be taken to imply that these kings were reigning at the same time or that one followed the other. Compare Daniel 1:21, where Daniel is said to have continued until the first year of King Cyrus. Of the two remaining references, 11:1 merely reiterates that Darius was a Mede, but 9:1 gives specific detail. He was son of Ahasuerus, by birth a Mede, who became king (lit. 'was made king') over the realm of the Chaldeans.

In the light of all this information it becomes clear that the writer was not short of facts about this ruler. Indeed, as J. C. Whitcomb writes, 'the Book of Daniel gives far more information concerning the personal background of Darius the Mede than of Belshazzar or even of Nebuchadnezzar. For he is the only monarch in the book whose age, parentage, and nationality are recorded'.[2] To assume that Darius the Mede did not exist, and so to dismiss the evidence provided by this book, is high-handed and unwise, especially in the light of its vindication in connection with Belshazzar, who at one time was reckoned to be a fictional character. Due consideration must be given to possible explanations of the apparent discrepancy before charges are made of mistaken identity.

The cuneiform historical texts which revealed the identity of Belshazzar also shed light on the events surrounding the fall of the Babylonian empire in 539 BC. Two previously unknown figures featured in the fall of the city of Babylon, Ugbaru, who died three weeks later, and Gubaru, who is frequently mentioned in different texts as governor of Babylon and the

[1] H. H. Rowley, *Darius the Mede and the Four World Empires in the Book of Daniel* (Cardiff, 1935), p. 52.
[2] J. C. Whitcomb, *Darius the Mede* (Eerdmans, 1959), p. 8.

District beyond the River.[1] Olmstead, writing of Gubaru under the Greek form Gobryas, made this assessment of his powers : 'In his dealings with the Babylonian subjects, Cyrus was "king of Babylon, king of lands". . . . But it was Gobryas the satrap who represented the royal authority after the king's departure. . . . Over the whole vast stretch of fertile territory (i.e. Babylon and the District beyond the River), Gobryas ruled almost as an independent monarch.'[2] Whitcomb's thesis is that Darius the Mede was an alternative name for Gubaru, and that the details of the incidents in Daniel would be fully satisfied by the person of this governor. Cyrus did not remain long in Babylon, but long enough, presumably, to commission the return of exiles to their own lands, and in particular the Jews to Jerusalem (Ezr. 1), but after a few months he returned to Ecbatana, leaving Gobryas to represent him.[3] If it be objected that in that case he should not have been called 'king', as he is twenty-eight times in Daniel 6, Whitcomb argues that in Aramaic the fine distinction between such Babylonian terms as *piḥatu* (district governor), and Persian *khshathrapâva* (satrap) could not be expressed except by using the foreign word. The fact is that the writer of Daniel did make these distinctions. This is a weakness in Whitcomb's case. The Aramaic *malkâ*, used also of Belshazzar, was capable of wider application than strictly 'king', and was appropriate for Gubaru, who was the effective ruler in the absence of Cyrus.

In the course of his closely-reasoned monograph Whitcomb clarifies several issues that are relevant to the history of the period, one of the most important being the situation in Media

[1] *Ibid.*, pp. 10–16. Unfortunately when the Nabonidus Chronicle was first published in 1880 the distinction was not made between the two names Ugbaru and Gubaru. The resulting confusion, unrecognized even after the correction made by Sidney Smith, in *Babylonian Historical Texts*, rendered invalid much scholarly work, including the argument of H. H. Rowley in *Darius the Mede and the Four World Empires in the Book of Daniel*; *cf.* J. C. Whitcomb, *op. cit.*, pp. 26ff. The Nabonidus Chronicle is now re-edited in A. K. Grayson's *Assyrian and Babylonian Chronicles*, pp. 104–111. On p. 109 he says, 'Whether Ugbaru is identical with the Gubaru of iii 20 is uncertain. Certainly neither can be identified with Gobryas, governor of Babylon, as Smith, BHT, pp. 121f. suggested.'
[2] A. T. Olmstead, *The History of the Persian Empire* (Chicago, 1948), pp. 71 and 56. Quoted by Whitcomb, p. 24.
[3] Olmstead, *op. cit.*, p. 71. Gobryas, governor of Babylon and Beyond the River, seems to have taken office in Cyrus's fourth year.

during the Neo-Babylonian empire. This was the country to which some Israelites had been deported after the fall of Samaria, for Media was at that time part of the Assyrian empire, but the Medes were prominent in the wars which brought the Assyrian empire to an end, and they succeeded in establishing an empire of their own. It was out of fear of the Medes that Nebuchadrezzar built a great chain of fortifications to make his kingdom impregnable. In 559 BC the vassal king Cyrus II, wishing to assert himself over his Median overlord, entered into an alliance with Nabonidus of Babylon. In 550 'Media ceased to be a separate nation and became the first satrapy, Mada. Nevertheless, the close relationship between Persians and Medes was never forgotten. . . . Medes were honoured equally with Persians. . . . Foreigners spoke regularly of the Medes and Persians; when they used a single term it was "the Mede".'[1] From this time on it was therefore a joint empire, though headed up by Cyrus. Important contemporary evidence is provided by the Harran stele, in which Nabonidus gives an account of the events of his reign. Writing in his tenth year (546 BC) he refers to 'the kings of Egypt, of the Medes and of the Arabs'. Professor D. J. Wiseman points out that the king of the Medes at this time, four years after his conquest of Media, can be none other than Cyrus, and concludes that 'in Babylonia Cyrus used the title "King of the Medes" in addition to the more usual King of Persia . . .'.[2]

This last quotation is part of Professor Wiseman's argument for his own theory concerning Darius the Mede, first put forward in 1957, which identifies Darius the Mede as Cyrus the Persian.[3] Whereas there is no evidence that Gubaru was a Mede, called king, named Darius, a son of Ahasuerus, or aged about sixty, Cyrus is known to have been related to the Medes, to have been called 'king of the Medes' and to have been about sixty years old on becoming king of Babylon. The suggestion requires that 6:28 be translated, 'So this Daniel prospered in the reign of Darius, that is, in the reign of Cyrus the Persian.' This is frequently the sense of the Hebrew particle which is usually the conjunction 'and', and indeed examples of it can be found elsewhere in this book : 'certain

[1] *Ibid.*, p. 37.
[2] *Christianity Today*, II. 4, 25 November 1957, p. 10. Quoted by J. C. Whitcomb, *op. cit.*, p. 47.
[3] See also *NBD*, article 'Darius', p. 293.

of the children of Israel, even of the seed royal' (1:3, RV); 'the document and interdict' (6:9) becomes simply 'the document' (verse 10), so proving that the writer regards these two words as synonymous. J. Barr, commenting on 7:1, notes, 'Some think *and* here is explicative, "he saw a dream, that is, visions of his head".'[1] Thus the usage is common, not only in Hebrew generally, but also in the style of the writer of Daniel.

While it is true that secular evidence has not yet verified the identification of Darius with Cyrus, there is some corroboration of it in the Greek Bible. In 11:1 the LXX and Theodotion have 'Cyrus' instead of Darius the Mede. This suggests that the Greek translator knew of the double name, and preferred to use the one that was better known to avoid confusing his readers. A second line of evidence is found in 1 Esdras 3:1 – 5:6, the story of the Three Guardsmen who were challenged by the king, Darius, to a competition, which Zerubbabel won. As part of his reward he asked that the king should remember his vow to build Jerusalem and to restore the Temple vessels. Zerubbabel was thereupon sent to fulfil this mission. Yet according to Ezra 4:1–5 Zerubbabel was certainly in Jerusalem before the reign of Darius Hystaspes. It is therefore probable that this story rightly preserves the name Darius, though 1 Esdras fails to distinguish between the two Dariuses, and also fails to recognize that Cyrus and the earlier Darius are one and the same person. The confusion in the Esdras account is generally recognized. J. Barr is of the opinion that the Darius of the Guardsmen story was originally Cyrus.[2] Just so if the two names belonged to the same person. This understanding of the situation also avoids the absurdity

---

[1] *IB*, p. 451. These examples and the suggestions that follow have been pointed out by D. L. Emery in correspondence with Professor Wiseman, which the latter has kindly shared with me. *Cf.* David W. Baker, ' "And" Makes all the Difference: Pleonasm in the Old Testament', a lecture given at the Tyndale Old Testament Study Group, Cambridge, 1978, and part of a forthcoming doctoral thesis. He cites several biblical texts in which recognition of an explicative *waw* would solve a textual problem. He concludes: 'The examples adduced range in date from the Ugaritic cases from the fourteenth century BC, Hebrew examples ranging from texts attributed to the tenth century (Gn. 4:4; 13:8) to those from the post-exilic period (*e.g.* Ne. 1:10; 2 Ch. 29:27), as well as fifth-century Aramaic (AP 11).' There is therefore no chronological reason why Daniel 6:28 should not be so interpreted.

[2] *PCB²*, p. 373.

that the same man authorized the Temple rebuilding, sent 1,000 horsemen and musicians to escort the builders (1 Esdras 5 : 1–3), presumably in his first year, and in his second year (1 Esdras 6 : 23) needed to send to search the archives to verify the alleged permission to rebuild. It is in the light of such misunderstandings that the careful documentation of the writer of the book of Daniel is fully appreciated. It was important for him to clarify that the Darius to whom he referred was 'the Mede'. D. J. Wiseman also points out that 'the description of the later Darius (II) as "the Persian" (Ne. 12 : 22) could imply the need to distinguish the king of that name from one who was already known in Babylonia as Darius the Mede" '.[1]

While it is true that the identity of Darius cannot be established for sure on the present state of our knowledge, there is too much evidence of him as a person in history for its total rejection. It will no longer do to dismiss him as a fiction and to build on this fiction the theory that the writer believed that there was a separate Median empire.[2]

d. Use of the term 'Chaldean'

The word 'Chaldean' is used in two senses in the book of Daniel : i. to designate the peoples of southern Babylonia, Semitic in origin, who settled round the Persian Gulf in the twelfth and eleventh centuries BC, and were called by the Babylonians 'Chaldeans' (Dn. 5 : 30; 9 : 1); ii. with reference to the astrology for which these people were famous (2 : 2, 4, 5, *etc.*), but this is not a Babylonian use of the term. Since Nebuchadrezzar was a Chaldean by race the ethnic use of the term in the book of Daniel is not surprising; its use by Herodotus[3] as a technical term for the priests of Bel in the fifth century BC shows it had already by then a secondary sense. There is nothing incongruous about the use of the term in both meanings, nor need it cause confusion, any more than our use in English of the word 'Morocco' to designate both the country and the leather for which it is famous. Needless to say the Moroccan would not use the name in both these senses.

---

[1] In *Notes on Some Problems in the Book of Daniel,* p. 14.
[2] See below, on chapter 8, p. 61.
[3] *History* i. 181, 183. For further information on the significance of the evidence of Herodotus see R. K. Harrison, *IOT,* p. 1113.

Though the term 'Chaldean' was used in an ethnic sense in Assyrian records of the eighth and seventh centuries, there is a complete absence of the word from Babylonian records of the sixth century in either of its senses, at least so far as available texts are concerned. The biblical usage is, therefore, up to the present unsupported,[1] but it is unwarranted to argue from silence that the word is anachronistic.

The difference between the Hebrew form of the word *kásdîm* and the Greek, which transliterates the Babylonian *kaldāyu* and becomes in English 'Chaldean', can now be accounted for on philological grounds. The Hebrew seems likely to preserve an earlier form of the word,[2] and not to be less accurate than the Greek form, as some commentators have assumed.[3]

In concluding this section on the historical assumptions of the writer of the book of Daniel I strongly assert that there is no reason to question his historical knowledge. The indications are that he had access to information which has not yet become available to the present-day historian, and that where conclusive proof is still lacking he should be given the credit for reliability.

III. THE ORIGINAL LANGUAGES

Like the book of Ezra, Daniel is partly in Hebrew (1 : 1 – 2 :4a; 8 :1 – 12 :13) and partly in Aramaic (2 :4b – 7 :28), a close cognate language to Hebrew, using the same script. There are two Aramaic words in Genesis 31 :47, which may indicate that the two languages had existed from early times side by side, and a short inscription on the Milqart Stele provides evidence of Aramaic belonging to the middle of the ninth century BC.[4] The Bible testifies to the use of Aramaic as an international language in the eighth century BC (2 Ki. 18 :26), and it was the official language of the Persian empire.

Various suggestions have been made to account for the change of language in the book of Daniel. The most cogent of these points out that chapters 2–7 contain the part of the

---

[1] A. R. Millard, 'Daniel 1–6 and History', *EQ*, XLIX, 2, 1977, pp. 69–71.

[2] A. R. Millard, *ibid.* He refers to W. von Soden, 'Grundriss der Akkadischen Grammatik', *Analecta Orientalia*, 33, 47 (Rome, 1969), para. 30 g.

[3] *E.g.* Porteous, p. 28.

[4] *DOTT*, p. 239.

book of interest to non-Jews, for whom it may have been published separately. H. H. Rowley also thought of this section as having circulated separately, but he postulated that a Maccabaean author used it to encourage resistance among his fellow Jews.[1] Another theory is that the author quite deliberately made use of two different languages in structuring his book, using the international language for chapters 2–7 which contained the message for the nations.[2]

In the past, however, interest has been concentrated not so much on the reason for the use of the two languages as on the evidence they provided for the date of writing. Needless to say the specialist knowledge that is required in order to assess the data and the arguments based on them keeps such a subject within a small circle of those equipped to make an independent judgment. All the same it is widely acknowledged that it is precarious to attempt to establish the date of a book on linguistic evidence, especially if the amount of comparative material is very limited, as is still the case with the Hebrew and Aramaic of the Old Testament.[3] Attempts to do so have been made, however, by several well-known scholars in this century, all of whom look back to the lead of S. R. Driver and his oft-quoted dictum : 'The Persian words presuppose a period after the *Persian* empire had been well established : the Greek words *demand,* the Hebrew *supports,* and the Aramaic *permits,* a date *after the conquest of Palestine by Alexander the Great* (B.C. 332).'[4] More recent commentators, without always giving reasons for their statements, have gone further : N. Porteous, for example, says of the Aramaic that it is 'not earlier than the third century BC, perhaps second century'.[5] David F. Hinson, writing largely for the younger churches, says : 'The language in which the book is written supports the idea that it was composed in the time of Antiochus IV.'[6] These

---

[1] For this and other evidence on the subject see conveniently *IOT,* p. 1133.

[2] A. Lenglet, 'La Structure Littéraire de Daniel 2–7', *Biblica,* 53, 1972, pp. 169–190. For further details see section vi, below, pp. 59f.

[3] See, *e.g.,* P. R. Ackroyd, 'Criteria for the Maccabaean Dating of the Old Testament', *VT,* III, 1953, pp. 113–132.

[4] *LOT,* p. 508, Driver's italics.

[5] Porteous, p. 7.

[6] D. F. Hinson, *Old Testament Introduction 2: The Books of the Old Testament* (Theological Education Fund Study Guide 10) (SPCK, 1974), p. 129.

are just two random examples of the way in which the linguistic argument is still being used, even though it has ceased to be so used by most scholars who specialize in the original languages, Hebrew and Aramaic.

So far as the Hebrew is concerned there is little that can be proved concerning its date. Though there must have been changes in Hebrew over the centuries, they are not easy to observe and 'Deborah does not talk so very differently from Qoheleth [writer of Ecclesiastes] though well over a thousand years separates them'.[1] A study of the thirty expressions listed by Driver in support of a late date has led W. J. Martin to the conclusion that 'there is nothing about the Hebrew of Daniel that could be considered extraordinary for a bilingual or, perhaps in this case, a trilingual speaker of the language in the sixth century BC'.[2] Clearly the Hebrew of the book cannot confidently be assigned to one century more than another.

In the case of the Aramaic, close study was given to the subject by several scholars earlier this century,[3] the most thorough being that of H. H. Rowley.[4] Further work constantly needs to be done, however, in the light of further Aramaic texts which are continually being published, and the increased understanding which they make possible; hence the long article by K. A. Kitchen, 'The Aramaic of Daniel'.[5] He looks at (a) vocabulary, (b) orthography and phonetics, (c) general morphology and syntax. It may be helpful to summarize the conclusions which Kitchen reaches as a result of his closely-reasoned and well-documented work.

In the first place the Aramaic of Daniel and of Ezra is shown to be Imperial Aramaic, 'in itself, practically undatable with any conviction within *c*. 600 to 330 BC'. It is therefore irrelevant to make distinctions between 'Eastern' and 'Western'

---

[1] D. Winton Thomas, 'The Language of the Old Testament', in H. W. Robinson (ed.), *Record and Revelation* (Oxford, 1938), p. 383.

[2] W. J. Martin, 'The Hebrew of Daniel', in *Notes on Some Problems in the Book of Daniel*, p. 30.

[3] Most easily accessible to the general reader is J. A. Montgomery's summary in *ICC*, pp. 15–20. This presents the subject as it was understood in 1927.

[4] H. H. Rowley, *The Aramaic of the Old Testament* (1929); but see also R. D. Wilson, in *Biblical and Theological Studies by Members of the Faculty of Princeton Theological Seminary* (1912), pp. 261–306.

[5] In *Notes on Some Problems in the Book of Daniel*, pp. 31–79.

Aramaic, which developed later.[1] The only indication of a place of origin arises out of the word order, which betrays Akkadian influence, and proves 'that the Aramaic of Daniel (and Ezra) belongs to the early tradition of Imperial Aramaic (seventh–sixth to fourth centuries BC) as opposed to later and local, Palestinian derivatives of Imperial Aramaic'.[2] He lists a number of scholars who today consider an eastern (Mesopotamian) origin for the Aramaic part of Daniel as probable, though absolute proof cannot be given within the relative unity of Imperial Aramaic. The conclusion of P. W. Coxon, in a philological note on the verb 'they drank' in Daniel 3:5, is that the form belongs unequivocally to Official Aramaic, and is a specifically *eastern* feature.[3] Incidentally, and not in connection with Daniel at all but on the subject of the date of the book of Enoch, R. H. Charles wrote, many years ago, 'The fact that VI–XXXVI were written in Aramaic is in favour of a pre-Maccabean date; for when once a nation recovers, or is trying to recover, its independence, we know from history that it seeks to revive its national language.'[4] What is true for Enoch is presumably applicable also to Daniel.

Attention has also been given to the loan words in the Aramaic of Daniel, particular significance being attached to those from Persian and Greek. H. H. Rowley listed twenty words which he considered to have a Persian derivation,[5] and by checking to see how many of these were used in the Jewish Targums (about the first century BC and later) he found that twelve persisted. For comparison he drew attention to twenty-six Persian words in A. E. Cowley's collection of fifth-century Aramaic papyri,[6] of which only two occur in the Targums, and two in Daniel. He concluded that the survival of Aramaic

---

[1] *Ibid.*, p. 75.

[2] *Ibid.*, p. 76. Evidence for Palestinian Aramaic is found in the Dead Sea Scrolls, especially *Genesis Apocryphon* and *Targum of Job*.

[3] *ZAW*, 89, 1977, p. 276. He refers to the argument of E. Y. Kutscher that the Aramaic of Daniel is shot through with eastern forms both in grammar and syntax (in T. A. Seboek (ed.), *Current Trends in Linguistics*, 1970, pp. 362–366), and suggests 'that the so-called prosthetic spellings in Dan corroborate his thesis of the early and eastern provenance of the Aramaic of the book'.

[4] R. H. Charles, *The Apocrypha and Pseudepigrapha* (OUP, 1963), p. 170.

[5] H. H. Rowley, *The Aramaic of the Old Testament*, p. 138.

[6] A. E. Cowley, *Aramaic Papyri of the Fifth Century B.C.* (Oxford, 1923).

words in Daniel pointed to a date nearer the Targums than to the fifth century. In reply K. A. Kitchen[1] points out that a score or so of words 'is altogether too fragile a basis for statistical argument'; that a comparison must also be made with the vocabulary of Imperial Aramaic, including that of Aramaic documents which have been published since 1923; that the type of word needs to be taken into account, for there are six terms that have not so far been found to occur after *c.* 330 BC, and certain terms were not understood by the Old Greek translators. He makes one further point, namely that the Persian words in Daniel are *Old Persian* words, that is, belonging to the period before *c.* 300 BC. The evidence is thus in favour of an earlier rather than a later date, and Kitchen concludes (p. 77): 'These facts suggest an origin for the Persian words in the Aramaic of Daniel before *c.* 300 BC.'

Much has been made of the occurrence of Greek words, and to the non-specialist the inference might seem conclusive that they point to a period after the conquests of Alexander the Great until it is made clear that there are only three such words, and that they are all the names of musical instruments.[2] Greek wares were being traded all over the Ancient Near East from the eighth century onwards; Greeks were apparently employed in Babylon in the time of Nebuchadrezzar, and there is nothing surprising about there being instruments of Greek origin and bearing Greek names in the Babylon of the sixth century BC. What *is* significant is that there are so few Greek loan words in the Aramaic of Daniel. According to M. Hengel, 'From the time of the Ptolemies Jerusalem was a city in which Greek was spoken to an increasing degree.'[3] 'It can be demonstrated from the Zeno papyri that the Greek language was known in aristocratic and military circles of Judaism between 260 and 250 BC in Palestine. It was already widespread at the accession of Antiochus IV in 175 BC and would hardly have been suppressed even by the victorious freedom fight of the Maccabees.'[4] 'From the third century we

---

[1] K. A. Kitchen, in *Notes on Some Problems in the Book of Daniel*, pp. 35–44.

[2] On the identification of *symphōnia* ('bagpipe', RSV) see *Notes on Some Problems in the Book of Daniel*, pp. 25f.

[3] Martin Hengel, *Judaism and Hellenism*, I (Fortress Press, Philadelphia, 1974. Tr. by John Bowden from the German *Judentum und Hellenismus*², 1973), p. 104.

[4] *Ibid.*, p. 103.

find almost exclusively Greek inscriptions in Palestine.'[1] On this evidence the fact that no more than three Greek words occur in the Aramaic of Daniel (and those are technical terms) argues against a second-century date for the writing of the book. 'One would – on the Greek and Persian evidence . . . – prefer to put the Aramaic of Daniel in the late sixth, the fifth, or the fourth centuries BC, not the third or second. The latter is not ruled out, but is much less realistic and not so favoured by the facts as was once imagined.'[2]

The reason why Kitchen comes to a different conclusion from Rowley on the dating of the Aramaic lies not only in the amount of new Aramaic literature which has become available since 1929, but also in a distinction which Kitchen makes, and which Rowley did not make, between orthography and phonetics. 'Old and Imperial Aramaic texts started off with a Phoenician orthography that, in some respects, only *approximated* to the phonetics of Aramaic as spoken; sound-shifts in Aramaic within the eighth–fifth centuries BC turned these approximate spellings into purely *historical* spellings. These phenomena are betrayed by sporadic phonetic writings and false archaisms in Imperial Aramaic documents of everyday business. By contrast, in Daniel and Ezra, which are scribally transmitted literary texts, the phonetic changes have shown themselves in modernization . . . of spelling, probably in or after the third century BC.'[3] If proper allowance is made for this modernization, the Aramaic of Daniel could have been written at any time between the late sixth and the second centuries BC.

In the continuing debate, though H. H. Rowley contested Kitchen's findings,[4] they were supported, and Rowley's arguments refuted, by the leading Israeli Aramaist E. Y. Kutscher in his major survey of the state of research on early Aramaic, and have been favourably received by other linguists.[5] It is

[1] *Ibid.*, p. 58.
[2] K. A. Kitchen, in *Notes on Some Problems in the Book of Daniel*, p. 50.
[3] *Ibid.*, p. 78.
[4] In a review, *JSS*, 11, 1966, pp. 112–116.
[5] E. Y. Kutscher in T. A. Seboek (ed.), *Current Trends in Linguistics*, pp. 400–403; M. Sokoloff, *The Targum of Job from Qumran Cave XI* (Ramat Gan, 1974), p. 9, n. 1. A. R. Millard, *EQ*, XLIX, 2, 1977, pp. 67–68. See also L. Dequeker, *The 'Saints of the Most High' in Qumran and Daniel* (Leiden, 1973), p. 131, and Delcor, pp. 31–33, in both of which Kitchen's argument is noted.

becoming an accepted fact that the date of Daniel cannot be decided on linguistic grounds, and that the increasing evidence does not favour a second-century, western origin.

IV. DATE AND UNITY OF THE BOOK

Having argued that the history recorded in Daniel 1–6 is not after all unreliable, and that the evidence from the original languages in which the book was written does not require or even support a second-century date, we look more specifically at the question of date and unity.

An obvious starting-place is the information provided by the author. According to 1 : 1 Daniel was taken to Babylon in 605 BC,[1] and lived at least until 537 (10 : 1), by which time he must have been over eighty years of age. But though 537 is the last date given in the book, it is not the last recorded event, for the 'prophecies' cover the fifth, fourth and third centuries and some of the second. Since it is axiomatic that the date of the final form of a historical book cannot be earlier than the last event it includes, those who think that most of chapter 11 is recording history and not prophecy are committed to a date around 167–165 BC in Palestine. Heaton, for example, marks the change from history to prophecy at 11 : 40, and argues that this gives us the date of the final composition of the book. 'Writing in 165/4 BC, he [the author] looked for the imminent destruction of the fourth kingdom, when God would finally take the power and reign.'[2] Whereas the writer had been accurate up to 165, from that point on he revealed ignorance of the movements of Antiochus, so betraying the fact that he was writing prophecy and not history. If this is sound reasoning the book of Daniel proves to be the only book of the Bible whose date of writing can be fixed to within a year. Neat though the reasoning may be, the matter cannot be allowed to rest there, for the date of the book is inextricably linked with its place of origin and unity of authorship.

---

[1] D. J. Wiseman, in a review of A. K. Grayson's *Assyrian and Babylonian Chronicles* for *Bibliotheca Orientalis* (forthcoming), has suggested that a passage in the Babylonian Chronicle (BM 21946, rev. 4, p. 105) which relates that Nebuchadrezzar took many prisoners from Syro-Palestine in 602 BC may indicate that Daniel and his companions could have been among them. If this were so, the exile and return could have been dated from after 605, allowing time for Cyrus's decree and the arrangements for the return.

[2] *TBC*, p. 240.

INTRODUCTION

a. Is there a single place of origin?

We have already seen that the evidence from the Aramaic of Daniel favours an eastern rather than a Palestinian origin. Writing as long ago as 1895 F. Lenormant noted 'the very decided Babylonian tint, and certain features of life at the court of Nebuchadrezzar . . . pictured with a truth and exactitude, to which a writer a few centuries later could hardly have attained'.[1] Montgomery was impressed by the orientalism of chapters 1–6 and saw their essential historical value in their 'reflection of the conditions of that Oriental complex of life on which we are too ill informed'.[2]

Since 1926 a good deal more information has become available. In 1941 R. H. Pfeiffer allowed the writer of Daniel two genuine echoes of Babylonian history: 'We shall presumably never know how our author learned that the new Babylon was the creation of Nebuchadnezzar (4:30 [H. 4:27]), as the excavations have proved (see R. Koldewey, *Excavations at Babylon*, 1915), and that Belshazzar, mentioned only in Babylonian records, in Daniel, and in Bar. 1:11, which is based on Daniel, was functioning as king when Cyrus took Babylon in 538 (ch. 5).'[3] Given a sixth-century witness to these events there would be no problem.

The case for the Babylonian provenance of chapters 1–6 is strengthened by the discovery at Qumran of the 'Prayer of Nabonidus', according to the judgment of D. N. Freedman: 'Behind Daniel 4 there is a story of the third (or an earlier) century, originating in Babylon . . . the materials in chaps. 3–5, at least, had already assumed substantially their present form in the pre-Palestinian period, and were incorporated as a unit by the author of Daniel (though with necessary changes).'[4] William Brownlee is of the same opinion: 'These points are based upon the assumption that the traditions really originated

---

[1] *ICC*, p. 74, where Montgomery is quoting F. Lenormant with approval, though he proceeds to argue that Babylonian religious practices survived long after the fall of the empire and were only slightly altered by the successive political phases.

[2] *Ibid.*, p. 76. See also W. F. Albright (*JBL*, 40, 1921), who notes the Babylonian atmosphere that enshrouds chapters 1–7 (p. 116) and argues that these chapters were written in Babylonia (p. 117).

[3] R. H. Pfeiffer, *Introduction to the Old Testament* (Black, 1952), pp. 758–759.

[4] D. N. Freedman, 'The Prayer of Nabonidus', *BASOR*, 145, 1957, pp. 31–32. See also the Additional Note, p. 116, below.

in the Exile and are not wholly fictional – a position to which the Prayer of Nabonidus has led us.'[1] These writers have assumed that the name Nebuchadrezzar had been substituted for that of Nabonidus in Daniel 4 in the traditions which came down to the (Palestinian) author of our present book.

A number of details which support a Babylonian background to chapters 1–6 are pointed out in the course of the commentary on these chapters. At the same time there are aspects of these chapters which would not have been appropriate for the reign of Antiochus IV. The point is well made by W. Lee Humphries : 'As a series of tales these would not, in and of themselves, be at home in Palestine in the crisis of the period of Antiochus IV Epiphanes, and it is difficult to understand how they could have been created at that period when the line between things Jewish and things pagan was being so sharply drawn. For in these tales the possibilities of life in contact and interaction with things foreign is affirmed; there has been no polarization of the situation.'[2] There is, therefore, no lack of scholarly support for the contention that chapters 1–6 have a Babylonian provenance and belong best to a period earlier than the time of Antiochus IV. How much earlier is a debated matter : few would date them before the fourth century,[3] but the late Neo-Babylonian or early Persian period best accounts for the exact information about the Babylonian empire which we have shown to be preserved in these stories.

Chapter 7 has been the subject of special study because, though it belongs among the visionary chapters and on that account to the second part of the book, it is the last of the Aramaic chapters, and it has affinities with chapter 2. It has been argued that chapter 7 belongs to part one of the book, and that, at least in its original form, it belongs to its pre-Maccabean stage.[4] Only so can justice be done to the differences between chapters 1–7 and 8–12. M. Delcor takes up the argument for Canaanite influence behind the imagery

[1] W. H. Brownlee, *The Meaning of the Qumran Scrolls for the Bible* (OUP, 1964), p. 42.

[2] W. Lee Humphries, 'A Life-Style for Diaspora: a Study of the Tales of Esther and Daniel', *JBL*, 92, 1973, p. 221.

[3] P. R. Davies ('Daniel Chapter Two', *JTS*, XXVII, 1976, pp. 392–401) has argued, however, that the origin of the story of Daniel 2 should be ascribed to the end of the exilic period or just after it (p. 400), that is, the sixth century.

[4] L. Dequeker, *The 'Saints of the Most High' in Qumran and Daniel*, p. 111.

37

of chapter 7, which suggests an earlier rather than a later date for this chapter. 'The influence of the religion and literature of Canaan on Israel . . . must have continued to be exercised after the exile.'[1]

A certain amount of evidence has been adduced to support a theory that the vision of chapter 7 has a parallel in the 'Near Eastern opposition history'.[2] 'Oriental historiography was based for many years on the succession of the Assyrian, Median and Persian empires. The three empires were oriental; they were cited by the historians in order to glorify the oriental Persian kings.' 'In the exegesis of Daniel the situational context of oriental opposition history against Hellenism can no longer be hidden. The Maccabean revolt is only part of it; it must be understood in connection with the religious resistance to Hellenism, which began in the Orient at least a hundred years earlier.'[3] Since chapter 8 of Daniel also is explicitly anti-Greek, this could on the same argument be dated long before the Maccabean period.

b. *Is there more than one author?*

One way of accommodating an early date for the first six or seven chapters and yet retaining a Maccabean date for the latter part of the book is to assume more than one author. Montgomery, for example, postulated that the first author, writing in Babylonia, composed chapters 1–6 in roughly the third century BC; chapters 7–12 were written in the second century, well before the recapture by the Jews of the Temple, because the Maccabees are referred to as a 'little help'. He thinks there is an element of prediction which may have contributed to the success of the Maccabean heroes.[4]

---

[1] Delcor, p. 32. *Cf.* 'Les sources du chapitre VII de Daniel', *VT*, XVIII, 1968, pp. 290–312.

[2] J. W. Swain, 'The Theory of Four Monarchies. Opposition History under the Roman Empire', *Classical Philology*, 35, 1940, pp. 1–21; and S. K. Eddy, *The King is Dead. Studies in Near Eastern Resistance to Hellenism 334–331 BC* (Lincoln, Nebraska, 1961), especially pp. 183–212.

[3] L. Dequeker, 'The Saints of the Most High', *Oudtestamentische Studien*, XVIII, pp. 132, 133.

[4] *ICC*, pp. 96–99. Eissfeldt makes the same distinction, but tends to assign the last chapters to the years 167–163, so allowing for adaptation by the author as the course of events demanded. For a concise summary of the history of this composite way of regarding the book, see R. K. Harrison, *IOT*, pp. 1107–1109.

INTRODUCTION

The argument that diversity of language indicates diversity of authorship continues to be used,[1] but the literary device of enclosing the central portion of a work in a framework of different style was commonly employed in the Ancient Near East and is illustrated by the Law Code of Hammurabi as early as the seventeenth century BC.[2] Referring to the books of Job and Daniel, Gordon remarks: 'The possibility of an intentional ABA structure deserves earnest consideration and should deter us from hastily dissecting the text.' Thus in this case evidence for composite authorship is turned in favour of the unity of the book.

Many recent scholars, acknowledging the Babylonian provenance of the first six or seven chapters, believe that a second-century author made use of earlier material which came to him in a relatively fixed form. Though he may have been responsible for some editorial insertions (there is little agreement as to detail because of the lack of solid evidence), on the whole he left the stories as he found them. Thus the fact is accounted for that they do not in every respect suit the purposes of a second-century author opposing Greek domination. At least one recent writer argues for three primary stages in the development of the book, and sees its original intention modified in accordance with the shifting historical circumstances of the Jewish community.[3] Thus there may have been several redactors, each of whom would adapt the material to his own time, and the last would be the Maccabean redactor who created the last vision of chapters 10–12.

The problem with composite authorship is that the book bears so little trace of the allegedly differing viewpoints. As a literary work it manifests unity of purpose and design. S. R. Driver assumed that one author was responsible for the whole, and R. H. Pfeiffer saw no reason for questioning the unity of the book, but, like many others, found 'in both its parts the same aim and the same historical background'.[4] The classical

MORE THAN TWO

[1] *E.g.* J. A. Soggin, *Introduction to the Old Testament* (Rome, 1967; ET, SCM Press, 1976), p. 410.
[2] Cyrus H. Gordon, *The World of the Old Testament* (London, 1960), p. 83. In Hammurabi's Code the prologue and epilogue are in semi-poetic Akkadian, whereas the laws are in prose.
[3] John G. Gammie, 'The Classification, Stages of Growth, and Changing Intentions in the Book of Daniel', *JBL*, 95, 1976, pp. 191–204.
[4] R. H. Pfeiffer, *Introduction to the Old Testament*, p. 761.

39

statement of the case for the unity of the book, though postu-
lating a second-century date, was made by H. H. Rowley in
his paper entitled 'The Unity of the Book of Daniel', read as
a Presidential Address to the Society for Old Testament Study
in 1950.[1] He first exposes the weaknesses, as well as the variety,
of the rival views, to which others have since been added;
and he comments that 'there is no positive view which can
claim anything like a consensus of opinion' and postulates that
'none of the divisive theories can offer an answer to the case
for the unity, or avoid greater difficulties and embarrassments
than those it seeks to remove'.[2] He then proceeds to argue the
inter-relatedness of the very chapters which are usually separated by those who would divide the book. Perhaps his most
telling sub-section is that headed 'The mental and literary
characteristics of the book are the same throughout'. He notes
a fondness for 'resounding lists of words' (such as the classes
of wise men in chapter 2, the musical instruments in chapter
3 and the repetition in 7 : 14), a habit of introducing new
elements in later repetitions and interpretations, and in at
least two instances (in chapters 4 and 8) what he sees as confusion between the symbolical and the real. 'A quality of mind,
or mental habit, is not . . . easily borrowed', and it is this
unconscious idiosyncrasy, observable throughout, that gives the
lie to diversity of authorship.

Rowley's forceful conclusion still stands : 'the onus of proof
lies upon those who would dissect a work. Here, however,
nothing that can be seriously called proof of compositeness
has been produced. On the other hand evidence for the unity
of the work that in its totality amounts to a demonstration
is available.'[3] Since Rowley accepted a Maccabean date for
the completion of the work, and so found himself in agreement with the majority of the scholars he was dealing with,
he did not go into the possibility that parts of the book
belonged to an earlier century. It is here that difficulty arises,
because his argument for the unity of the book is such that it
presupposes one author. Prove that part of the book comes
from an earlier period, and the Maccabean dating becomes
untenable unless its unity is abandoned.

[1] Published in *The Servant of the Lord*[2] (Oxford, 1965), pp. 249–
280.
[2] *Ibid.*, p. 249.
[3] *Ibid.*, p. 280.

c. The case for and against a second-century date

Though several arguments are adduced with the intention of giving cumulative force to a second-century date, there is basically one reason for the tenaciously-held opinion, and that is the content of chapter 11. Here we have a survey of the future, beginning briefly with the Persian era, continuing with the Greek, and becoming more and more detailed as it approaches the time of Antiochus IV. Old Testament history ended with the period of Nehemiah and the genealogies of Nehemiah 12; nowhere else in Scripture is there any reference to the second century BC. Given a thorough knowledge of the ancient historians of the period, Herodotus, Polybius and the books of the Maccabees, Josephus, Livy and Tacitus, a commentary on the chapter can become a maze of information which bewilders the reader. Can it be possible that so much scholarly information is necessary in order to appreciate the significance of this recital of events? As we point out in the commentary, not all the events in Daniel 11 fit into the evidence culled from other sources; on occasions there is additional information in Daniel; sometimes more than one interpretation of an incident is possible and sometimes the meaning cannot be known, given the present state of knowledge of the period. This is what might be expected, but we ought not to exaggerate the extent to which the Daniel narrative fits into known history of the period.

On the other hand there can be no doubt about the primary reference of the chapter: it has to do with the confrontation between the mighty Antiochus IV, with his intention to impose Greek worship and lifestyle throughout his empire, and the struggling people of God, who lacked political identity and were further weakened by division among their own ranks. For the first time in their history an emperor was going to have his way and impose his will, not as in the time of the exile because God was bringing well-deserved judgment on his people, but because conflict between world rulers (or, as Paul was to put it, the 'world rulers of this present darkness' whom he parallels with 'spiritual hosts of wickedness in the heavenly places'), backed by opposition in the heavenlies, was to try to wipe out the people of God. The two great world powers, Egypt and Syria, had between them a monopoly of political and military strength. There was every human reason why they should succeed, but the message of this chapter, which reiterates that of the whole book, is that, however mighty the rulers of the earth, they 'stumble and fall, and shall not be found' (11 : 19). The last of the sequence has the fullest treatment, not because the writer is contemporary with him and so knows him better than the others, but because he will ride roughshod over the people of God and make himself out to be God incarnate. But there will be an end to his empire as to others; history is foreshortened so that the end of history appears to follow the overthrow of the last tyrant. When that will be is not disclosed.

At this point the question has to be asked whether the contents of this chapter can reasonably be regarded as prophecy, or whether, whatever date may be postulated for the remainder of the book, 11 :2–39 at least forces itself on the reader as history written after the event. In the first place there appears to have been something like predictive prophecy in Babylon,[1] and a revelation surpassing the foretelling of the local wise men is to be expected. In the second place the earliest interpreters, both Jewish and Christian, took the prophecy at its face value, and accepted it as a product of the period immediately following the exile.[2] One corner-stone of Christians' witness in the first two centuries of the church was the fulfilment of prophecy. Little wonder, therefore, that the attack of their opponent Porphyry (died *c*. AD 305) centred on this very issue, and declared that this chapter was not prophecy at all, but history written in the time of Antiochus IV. Since the end of the eighteenth century this has been 'an assured position of scholarship', though there have been some scholars who have argued in favour of the traditional date and have regarded the whole chapter as prophecy.[3] According to

[1] In the so-called Dynastic Prophecies, published by A. K. Grayson in *Babylonian Historical-Literary Texts* (Toronto, 1975), p. 21. A fuller reference to these texts is made on pp. 55f. of this commentary. W. W. Hallo (*IEJ*, 16, 1966) prefers to call them 'Akkadian Apocalypses'. The point is that the genre was known in Babylon and in a Sumerian 'prototype' (p. 242 footnote). He makes it clear that the distinctive character of biblical prophecy and apocalyptic is in no way compromised by this literature. The significance of Akkadian prophecy for the book of Daniel has been assessed in the author's 1978 Tyndale Old Testament Lecture, 'Some Literary Affinities of the Book of Daniel', to be published in the 1978 *Tyndale Bulletin*.

[2] See section VII, below, p. 64.

[3] *E.g.* E. B. Pusey, *Daniel the Prophet* (1885); C. H. H. Wright, *Daniel and his Prophecies* (1906); R. D. Wilson, *Studies in the Book*

Eissfeldt, among certain Continental scholars there are those 'moving back towards the tradition of Synagogue and Church, in that the book of Daniel, or at any rate its basic material, is ascribed to the exilic period'.[1]

These are signs that the 'assured position' is being challenged, and in the New Testament the same may well be true of Jesus' apocalyptic discourse (Mt. 24; Mk. 13; Lk. 21 :5–36). In many ways this discourse is similar to Daniel 11 in that it gives what purports to be a prophecy about the impending fall of Jerusalem, and together with that blends signs and warnings about the end of all things. Many scholars have taken it as axiomatic that these chapters must have been written after the fall of Jerusalem by disciples of Jesus who wrote what they remembered of His sayings in the light of their experiences at the hands of the Romans. Now several scholars are agreeing that Mark 13 fits better *before* the destruction of the Temple it purports to prophesy.[2] As long ago as 1947 C. H. Dodd was arguing that the language in Luke 21 deals with the regular commonplaces of ancient warfare : 'So far as any historical event has coloured the picture, it is not Titus's capture of Jerusalem in AD 70, but Nebuchadrezzar's capture in 587 BC. There is no single trait of the forecast which cannot be documented directly out of the Old Testament.'[3] We contend that in Daniel 11 likewise there is no feature which requires that the prophecy must have been written after the event.

Chapter 11 is closely bound up with chapters 2, 7 and 8, of which 2 and 7 show signs of Babylonian origin and pre-Maccabean authorship, as we have seen.[4] Whereas chapters

---

of *Daniel* (1907); A. C. Welch, *Vision of the End* (1922); E. J. Young, *The Prophecy of Daniel* (1949); Bruce K. Waltke, 'The Date of the Book of Daniel', *Bibliotheca Sacra*, 133, Oct.–Dec. 1976, pp. 319–329.

[1] O. Eissfeldt, *The Old Testament* (Oxford, 1966), p. 519.

[2] J. A. T. Robinson, *Redating the New Testament* (SCM Press, 1976), p. 19. In support of his thesis he refers (p. 18, footnote) to W. Marxsen, *Mark the Evangelist* (ET, Nashville, 1969), p. 170 (*cf.* 166–189); E. Trocmé, *The Form of the Gospel according to St. Mark* (ET, 1975), pp. 104f., 245.

[3] C. H. Dodd, 'The Fall of Jerusalem and the "Abomination of Desolation" ', *Journal of Roman Studies*, 1947, pp. 47–54; reprinted in C. H. Dodd, *More New Testament Studies* (Manchester University Press, 1968), pp. 69–83.

[4] In addition to other evidence already cited an attempt has recently been made to postulate a Persian source for Nebuchadrezzar's dream in chapter 2 by D. Flusser, 'The Four Empires in the Fourth Sibyl and in the Book of Daniel', *Israel Oriental Studies*, 2, 1972, pp. 148–175.

2 and 7 terminate with divine intervention into the fourth empire, chapters 8 and 11 culminate in the third (see pp. 61f.), and in the case of the latter the spotlight is upon the suffering which will come to the people of God as a result of political and military reverses on an over-ambitious despot. If the main outline of history could be revealed in chapters 2 and 7, which seem to have originated in Babylon, there is no reason why more detail such as chapter 11 contains should not have been revealed in the same general area long before the Maccabean period.

d. Evidence from Qumran

One further factor needs to be considered and that is the evidence for the book in the literature from the Dead Sea area. Study of the scrolls from Qumran and the surrounding district is continuing to bring to light new information, though unfortunately much remains as yet unpublished. Whereas before 1947 there were no available manuscripts of Old Testament books earlier than the Middle Ages, now for Daniel there are several fragments dating back to the pre-Christian era, as well as many other documents of relevance to background study of this and other biblical books. At the very least the new evidence should enable the expositor to come up with better answers to the old questions, including the date of the book.[1]

Study of the scripts in which texts from Qumran were written has provided new criteria on which to base their date. One result has been to vindicate in general the accuracy of the scribes of antiquity, despite the occasional mistake. Another has been to show that no one master text was in use at Qumran, and in the case of certain books such as Chronicles the result has been to place the original earlier than had previously been supposed.[2]

In the case of MSS of Daniel[3] the texts represent several different periods, the earliest being 4QDn^c. It was of this fragment that Cross wrote : 'One copy of Daniel is inscribed in the script of the late second century BC; in some ways its antiquity is more striking than that of the oldest MSS from

[1] On the book of Daniel in the light of the Dead Sea scrolls see Alfred Mertens, *Das Buch Daniel im Lichte der Texte vom Toten Meer* (Stuttgart, 1971).
[2] F. M. Cross, *The Ancient Library of Qumran and Modern Biblical Studies* (New York, 1958), p. 189.
[3] See the list below, p. 73.

Qumran, since it is no more than about half a century younger than the autograph of Daniel.'[1] Three years later he modified this slightly to a date between 100 and 50 BC.[2]

Now it is a fact that the Maccabean dating of certain Psalms has been questioned as a result of their appearance in a Psalms manuscript at Qumran.[3] Millar Burrows, arguing from the scrolls of Ecclesiastes found in Cave 4 and dated about 150 BC, reasons that 'the probability of its composition in the third century, if not earlier, is somewhat enhanced by finding the manuscript probably not written much after 150 BC'.[4] By the same token the discovery of several Daniel MSS at Qumran might be expected to push the date of the autograph earlier than the Maccabean period; yet Brownlee states that 'None of the Dead Sea Scroll copies of Daniel are so early as to dispute the usual critical view of the book's authorship'. R. K. Harrison is of the opinion that the Maccabean dating of Daniel is 'absolutely precluded by the evidence from Qumran . . . there would have been insufficient time for Maccabean compositions to be circulated, venerated, and accepted as canonical Scripture by a Maccabean sect'.[5]

In short, scholarly opinion is divided on the question both of unity and date. On the one hand the second-century dating continues to be held tenaciously by most scholars, despite cogent arguments against it. Others acknowledge the weight of evidence for an earlier, Babylonian origin of chapters 1–6 (7), and postulate a date from the fifth to the third century. Most of these would abandon the idea of the unity of the book,

[1] F. M. Cross, *op. cit.*, p. 33.

[2] F. M. Cross, 'The Development of the Jewish Scripts', in G. E. Wright (ed.), *The Bible and the Ancient Near East: Essays in Honour of W. F. Albright* (London, 1961), p. 140.

W. H. Brownlee, *The Meaning of the Qumran Scrolls for the Bible*, p. 30: '. . . it would seem that we should abandon the idea of any of the canonical Psalms being of Maccabean date, for each song had to win its way in the esteem of the people before it could be included in the sacred compilation of the Psalter.'

[4] Millar Burrows, *More Light on the Dead Sea Scrolls* (New York, 1958), p. 171.

[5] *IOT*, p. 1127. J. A. Soggin (*Introduction to the Old Testament*, p. 409) apparently agrees: '. . . many fragments of it [Daniel] have been found among the writings of the Qumran sect, which is an evident sign that the book had acquired considerable importance at the earliest in the third century and certainly in the second.' On p. 410, however, he favours a date of writing between 168 and 164.

and would suppose that a second-century editor used the earlier material and added to it the visions of chapters 8–12. The unity of the book continues to demand recognition, yet, in the light of recent studies, 'if the book in its present form stems from the Maccabean period its unity ceases utterly'.[1]

Though, to judge by its popularity, the second-century date seems assured, unresolved problems remain. Manuscript evidence alone is disturbing because it leaves too little time between a mid-second-century autograph and the acceptance of the book as canonical. An increasing number of scholars are arguing in favour of a Babylonian source of much of the book, to which they think that Maccabean material was added. When all the relevant factors are taken into account, including the arguments for the unity of the book, a late sixth- or early fifth-century date of writing for the whole best suits the evidence.

V. LITERARY GENRE

Scholars are generally agreed that the book of Daniel is the example *par excellence* of apocalyptic in the Old Testament, and yet, on most definitions of the term, it proves to be an exception. There is, for example, little that strikes the reader as apocalyptic in style or in content in the first six chapters. Babylon is the historic city of the Neo-Babylonian empire; its kings are real men with awesome power. Nowhere is there any hint that Babylon is to be taken as in any way symbolic of something else, although there was symbolism ready to hand in Genesis 11 :9, and developed as such in major prophetic books (Is. 13 :19; Je. 51 :7; *cf.* Rev. 17 :5). Compared with the vivid apocalyptic imagery of Ezekiel's description of Tyre (Ezk. 26 – 28), which reappears in Revelation 18 as the description of the fall of Babylon, these chapters of Daniel are positively prosaic.

Accordingly a number of scholars have preferred to classify the stories of Nebuchadrezzar, Belshazzar and Darius as court tales,[2] popular romances[3] or Wisdom-style dramas, after the

---

[1] A. Jepsen, 'Bemerkungen zum Danielbuch', *VT*, XI, 1961, p. 386.

[2] So, *e.g.*, A. Jeffery, *IB*, pp. 359–360; W. Lee Humphries, *JBL*, 92, 1973, pp. 211–223.

[3] E. W. Heaton, *TBC*, pp. 37–41: 'The most obvious of the romances dealing with the Jew among the gentiles is one of the strands of the saga of Joseph (Gen. 40, 41).'

model of the Joseph stories in Genesis.[1] The affinities between Wisdom literature and apocalyptic particularly deserve to be noted, and will be taken up later. But to accept any one of these classifications is to deny the unity of the book which we have defended, or its definition as apocalyptic which we have so far assumed. Heaton follows A. C. Welch[2] in refusing to see Daniel as a typical specimen of apocalyptic literature, and there is much to be said for recognizing its distinctiveness.

The reason why a distinction becomes necessary is not far to seek. Between about 200 BC and AD 100 a large number of works were written which come into the category of apocalyptic. At the end of the document known as *4 Ezra* reference is made to seventy apocalypses, and by the end of the period this number may well have been near the mark. Some of these documents have long been known; others have come to light amongst the Dead Sea scrolls; yet others are known only by name from references to them in early Christian books. Now it goes without saying that this literature is a study in itself. The fact that it spans three hundred years or more means that it has a history; one book differs greatly from another, and a definition which attempts to characterize so diversified a collection of works will either be very general, or will include specific marks which are true for some but not for all apocalyptic. The book of Daniel is on any reckoning one of the earliest examples of this genre; indeed it might be regarded as a prototype or model from which later writers drew their inspiration.[3]

The traditional view has not so regarded the book, for it has been usual to postulate that apocalyptic is a late, foreign element in religion, transported from Persia, and of little real worth as compared with Old Testament prophecy. The book of Daniel was to be seen as the one example of this body of

---

[1] G. von Rad (*Old Testament Theology*, 2 [ET, Oliver and Boyd, 1965], p. 307) points out that from earliest times the interpretation of dreams 'fell in the province of Wisdom (Gen. xli. 8, 39)'.

[2] A. C. Welch, *Visions of the End* (James Clarke, 1922), pp. 101f., quoted by Heaton (*TBC*, p. 35).

[3] Other early works are the *Book of Jubilees*, usually dated mid-second century, but put considerably earlier by some scholars, *e.g.* W. F. Albright, *FSAC*, p. 347, who contends that it is pre-Hellenic and so attributes it to the late fourth or early third century; 1 *Enoch* 1–36 may be mid-third century BC; *cf.* T. F. Glasson, *NTS*, 23, 1976, pp. 82–90.

literature to be accepted into the canon. It has been assumed
that it had more in common with the extra-biblical apocalyptic books than with 'the Law and the Prophets'. Because
pseudonymity, for example, applies in the case of such books
as the *Psalms of Solomon* or the *Apocalypse of Abraham,*
Daniel must be pseudonymous. 'Apocalyptic literature is not
anonymous; the various individual works always name an
author. It is pseudonymous; for undoubtedly none of the
apocalyptic writings has any justification for the author's
name which it bears.'[1] But does it necessarily follow that the
book of Daniel must be pseudonymous merely on the ground
that it is an apocalyptic kind of book? It is the methodology
which is questionable.[2]

A welcome reappraisal of apocalyptic takes account of the
need to see the subject afresh in its historical and sociological
dimensions.

a. Origins of apocalyptic

We begin by considering the view that foreign elements,
especially Persian, are responsible for the distinctive marks of
apocalyptic. One typical definition of apocalyptic runs thus :
'A type of religious thought which apparently originated in
Zoroastrianism, the ancient Persian religion; taken over by
Judaism in the exilic and post-exilic periods . . . .'[3] What
seems to have been overlooked in the past is the late date of the
sources for Zoroastrianism. The *Avesta* may be as late as the
fourth century AD,[4] and the *Dinkart,* to which Frost refers, is
on his own admission a work of the ninth century AD.[5] 'Indeed

---

[1] Walter Schmitals, *The Apocalyptic Movement: Introduction and
Interpretation.* Translated by John E. Steely (Nashville, 1975), p. 15.

[2] James Barr (*Jewish Apocalyptic in Recent Scholarly Study* [Man-
chester, 1975], p. 35) expresses the opinion that other generalizations
will be upset. 'The standard formulae, which speak about the "dualism"
of apocalyptic, its "determinism", its "doctrine of the two ages" and so
on, all require careful retesting. Some of them are probably inaccurate
in any case, or too vague to be useful.' The assertion of pseudonymity
has been tested in J. G. Baldwin, 'Is there pseudonymity in the Old
Testament?', *Themelios,* 4.1, September 1978, pp. 6–12.

[3] M. Rist, *IDB* I, 'Apocalyptic', p. 157. S. B. Frost (*Old Testament
Apocalyptic* [London, 1952], pp. 19, 44, 73ff.) took for granted Iranean
influence.

[4] Ninian Smart, *The Religious Experience of Mankind* (Fontana,
1971), p. 304.

[5] S. B. Frost, *op. cit.,* p. 187.

Zoroastrianism is more likely to be indebted to the Bible than the other way round.'[1]

Paul D. Hanson has further opposed a Persian origin, concluding that both Persian and Hellenistic influences were late, 'coming only after the essential character of apocalyptic was fully developed, and were thus limited to peripheral embellishments'.[2] It has been pointed out that if Daniel owes anything to Persian eschatology, it is remarkably odd that Satan finds no place in the book. Moreover the names given in Daniel to angels owe nothing to Persia.[3] It seems clear that we may reject supposed Iranian influence and turn next to explore the possibility of biblical sources of apocalyptic in general and of Daniel in particular.

The book opens with Daniel and his friends receiving special training among the wise men of Babylon. The reminder that Wisdom was an international movement, appreciated in Egypt, sought by the Queen of Sheba, practised throughout the East (1 Ki. 4:29–31) for centuries before the exile, makes Wisdom a logical starting-point for a search into the origins of apocalyptic. Those who find in the book a legendary treatment of history put this down to a Wisdom source, similar to that which is said by some to lie behind the stories of Joseph (Gn. 40 and 41), the *Story of Ahikar*[4] and tales such as those of Tobit and Judith in the Apocrypha. Another alleged link with Wisdom is through the parable or allegory (Heb. *māšāl*), in which stories from the past were used as a teaching medium. The listener was expected to look for some practical application to his own situation, much as we do today in sermons.

A Wisdom source for the book of Daniel is argued by Heaton in his commentary, and has been exhaustively pursued by von Rad.[5] He argues that knowledge is the nerve-centre of

---

[1] J. H. Moulton, *HDB* IV, 'Zoroastrianism'.

[2] P. D. Hanson, *RB*, 1971, pp. 31–58.

[3] David Payne, 'The Place of Daniel in Old Testament Eschatology', *Themelios*, 4, 1967, pp. 33–40.

[4] This tale, echoed over a number of widely separated literatures, is first attested in Aramaic papyri of the fifth century BC found at Elephantiné on the Nile. It is set in the Assyrian court. Later it was partly utilized in the apocryphal book of Tobit. See *DOTT*, pp. 270–275; *ANET*, pp. 427–430.

[5] G. von Rad, *Old Testament Theology*, 2, pp. 306–308; *Wisdom in Israel* (ET, SCM Press, 1972), pp. 263–283.

apocalyptic literature and that the matrix from which it originates is Wisdom, understood as 'the effort made by the people of Israel to grasp the laws which governed the world in which she lived, and to systematize them'.[1]

Von Rad undoubtedly has a point of substance here. He has drawn attention to important links between Wisdom and apocalyptic, but he has not succeeded in convincing the majority of scholars that Wisdom is the one and only root of apocalyptic. By rejecting out of hand the possibility that apocalyptic was the child of prophecy he put that theory to the test, from which it has emerged more strongly supported than before.

The very fact that prophetic books contain sections with apocalyptic features (*e.g.* Is. 24 – 27) should be sufficient proof that there is a close connection between them. S. B. Frost based his book on the thesis that 'the [apocalyptic] writings grew and developed naturally from prophetic and liturgical origins'.[2] Both H. H. Rowley and D. S. Russell saw apocalyptic as reinterpreting Old Testament prophecy, and Rowley traced its roots far back into Israel's history, convinced 'that apocalyptic is the child of prophecy, yet diverse from prophecy'.[3] Paul Hanson, using what he calls the 'contextual-typological' approach, concluded, 'Jewish apocalyptic literature emerged in an unbroken, inner-Israelite development out of pre-Exilic and Exilic prophecy.'[4] Most writers agree that the connections can be traced, particularly in books such as Isaiah, Ezekiel and Zechariah, where early forms of apocalyptic are an essential part of the form and content.

The form of Daniel has characteristics in common with a book such as Zechariah. Both divide into two parts, the former with a given historical setting, the latter problematic because of unfamiliar historical allusions and highly symbolic language. In the New Testament the book of the Revelation was to begin from a specific historical situation, the seven churches of Asia (Rev. 1 – 3), and only after that was it to reveal the open door in heaven and the visions associated more closely with apocalyptic. We note that these books are

---

[1] G. von Rad, *Old Testament Theology*, 2, p. 306.
[2] S. B. Frost, *Old Testament Apocalyptic*, p. 3.
[3] H. H. Rowley, *The Relevance of Apocalyptic* (London, 1944), p. 15.
[4] P. D. Hanson, *RB*, 1971, p. 33.

not uniform in their contents, and that they bear witness to careful arrangement.[1] In the light of this evidence the stories of chapters 1 – 6 do not after all have to be regarded as belonging to another genre; apocalyptic is able to take many different literary forms and weld them into a whole.[2] This is one of the reasons why it is difficult to arrive at a satisfactory definition of apocalyptic.

One recent writer has drawn attention to the likelihood of the sixth century as the period for the rise of apocalyptic : 'The origins of apocalyptic must be searched for as early as the sixth century BC. In the catastrophe of the exile the older forms of faith and tradition came into crisis, and Israel's institutions, including her religious institutions, collapsed or were transformed.'[3] While earlier forms of law and history were being worked into their final shape, the presuppositions on which this older literature was based were being called in question. Transformations were taking place in the style of the prophetic oracle in the later part of Ezekiel. Cross ends his paper with the words, 'I think it is accurate to say that it is in this late exilic and early post-exilic literature that we detect the rudimentary traits and motives of apocalypticism'.

We have already argued that there are connections between the prophets of the sixth century and apocalyptic; what we have not done is to examine the possibility that the exile is the likely period of its birth. The importance of culture clash, internal conflict, political oppression, foreign imperialism, economic crisis, psychological stress in religious change is currently being appeciated and explored.[4]

---

[1] The argument that Zechariah is to be regarded as apocalyptic in structure is worked out in J. G. Baldwin, *Haggai, Zechariah, Malachi* (*TOTC*, 1972), pp. 74–81. *Cf.* p. 70.

[2] John G. Gammie ('The Classification, Stages of Growth, and Changing Intentions in the Book of Daniel', *JBL*, 95, 1976, pp. 191–204) claims that one characteristic of apocalyptic is that it contains at least three or four sub-genres, and draws upon earlier literature. 'Full recognition may be given to the variety of sub-genres within the book [of Daniel] without denying the overall classification "apocalyptic" ' (p. 193).

[3] F. M. Cross, 'New Directions in the Study of Apocalyptic', *JTC*, VI, 1969, p. 161. The contribution of Akkadian texts to the study of apocalyptic was referred to above (p. 42, footnote 1). See also p. 55.

[4] See, for example, Gottfried Oosterwal, *Modern Messianic Movements* (Elkhart, Indiana, 1973), especially pp. 13, 14.

INTRODUCTION

b. The significance of the exile

Now this link between the end of the exile and the birth of apocalyptic writing is extremely significant, and deserves further investigation.[1] The prophecy of Ezekiel, with its distinctively apocalyptic traits, belongs in the early part of the exile. If it be true that there is a connection between adversity and apocalyptic there could be no more likely time for it to come to fruition than the sixth century, when every visible expression of Israel's very existence collapsed, and the shape of the future was completely unknown. In this setting it is easy to see how eagerly Ezekiel's plan of the new temple and city, surrounded by the traditional tribes in an orderly array, would be studied by his contemporaries. The sense of uncertainty and bewilderment persisted even after the return from exile, and the prophet Zechariah, by means of visions and oracles (chapters 1 – 8), showed both the divine pattern in Israel's past and the divine purpose for the future. Nothing less than blessing for all nations is the culmination of both parts of the book (Zc. 8 :20–23; 14 :9, 16). Despite this inclusion of all the peoples of the earth, these prophetic books are Israel centred and covenant based. Ezekiel describes an eschatological battle (38; 39), but he ends with the assurance that his people will all be gathered back to their own land, there to be recipients of God's Spirit. Zechariah 14 pictures cataclysmic events, but the final picture is limited to sacrificial worship in the confines of Jerusalem.

What was lacking was a genuine world-view and a more comprehensive understanding of history, which would take account of other nations and their part in God's overarching purpose. This is where the book of Daniel comes into its own, and who could be better fitted to receive it than a well-instructed Jew who had lived the major part of his life as royal adviser in the court of the Babylonian world empire? His duties had

[1] In the development of his thesis that a tension between vision and reality resulted in polarization at times of crisis, Paul Hanson sees that process reaching 'its extreme in the late sixth and again in the early second centuries' (*op. cit.,* p. 43, footnote). These then would be the likely times for the development of apocalyptic. W. R. Millar, in *Isaiah 24–27 and the Origin of Apocalyptic* (Harvard Semitic Monograph Series, Missoula, Montana, 1976) concludes, 'We can with reasonable confidence date the entire apocalypse to the last half of the sixth century BC. It was in the years of exile and shortly thereafter that the apocalyptic movement was born' (p. 120).

forced him to break away from the thought-patterns of his childhood and, while maintaining his own faith, to see the application of its truths in an alien and powerful state. He lived through the fall of both the Assyrian and Babylonian empires, and in his old age would have been made ready to receive the visionary revelations concerning the final over-throw of God's enemies. As the days of past empires had been numbered, just as surely would those of the future be num-bered. Though Jerusalem and 'the glorious land' are of central importance in the last four chapters, the setting in which the visions are received remains to the end the river Tigris (10:4; 12:5; are we to think of a riverside Jewish settlement? *cf.* Ezk. 1:1) and the identity of 'the wise' (12:3) is left open-ended. Despite many attempts that have been made to identify them with one and another group of Jewish society, the possi-bility remains that the author may have had in mind others besides Jews who would 'turn many to righteousness'.

c. Distinctiveness of Daniel

It is due to this 'secular' background to the book that there is considerable discontinuity between Daniel and what has been termed 'prophetic apocalyptic'.[1] Missing from our book are the characteristics of 'that day' as it is referred to from the time of Amos onwards. We look in vain for cosmological up-heavals symbolized by earthquakes, the famine theme as a divine warning, utter silence as the ominous moment before judgment strikes. All these were warnings to the covenant people, calling them to change their ways before it was too late. They were part of an accepted interpretation of past history, each vibrant with memories and emotions. To any other people 'natural' disasters would lack any such specific message, and we do not find them in Daniel. On foreign soil, in a missionary situation, the God of gods revealed Himself in ways meaningful to the new culture and background. Where dreams were revered as a vehicle of revelation, there dreams were used; where barbaric punishments were meted out, there this God miraculously delivered His servants; where pride defied the living God, there pride was abased.

Nevertheless there was new revelation also for the chosen people in all this. It concerned their history, which from this

[1] G. E. Ladd, 'Why not Prophetic-Apocalyptic?', *JBL*, 77, 1957, pp. 192ff.

time on was to be bound up with that of the great world empires. For this reason the Deuteronomic interpretation of history, based on national faithfulness to the covenant, was no longer adequate. The world had become too big and Judaism too fragmented for older formulae to apply. If any sense was to be made of the world-scene, a more comprehensive coverage was needed, in which other great nations were not only included but also played a major role. Prophets had proclaimed Yahweh the divine warrior, victor over mighty enemies (*e.g.* Is. 25 : 1–3; Ezk. 38 : 3, 4; Zc. 9 : 14), but they had used poetic imagery which, while it was clear as to its main message, was sometimes obscure and difficult in application. The author of Daniel employs an entirely different idiom, which first appears in the dream of Nebuchadrezzar (Dn. 2), involving the division of subsequent time into four periods. Like the dreams of Pharaoh this dream was a means of revelation and originated in the purposes of God (Dn. 2 :28).

When the time came for Daniel to receive 'a dream and visions of his head' (7 : 1), a similar fourfold pattern was presented; though under different symbolism, in both chapters the dream spanned the whole of time from the exile to the establishment of God's kingdom. The bold simplicity of the idea makes it strikingly memorable, and it effectively conveyed certain basic truths. In the first place human kingdoms were shown to be short-lived. This was nothing new, but put in this pictorial way it registered in the mind. In the second, far from evolving towards a Utopia, human kingdoms were declining in value (chapter 2) and becoming more beastly (chapter 7). Less obvious, but still part of the symbolism, is the sovereignty of God controlling the pattern of history. The dream image, though sliced into metals of different colours and values, still formed a recognizable shape; in the vision of the beasts an invisible master-hand was at work, removing grandiose illusions of power and cutting human rulers down to size. But that is not all. The heavenly world breaks into both scenes : in the former to consume human kingdoms and to bestow in their place one heavenly kingdom which will fill the earth; in the second to reveal the judgment throne of God, the destruction of the fourth beast and the setting up of a kingdom given to 'one like a man'. This unveiling (Gk. *apokalypsis*) is thus intended not only to give a glimpse of heaven, but also to summarize human history as it looks in divine perspective.

It has long been recognized that the author of Daniel was not the originator of the four kingdom sequence, followed by a fifth which would be lasting (*cf.* the Additional Note on 'Nebuchadrezzar's dream statue', p. 96). Herodotus, who wrote in the third quarter of the fifth century BC, seems to have had a Persian source for his sequence : Assyrians, Medes, Persians (Babylonians would have said Assyria, Chaldea, Persia); when Alexander came to power it would be natural to add the Greeks. Oriental dissatisfaction at being ruled by Westerners raised hopes of a reversal under a fifth empire. 'It is perhaps not too much to suggest that, even in the days of Antiochus III, the Daniels of these other Judases sometimes spoke of four empires to be followed by a fifth that would be universal and eternal under the hand of God.'[1] Basing his argument on a passage in Aemilius Sura, the date of which he shows to be between 189 and 171 BC, Swain demonstrates that 'the philosophy of four empires and a fifth was known in Rome several years before the rise of Judas Maccabaeus and the composition of the Book of Daniel'.[2]

That the basic idea came from the Ancient Near East is supported by texts, all of which came from Persian or Seleucid Babylon, and which have been classified by A. K. Grayson as Akkadian prophecies.[3] These are not to be confused with biblical prophecies, which are quite different (p. 14). Of special significance is the so-called Dynastic prophecy, published here for the first time by Grayson. It had already been noted that 'there is similarity between the Babylonian genre and certain parts of the Book of Daniel (8 :23–5 and 11 :3–45). In style, form and rationale there is a striking resemblance'.[4] Interestingly some of this literature dated back at least to the time of Nebuchadrezzar (*c.* 1126–1105 BC) and would presumably have been known in sixth-century Babylon. Grayson goes on, 'The appearance of the Dynastic prophecy now adds significant evidence of this close connection. In the Dynastic

[1] Joseph Ward Swain, 'The Theory of Four Monarchies: Opposition History Under the Roman Empire', *Classical Philology*, 35, 1940, p. 9.

[2] *Ibid.*, p. 5. Swain, of course, assumes a second-century date for the writing of Daniel.

[3] A. K. Grayson, *Babylonian Historical-Literary Texts*, especially pp. 13–27.

[4] Grayson and Lambert, *JCS*, 18, 1964, p. 10; and *cf.* W. W. Hallo, *IEJ*, 16, 1966, pp. 240–242, given in a footnote by A. K. Grayson, *Babylonian Historical-Literary Texts*, p. 21.

prophecy the concept of the rise and fall of empires, which must have its roots in the dynastic tradition of Mesopotamian chronology, is mirrored by the similar concept in Daniel.'

The main tablet, which is not complete, contained a description of the fall of Assyria and the rise of the Chaldean dynasty, written as though future, and the monarchs who feature in the story are not named, though they can be identified by the length of their reigns. Cyrus, called a 'king of Elam', can be recognized, as can Alexander the Great, called here 'the Hanaean', archaic for an inhabitant of Thrace. The Dynastic prophecies raise many questions, but they at least establish the existence of a genre, well known in the Ancient Near East, with which the book of Daniel has important links.

The document ends with an attempt to predict the fall of the Hellenistic kings and thus fulfils a purpose similar to that of political propaganda. The underlying hope is that the bad regime will be overthrown and that a more just and lasting kingdom will take its place, but Grayson is emphatic that there is no suggestion in any Akkadian prophecy of a climactic end to world history.

To return to Daniel, where the end of world history *is* expected, it is not altogether true to describe the historical slant of this book as pessimistic, though to be sure no human kingdom is to be viewed with any optimism. Even the best are short-lived and destined to be followed by inferior systems. But if history is man-shaped, like the image of chapter 2, it is also true that the one to whom the dominion is finally given is 'one like a son of man' (7 : 13). The imagery, if we may anticipate the exposition of the text, shows that God has not given up on man. Marred though he is, and bluster as he may to cover his deficiencies, man will yet receive what God intended for him at creation (Gn. 1 : 26) and be what God intended him to be.[1] This is the best of good news and Daniel's way of spelling out the gospel, though he could not have appreciated it to the extent that the Christian does, in the light of Christ's finished work. Once more there is universal application. All mankind and not just a section of mankind is eligible to receive this good news.

In the Old Testament there is then a distinction to be made between Daniel and what we have called 'prophetic apocalyp-

---

[1] *Cf.* the Additional Note on 'Son of man', p. 148.

tic', that is, those poetic passages in the prophets which look to the end time and give an account of God's covenant promises to Israel as seen from that angle. Apocalyptic such as we have in the book of Daniel is viewing secular world empires in the light of God's purposes for world history. On this wider canvas the covenant people is still central, but the largest figures are the rulers of the nations and their empires. To them the living God disclosed Himself so that Daniel was able to rehearse for Belshazzar 'the deeds of the Lord' (Dn. 5 : 18–21) in much the same way as the prophets of Israel would rehearse the history of the exodus as a means of bringing Israel back to faith. By and large these rulers accepted the advantages of having a man of God among them, but rejected the call to repentance and commitment to Him. In this they were no different from Israel. As Paul saw so clearly, there was nothing to choose between Jew and Greek (Rom. 3 : 9ff.). But in the case of Israel there was a covenant promise to which appeal could be made, and the certainty of a righteous God who was at the same time full of compassion and mercy, whereas so far as the nations were concerned it was not clear how salvation would come to them. The fact that the kingdom was given to one like a son of man, a representative of the human race, was one source of hope, and designation of the 'wise' as those who would awake to life was another, for there could be wise men outside of Israel.

It is Christ who makes possible an apocalyptic outlook that brings together both the prophetic longings for the fulfilment of Israel's covenant relationship with the Lord and extends its reach to include the nations. Already in Mark 13 prophetic apocalyptic is combined with concepts taken from Daniel, and all is used with a future reference. The Revelation of John does the same thing on a grand scale, recapitulating all that has gone before in the Bible to stage a final panorama of human history, by comparison with which Daniel is merely a kind of first draft. With hindsight we can see that part of the Danielic vision was enacted first at the time of Antiochus IV and again in AD 70, and yet as a whole it remains unfulfilled and therefore still has a future reference. In the apocalyptic presentation of history there are clear indications that cyclical concepts of repeated patterns are not without their contribution to the truth. Nevertheless history is not an ever-turning wheel getting nowhere, but is more like a spiral working to a climax, or rather a nadir, an all-time low, at which point God will intervene to make all things new. Here the prophets and apocalyptic writers are at one.

One further characteristic of Daniel is its use of numbers in a symbolic way that is particularly puzzling to the western mind. Coupled with that is the idiomatic use of the word 'time' in such phrases as 'time, times and half a time'. The question 'how long?' in Daniel appears to have its answer, but in the detailed application the sequence is always cut short. Sixty-nine and a half weeks just fall short of seventy (Dn. 9 : 24–27), as if to say 'the end is not yet'. In chapter 7, though judgment had fallen on the fourth beast, the rest continued to live 'for a season and a time' (7 : 12); evidently history had not yet come to an end.

While Wisdom writers were aware of set times in human life (Ec. 3 : 1–8, 17; 8 : 6), the prophets used the word with a more historical connotation. For Hosea, for example, a time of seclusion was a necessary part of the Lord's dealings with Israel (Ho. 3 : 3, 4), but it was to have as its sequel a new age (3 : 5). ' "Then" (*'aḥar*) very clearly denotes Hosea's two-phased eschatology that appeared already in 2 : 9, 17 . . . here one root of apocalyptic with its division of history into periods becomes visible . . .'[1] The new message after a time of judgment is illustrated particularly clearly in Ezekiel, who, after the fall of Jerusalem, would no longer be dumb (Ezk. 24 : 27), but would be able to complete what had been a ministry of doom with a word of hope. Habakkuk's vision awaited its time (Hab. 2 : 3). It is significant that Jesus began His ministry with the words 'The time is fulfilled' (Mk. 1 : 15). 'Then' had become 'today'.

Without doubt the 'time' to which Jesus referred was that of both prophets and apocalyptists. The kingdom of the God of heaven was at hand (*cf.* Dn. 2 : 44), but though a new era had dawned the long-awaited 'end' was 'not yet' (Mt. 24 : 6). There was a limit to what even the most enlightened visionaries of Old Testament times could discern, and what they did discern was foreshortened like a view of distant hills, lacking any indication of the gap that separated one range from another. In the teaching of Jesus the timetable is no more definite, but the future is set in a completely renewed context because

[1] H. W. Wolff, *A Commentary on the Book of the Prophet Hosea* (ET, Philadelphia, 1974), p. 62.

of all that He was to accomplish through the cross and resurrection. The preaching of the gospel to all nations provided the programme (Mk. 13:10), tribulation such as Daniel had depicted would be the experience of the messengers (Mk. 13:7, 8, 11–20); endurance and watchfulness must continue till the end (Mk. 13:13; *cf.* Dn. 12:12).

To sum up, the book of Daniel is thoroughly integrated with the Old Testament as a whole, but at the same time presents its truth from a world standpoint to an extent which was never attempted by a prophet. By means of a schematized presentation all subsequent history was outlined and its end depicted. Of necessity then the future is to some extent predetermined, though the numbers given cannot be used like historical data. It is rather that, given a framework which this book provides, human rulers will unwittingly fit into a pattern of behaviour and will implement policies recognizable from this book. The people of God will be victims of these policies and, being forewarned, must set themselves to endure in the knowledge that their God is still in control and will vindicate His own. This is the significance of Old Testament apocalyptic, as it is outworked in the book of Daniel.

VI. STRUCTURE

We have argued that the book of Daniel is a unity and that it should be regarded in its entirety as an apocalyptic book. If this is so its structure should demonstrate that unity, and we believe that it does so in at least two ways.

a. *The book has a discernible pattern*
This has already been argued in the discussion of the unity of the book.[1] Here we do no more than state that the change of language from Hebrew to Aramaic and back to Hebrew is deliberate on the part of the author, who is adapting a literary device found in other books from the Ancient Near East.

In addition to an ABA pattern in the over-all structure, there is a clear literary arrangement in the Aramaic part of the book, as A. Lenglet has shown in a recent study of the subject.[2] He

[1] See above, p. 39.
[2] A. Lenglet, 'La Structure Littéraire de Daniel 2–7', *Biblica*, 53, 1972, pp. 169–190. Lenglet's thesis receives appreciation in J. C. H. Lebram, 'Perspektiven der Gegenwartigen Danielforschung', *JSJ*, V, 1975, p. 9.

points out what he calls the concentric arrangement of the subject-matter, with the extremities, chapters 2 and 7 presenting four kingdoms, chapters 3 and 6 narratives which demonstrate God's power to deliver His servants, and the middle two chapters God's judgment on proud rulers. He contends that the central section is the climax of the message, for the God of heaven wants to be acknowledged as such by the princes of the world. The six chapters as a whole form a theology of history, addressed to the kings of the earth and therefore written in the international language. Lenglet's thesis presupposes an intentional arrangement of the material, with the remaining chapters written in Hebrew quite deliberately because they are addressed to Jews.[1] This ABC CBA structure draws attention to the completeness of the Aramaic section within the larger book. It starts with a problem in the Babylonian court and proceeds to show that the man of God is equipped with the solution. The king's dream is interpreted as a relatively straightforward survey of the remainder of human history, seen as a succession of four world empires. The concluding Aramaic chapter recapitulates that history, but describes more explicitly the character of the world rulers. It also enlarges on the kingdom which the God of heaven is to set up (2 :44), and concludes with all earth's dominions worshipping the Most High (7 :27).

In the Hebrew which provides the frame for the Aramaic section the first chapter is introductory, supplying the historical details to account for the presence of Daniel and his friends at the court of Nebuchadrezzar. It illustrates both their single-minded devotion to their God and God's vindication of their self-discipline by giving them acceptance with the officials set over them. The transition from Hebrew to Aramaic (2 :4b) is made at an appropriate point, and so is not forced. It presupposes that the readers were bilingual (*cf.* 2 Ki. 18 :26). Chapters 8–12 relate the visionary material under new symbols with the express purpose of revealing in increasing detail the

[1] In the course of his argument Lenglet claims that concentric arrangement is not limited to the Bible or even to Greek and Latin, but is common to Hittites, Egyptians, Anglo-Saxons and Africans. He also refers in a footnote to A. Vanhoye, *La Structure Littéraire de l'Épitre aux Hébreux* (Paris–Bruges, 1963), pp. 37, n.1; 60-63, and to C. H. Talbert, 'Artistry and Theology: An Analysis of the Architecture of John 1 :19 – 5:47', *CBQ*, 32, 1970, pp. 360, 361. *Cf.* J. G. Baldwin, *Haggai, Zechariah, Malachi (TOTC)*, pp. 74–80.

bearing of world empires on Jerusalem, the holy city, and the time of the end (Dn. 8 :17, *cf*. 19; 11 :35, 40). Even when the city had been restored after seventy years in ruins it would not be secure against enemies who would sweep through the land. But God's treasure, listed in His book, consisted of people and not of lifeless monuments; those who belonged to Him could look even beyond death to a glorious future (12 :2, 3).

Though chapter 8 is dated in the reign of Belshazzar, the Babylonian empire is omitted from consideration; it is already as good as finished. The prophet is in Susa, capital of Elam and one of the royal cities of the Persian empire (Ne. 1 :1; Est. 1 :2). For the first time in the book (apart from 2 :38) names are given to the empires intended by the symbols. The ram with the two horns (8 :3) is expressly said to be 'the kings of Media and Persia' (8 :20; *cf*. Est. 1 :3, where Persia is named before Media). If the book was written in the Persian period no mistake could have been made at this point; if it was a second-century work the evidence of Ezra 1–6 would have been at hand as a source of historical information, even if the text of Esther was not known. The writer did not think of the ram as representing two empires (erroneously Median and Persian, as many insist), but one, for Media and Persia had become one kingdom. 'The he-goat is the king of Greece' (8 :21) and all that follows in that chapter belongs to the Greek period.

In relation to the four sections of the image in chapter 2 the two animals of chapter 8 correspond, therefore, to the silver (Persian) and bronze (Greek). The iron, later to be inter-mingled with clay, is not covered by chapter 8. In relation to the four beasts of chapter 7 the ram corresponds to the bear (7 :5, Persian) and the goat to the leopard (7 :6, Greek). Again in chapter 7 there is a fourth animal left in the sequence, indicating that the end of time was not to be expected during the Greek period. Indeed chapter 8 does not mention the end of time or the coming of the heavenly kingdom, but concentrates on the cleansing of the sanctuary (8 :14).

Chapter 9 goes further under the symbolism of seventy weeks. At the end of sixty-nine weeks the sanctuary is not merely desecrated but destroyed. Half of the last week is accounted for under the heading of persecution and sacrilege (9 :27), but nothing is said of the final half of the week. Though the persecutor comes to his deserved end, the revelation goes no further. Chapter 11 retraces the period symbolized by the two beasts of chapter 8, dismisses the Persian period in one verse, and concentrates on the Greek period, beginning with Alexander the Great, as we know him, down to an indeterminate period when, after unprecedented persecution, a general resurrection of the dead will bring history to its completion. At the end of the book the writer once again, as in chapters 2 and 7, takes us to the end of time.

b. There is progressive parallelism

In addition to the deliberate pattern discernible in the book there is in particular an apocalyptic form, present in its simplest stage in Zechariah[1] and most fully developed in Revelation. The term 'progressive parallelism' is used by W. Hendriksen in his commentary on Revelation,[2] but we have already begun to introduce the idea in the previous paragraph, for chapters 2, 7, 8, 9 and 11 are to some extent parallel. They review a period of history by means of different symbols; in chapters 2 and 7 this period is identical, whereas in chapters 8, 9 and 11 the starting-point is later, and there is concentration on one theme. Chapter 2 is least complex; chapter 11 is very detailed. The dream image has nothing to say about the future of God's people beyond assuring them that God is ultimately going to have His way in the affairs of the nations; but the vision of the four great beasts ends with 'the saints of the Most High' receiving the kingdom; subsequent visions lay stress on the fearful destruction which will lay waste the sanctuary and defeat God's cause before the appointed end comes. The revelation is thus progressive, though it remains within the general frame of reference given in the first of the series.

It follows that the book must have been the work of one person, who planned the presentation of his theme with meticulous care. First there was the selection of five incidents from what must have been a profusion of events, known from the reigns of Neo-Babylonian and Persian kings. Such bold

[1] See *Haggai, Zechariah, Malachi (TOTC)*, p. 71.
[2] W. Hendriksen, *More than Conquerors* (Tyndale Press, 1962), pp. 34–36. *Cf.* John J. Collins, 'The Son of Man and the saints of the Most High in the Book of Daniel', *JBL*, 93, 1974, pp. 54–55, which sets out four parallel accounts in chapters 7–12, centring on the career of Antiochus Epiphanes.

selectivity is the mark of the artist : by this means he proclaims his message. The skilful use of literary pattern and progression reaffirms the unity of the book, with its one main theme : the cost but final vindication of witness in a hostile society.

VII. INTERPRETATION

The earliest interpreters of Daniel to whom we have access are the writers of the New Testament (*cf.* specifically Mt. 24 : 15) and Josephus (AD 37–*post* 100). Josephus regards Daniel as 'one of the greatest prophets' who 'was not only wont to prophesy future things, as did the other prophets, but he also fixed the time at which these would come to pass'.[1] In his summary of Daniel 11–12 Josephus comments, 'And these misfortunes our nation did in fact come to experience under Antiochus Epiphanes, just as Daniel many years before saw and wrote that they would happen.' Countering the viewpoint of the Epicureans, who denied that any wise being directed human affairs, Josephus argued that if they were right 'we should not have seen all these things happen in accordance with his prophecy'.[2] There is no evidence at this period of any doubt about the historicity of the sixth-century Daniel, nor of the genuineness of his prophecy.

Jewish expositors in the Talmud (containing the teaching of Jewish doctors up to the end of the fifth century AD) regarded Daniel very highly. Though its core, the Mishnah (the record of Jewish scribes and teachers of the Oral Law) aimed to preserve, cultivate and apply to life the Torah, 'the Law' or instruction of the Old Testament, yet even so Zechariah ben Kabutal, speaking of preparation of the High Priest for the Day of Atonement, says, 'Many times I read before him [the High Priest] out of Daniel.'[3] Daniel was highly regarded as an example to follow, though not as a source of authoritative teaching. Jewish scholars of the medieval period and later regarded Daniel as inferior to the Prophets, probably because there was reaction against Christian Messianic interpretation of the book.

---

[1] *Jewish Antiquities* x. 266, 267.
[2] *Ibid.*, sections 276 and 280.
[3] Herbert Danby, *The Mishna: Translated from the Hebrew with Introduction and Brief Explanatory Notes* (OUP, 1933), Yoma 1:6, p. 163.

INTRODUCTION

Early Christian commentators on Daniel, Hippolytus of Rome, Polychronius and Theodoret, whose works have survived in whole or in part, are referred to by Montgomery who notes their sane, historical exegesis.[1] Jerome (c. 345 – c. 419), however, is the best known. His commentary was intended to refute an attack on the historicity of Daniel by the Neoplatonist Porphyry (232 – c. 305), who, as we know from Jerome, considered the prophetic passages in Daniel to be the narration of an unknown author during the time of Antiochus Epiphanes. This conclusion he reached from the premise that the author could not have known the future. If it had not been for the careful quotations by Jerome the work of Porphyry would not have survived, and it is ironical that at the present time it is the position of Porphyry and not that of the Christian apologist which dominates most works of scholarship. In the early centuries of the Christian era Christians accepted without question the authenticity of Daniel and his prophecy.

With the beginning of biblical criticism in the seventeenth and early eighteenth centuries the viewpoint of Porphyry was widely adopted by biblical scholars under the influence of rationalism. The book was held to be the product of the Maccabean period, and to be pseudepigraphic, that is, attributed to Daniel though not in fact written by him. A number of able scholars opposed this trend, among them the English commentators Pusey (1864) and C. H. H. Wright (1906), the American M. Stuart (1850) and the German C. F. Keil (1867), whose works are available in English, R. D. Wilson, *Studies in the Book of Daniel* (1917, 1918) and E. J. Young, *The Prophecy of Daniel* (1949). J. A. Montgomery already in 1927 pointed out that 'Archaeology has . . . inspired a considerable revival of the defence of the authenticity of the book' and he supported 'the reaction toward recognition of a far greater amount of historical tradition in the book than the older criticism allowed'.[2] This trend has not for the most part been followed by more recent commentators, who have taken for granted its Maccabean date, its historical inaccuracies and the supposed lateness of its original text,[3] without making reference to any evidence to the contrary.

[1] *ICC*, p. 107.
[2] *ICC*, p. 109.
[3] So, *e.g.*, *TBC*, pp. 1 and 56ff., and Porteous, p. 20.

The standpoint of the commentator is immediately apparent in his interpretation. Those who think the book is the product of the Maccabean period assume that the writer has most detailed knowledge of the history of his own day, and that the fourth kingdom is to be identified with the Greek empire, of which Antiochus Epiphanes was the predominant ruler from 175 to 163 BC. That this necessitates the Medo-Persian empire to be split, contrary to historical fact, into two separate and successive empires, is put among the historical inaccuracies of the writer. Thus the four kingdoms become Babylon, Media, Persia, Greece rather than Babylon, Medo-Persia, Greece, with the fourth Rome, as was assumed in the section above on Structure.[1] The difficulty with this view is that the book itself identifies the ram of 8:3, 4 with the Medo-Persian empire (8:20), and the goat with Greece (8:21). Josephus saw this, but he also accepted, with his rabbinic contemporaries, that chapters 11 and 12 referred to the Romans as well as to Antiochus.[2] Thus, when the Romans destroyed Jerusalem, they too were seen to be fulfilling prophecy (*cf*. Mt. 24:2, 15–22). Early Christian exegetes were at one with Josephus in this.

The fact that Daniel is so controversial a book draws the modern commentator into current discussions about historicity, date of writing, literary genre and other interesting matters, to the extent that the whole purpose and intention of the writer can easily be overlooked. Considerations of interpretation, as we have seen, polarize into two possibilities: the fourth kingdom is either Greece or Rome. James Barr, commenting on the British contribution to an understanding of Apocalyptic, says, 'It has approached the complicated and obscure mixtures which form the apocalyptic books with rather clear and simple questions, to which in principle a yes-or-no answer may be

---

[1] See also the commentary, below, p. 161. Not all conservative scholars have interpreted the fourth kingdom as Rome. Gordon J. Wenham (*Themelios*, 2.2, 1977, p. 51) makes the important point that various conservative Christians, including the Westminster divines, held the Greek view long before it became the hallmark of liberal orthodoxy. Robert J. M. Gurney (*ibid*., pp. 39–45) argues from his understanding of the history of the period that the four kingdoms should be interpreted as the Babylonian, Median, Persian, Greek empires. John Goldingay, in the same issue, supports this interpretation, but on the ground that the author wanted to use a contemporary motif which could not be modified. Thus he had to stretch his material to fit the scheme, but he was not mistaken in his history (*ibid*., p. 46).

[2] *Jewish Antiquities* x. 276.

obtained. . . . This reduction of the very enigmatic material to essentially simple questions seems to me to be a feature of much of our British tradition of scholarship in apocalyptic.'[1] This discerning comment applies not only to apocalyptic in general but also to Daniel in particular, especially with regard to interpretation of the last kingdom in chapters 2 and 7 : is it Greece or Rome, which?

We have argued[2] that if the author was working in the second century BC, during the Maccabean struggle, it was already obvious to the observer without any supernatural gift of insight that Rome was gaining supremacy over Greece. If he was working in the sixth century and was genuinely receiving revelation from God, the fourth kingdom, on such interpretation as the book itself provides, turns out to be Rome. But why should this be so, particularly in view of the space given to events of the Greek period in chapter 11 ? What is the writer intending to say, or rather what is the impact intended by the Holy Spirit upon the church through the message of this book?

The predominant message is that God's people will experience suffering and be threatened with extinction, but that will not be the end of the story because their God is the living and all-powerful God who will get glory by vindicating His name and who will save them. In the first part of the book Daniel and his friends are caught in the conflict between Babylonian/ Persian imperialism and the claims of their God. Here the conflict is seen in its simplest terms : individuals, threatened with death because they do not conform to what is expected of them by the state, find miraculous deliverance. But the whole drama has yet to be worked out on other levels : the people of God as a whole are to find themselves at the mercy of a ruler who will systematically impose on them heathen ways and at the same time forbid them to worship the God of their fathers. This process came to a head in the time of Antiochus Epiphanes, and the book prepares them ahead of time so that faith does not falter when the test comes. Behind the struggle on earth, however, is a vital conflict taking place at a cosmic level 'in the heavenlies', and the visions reveal the reality of the fight in which angelic beings have their part. At

[1] James Barr, *Jewish Apocalyptic in Recent Scholarly Study*, pp. 32, 33.
[2] See below, pp. 184, 200.

this cosmic level also God will prevail and establish His kingdom. The stone 'cut out by no human hand' (2:34) was a kingdom set up by the God of heaven (2:44); in 7:21, 22 the fourth kingdom 'prevailed over the saints' and they were overcome until God intervened and a man was given dominion and glory and a kingdom that would not be destroyed (7:13, 14). Only after defeat would victory be achieved and the kingdom be given to the saints of the Most High (7:18).

Now it is likely that the author of Daniel, whenever he was writing, did not see further ahead than that, but he had grasped what mattered, namely that great conflict lay in the future for God's people so as to involve them to the death (*cf.* Zc. 14:1, 2). The Maccabean period saw the little state of Judea threatened as never before with the extinction of their faith, and indeed many faithful believers died. Freedom fighters under Judas achieved a marvellous initial deliverance and the Temple once again became the centre of worship. God had delivered His people, but the sequel was indecisive, for the state of Judea in the following centuries was no model of godliness. The cosmic aspect of the struggle had not yet come to a head, and the book ends with a mysterious time of waiting for 'the end'. Deliverance is promised but the wicked continue to 'do wickedly' (12:10). The kingdom has not yet been ushered in.

From the point of view of an Old Testament writer this assurance of ultimate deliverance was a marvellous revelation, and we do well to appreciate what to understand as much as this must have meant to him and to believers who had to go through times of persecution. But to return to the identity of the fourth kingdom, the interpreting angel did not give it a name, and to assume that if we in the twentieth century know whether Greece or Rome was intended we have therefore interpreted the book is to miss the point. We believe that the earliest Christian commentators were not mistaken in seeing the fourth kingdom as Rome, and the death and resurrection of Christ as the focal point to which chapters 2 and 7 were looking. They had Paul's Epistles on which to draw for evidence of the cosmic battle won on the cross (*e.g.* Eph. 1:19–22; Phil. 2:8–11; Col. 1:18–20; 2:15). But the days of conflict were not therefore over. Christians were engaged in a battle which required the whole armour of God (Eph. 6:11–18); wars and persecutions still lay ahead (Mt. 24:6–14) and Jesus went on to apply Daniel 9 :27; 11 :31; 12 :11 to a time still future. The book of Daniel had future relevance for the church, even if at one level the prophecy seemed to have been fulfilled in the second century BC. The end was 'not yet', for the task of proclaiming the kingdom throughout the world had yet to be carried out (Mt. 24 :14). If, therefore, our western minds want a yes-or-no answer to the question we ourselves pose, 'What does the fourth kingdom stand for?', we may be asking the wrong kind of question.

The four-kingdom scheme seems to have its significance in the four empires between the time of the exile and the death of Christ, but it may have a symbolic meaning also, representing the relationship between God's church and the world powers throughout time. The book of Revelation takes up the theme of conflict from where the book of Daniel leaves it, and looks to a final confrontation with the powers of evil who war against the church, though it does not end there. With his triumph accomplished the Lamb holds 'the keys of Death and Hades' (Rev. 1 :18); the powers of evil still persecute to the death God's witnesses (Rev. 11 :8), but their final triumph is sure because 'the kingdom of the world has become the kingdom of our Lord and of his Christ, and he shall reign for ever and ever' (Rev. 11 :15). Daniel sees to the first advent of Christ; John in the Revelation sees his second advent.

Meanwhile 'We would do well to look at what happens to us as individuals and as the church as part of the struggle between chaos and cosmos which is the world's story from its beginning to its end, and to see these things as the dealings of the eschatological God. In all the power, holiness, and love that belong to creation and to the end, he is with us in each crisis, and we can experience another foretaste of the final victory'.[1]

VIII. TEXT AND CANON

A reader who uses the Jerusalem Bible is immediately confronted by additional material in Daniel which does not appear in other versions : 3 :24–90, the song of Azariah in the furnace which appears in the Book of Common Prayer as the Benedicite; 13 :1–64, about Susanna and 14 :1–42, 'Bel and the

[1] John E. Goldingay, 'The book of Daniel: three issues', *Themelios*, 2.2, 1977, p. 48.

Dragon'. The reason is that the Septuagint (LXX) and Vulgate, on which the Jerusalem Bible is based, have this longer text, whereas the Hebrew/Aramaic has not. Since the Reformation the standard English versions have been translations from the Hebrew/Aramaic shorter text. This raises questions about the relationship between these two sources.

Hebrew/Aramaic

Little light has been shed in recent years on the Hebrew/Aramaic text of Daniel, except that the Daniel fragments among the Dead Sea scrolls for the most part support the Massoretic Text (MT) and provide testimony to the faithfulness with which the biblical text was handed down over the centuries. Individual variants, however, prove that at the time when these copies were written the Qumran community had no standardized 'canonical' text. There are places where a text follows LXX or 'Theodotion', but it is too early to be at all sure whether the Qumran scribes attempted a critical compilation out of available texts, or whether these represent different MSS which were already extant. Nevertheless, what can be said is that the texts are very close to the later text of MT, which is true of almost all the hand-written texts of Bible books found at Qumran.[1] It is especially providential that the points at which the language change takes place (2:4; 7:28/8:1) are included, so proving that it was a characteristic of the text in its earliest extant form.

One Hebrew MS which has recently been published, though not as ancient as the MSS from Qumran, 'reflects features of a text produced by a Babylonian school of Massoretes which flourished centuries earlier and was different from the Tiberian school of Massoretes responsible for the MT'.[2] In an English summary of an otherwise Hebrew work the author presents some of the similarities between this MS and the Qumran scrolls, with which it shares a tendency 'to make the book of Daniel linguistically more intelligible to his [the scribe's] contemporaries – namely, the members of the Jewish communities of Geonic Babylonia',[3] that is, of the fourteenth century AD.

---

[1] In this paragraph I have drawn freely on Alfred Mertens, *Das Buch Daniel im Lichte der Texte vom Toten Meer*, p. 166.

[2] John M. Bauchet in a review in *Scripture Bulletin*, 5. 1, 1974, of Shelomo Morag, *The Book of Daniel, A Babylonian-Yemenite Manuscript* (Jerusalem, 1974).

[3] Shelomo Morag, *op. cit.*, p. XV.

INTRODUCTION

Greek

The Old Greek (LXX) survives in only two MSS: Codex Chisianus (tenth century AD) and Chester Beattie papyrus 967 (third century AD).[1] The Syro-Hexaplar (AD 616–617) is a literal translation of the Greek column of Origen's text of the LXX, from which it is possible to guess at the original Greek translation; this is presumed to have been made in c. 100 BC. It was evidently a fairly free translation, marked, as we have seen, by textual expansions, and was superseded early in Christian writings by the more literal version of Theodotion (second century AD). His translation of Daniel entirely superseded that of the Septuagint.

Questions were raised when it was realized that readings like those of Theodotion appeared in literature written before his time, and it was supposed that there must have been an 'Ur-Theodotion' which he was revising.[2] Now, as the result of a study of Greek forms of text from Qumran and elsewhere, Barthélemy has shown that Greek fragments of the Minor Prophets from Naḥal Ḥever represent a rescension of the Old Greek (LXX).[3] He calls it Proto-Theodotion and suggests the date AD 30–50. Others prefer a first-century BC dating. New Testament quotations, especially in Hebrews and Revelation, appear to come from this version.

None of the LXX additions to Daniel is represented in the Qumran texts,[4] and since they were not in the Hebrew/Aramaic MSS either it has been assumed that they originated outside Palestine, possibly in Egypt. This would easily explain their acceptance in LXX, which was translated in Alexandria.

The absence of the LXX additions to Daniel is highlighted by the fact that other Daniel material has been found at Qumran. The *Prayer of Nabonidus*[5] is the most important

[1] The papyrus includes Dn. 3:72 – 8:27 with chapters 7 and 8 preceding 5 and 6 (the chronological order). The preserved text ends at 6:18. *Cf.* S. Jellicoe, *The Septuagint and Modern Study* (OUP, 1968), pp. 84, 231, 302.

[2] Montgomery, *ICC*, pp. 46-50. The prefix *Ur-* is a neat German method of expressing 'original', 'earliest form of . . .'.

[3] D. Barthélemy, *Les Devanciers d'Aquila, VT* Supplement 1963. Summarized by K. G. O'Connell, 'Greek Versions (Minor)' in *IDB* Supplementary Volume, p. 378.

[4] 1QDn^b includes 3:23, 24, but the song of Azariah is not inserted.

[5] See Additional Note, p. 116. A list of Daniel fragments and other documents relating to Daniel is appended at the end of the Introduction, below, pp. 73f.

70

document; others are fragments of three other Aramaic documents, sometimes referred to as Pseudo-Daniel, which contain
the four-kingdom scheme leading history to its end, and the
idea of resurrection. It is not easy to assess the significance of
these texts, but at the very least they indicate that a wider
circle of Daniel literature was known than is contained in the
canonical book, and that the biblical writer was highly selec-
tive, including only what exactly suited his purpose.

Canon

The Septuagint represented a different tradition from the
Hebrew in the order in which it placed the books of the Old
Testament, and the Christian church followed the general
pattern of the Greek versions. That is why the book of Daniel
is to be found in our Bibles among the prophets, whereas in
the Hebrew canon it was among the 'Writings', together with
books like Job, Psalms and Proverbs, which were neither 'Law'
nor 'Prophets'. Unfortunately little is known about the process
by which books became accepted as authoritative. It seems
likely that the Writings contained the books which were last
in order of canonization, and Driver argued that if the book of
Daniel had been known when the collection of 'Prophets' was
made it would have ranked among them.[1] The reference in
Daniel 9:2 to 'the books', amongst which is included the book
of Jeremiah, bears witness to prophetic works already regarded
as authoritative; though Daniel was spoken of as 'the prophet'
both at Qumran and in the Gospels, his book was in a
different category and for this reason did not belong among
the 'Prophets'. The fact that the Hebrew canon placed
Daniel among the 'Writings' did not necessarily indicate late
date.[2]

Study of the Qumran texts has demonstrated clearly that
the book of Daniel was extremely influential among the
Qumran community: 'there are grounds for thinking that a

---

[1] *CB*, p. xlviii. We have pointed out (p. 13, above) that the book of
Daniel did not in any case fit into the category of the 'Prophets'.

[2] *Cf.* John Gray, *Joshua, Judges and Ruth* (*Century Bible*, New
Series, Nelson, 1967), speaking of the position of the book of Ruth
among the Writings: 'Its place in the MT in the Writings certainly
indicates its late acceptance as canonical Scripture, probably no more
than two centuries before Christ, but that does not necessarily mean
late composition.'

century before the beginning of the Christian era at least one group of Jews – the men of Qumran – gave serious thought to the study and interpretation of the book of Daniel.'[1] Whether or not it was regarded there as canonical remains a moot point. Arguments based on the size of columns and whether or not papyrus or skin was used for the scroll have proved inconclusive. When texts were published in which words from Daniel were quoted as 'written in the book of Daniel the prophet'[2] the answer seemed to F. F. Bruce to be clear : 'This expression (*cf.* Mt. 24 : 15) should put an end to doubts about the canonical status of Daniel in the Qumran community.'[3] Perhaps in the end it will be more general considerations which prove to be most telling : 'One cannot carefully study the Qumran literature without noting the pervasive influence of Daniel upon the thought and language of the sect. Whatever the theory of canonicity, for all practical purposes Daniel was authoritative.'[4]

According to a recent study[5] the canon of the Old Testament was closed in Maccabean times and not at the end of the first century AD, as has generally been supposed. As Wenham points out, if this view finds scholarly acceptance, 'it will become the more difficult to explain how Daniel was ever accepted into the canon if it was written in the second century BC. It is a surprise to find an allegedly pseudonymous work being accepted as holy Scripture at all; it would be startling if it were accepted as Scripture as soon as it appeared, when everybody would at least have realized its novelty.' If Daniel had been accepted into the canon already in Maccabean times it ceases to be remarkable that the Qumran community found it authoritative or that it was so evidently regarded as Scripture in the time of Jesus.

---

[1] F. F. Bruce, 'The Book of Daniel and the Qumran Community', in *Neotestamentica et Semitica,* Studies in Honour of Principal Matthew Black (Edinburgh, 1969), p. 222.
[2] J. M. Allegro and A. A. Anderson, *Discoveries in the Judean Desert,* 5 (OUP, 1968), pp. 53–57, included the Florilegium (4QFl). The quotations were Dn. 12:10, 11; 11:32.
[3] F. F. Bruce, *art. cit.,* p. 235 footnote.
[4] William Brownlee, *The Meaning of the Qumran Scrolls for the Bible,* p. 48.
[5] S. Z. Leiman, *The Canonization of the Hebrew Scriptures* (Hamden: Archon Books, 1976), referred to by G. J. Wenham, *Themelios,* 2.2, 1977, p. 51.

IX. SOME DATES OF IMPORTANCE FOR THE BOOK OF DANIEL

	612	Fall of Nineveh. Effective end of Assyria.
BABYLON	605	Battle of Carchemish. Nebuchadrezzar defeated Egypt and deported Daniel and his friends (Dn. 1:1). Accession of Nebuchadrezzar II (605–562).
	597	Jerusalem taken by Nebuchadrezzar; many Jews exiled; city subjugated but not yet destroyed.
	587	Fall of Jerusalem.
	562–560	Amel-Marduk (Evil-Merodach 2 Ki. 25:27–30), King of Babylon.
	560–556	Neriglissar, son-in-law of Nebuchadrezzar.
	556	Labashi-Marduk.
	556–539	Nabonidus (Belshazzar acting in Babylon).
	539	Fall of Babylon.
PERSIA	539–530	Cyrus: the Achaemenid dynasty.
	530–522	Cambyses.
	522–486	Darius I.
	486–465/4	Xerxes I (Ahasuerus).
	464–423	Artaxerxes.
	423–404	Darius II.
	404–359	Artaxerxes II.
	359/58–338/37	Artaxerxes III.
	338/37–336/35	Arses.
	336/35–331	Darius III.
GREECE	334–331	Conquests of Alexander of Macedon (331–323).
	323	Death of Alexander, empire divided into four areas, of which the Egyptian and the Syrian become predominant.

EGYPT (Ptolemies)		SYRIA (Seleucids)	
323–285	Ptolemy I.	312–281	Seleucus I.
285–245	Ptolemy II.	281–260	Antiochus I.
247–221	Ptolemy III.	260–246	Antiochus II.
221–203	Ptolemy IV.	245–223	Seleucus II and III.
203–181	Ptolemy V.	222–187	Antiochus III 'the Great'
198	Syria took over Palestine from Egypt	187–175	Seleucus IV
		175–164	Antiochus IV 'Epiphanes'
ROME the rising power		168	Antiochus expelled from Egypt by Roman consul (Dn. 11:30)
		167	(Dec. 25) erection of Greek altar in the Jerusalem temple.

X. FRAGMENTS OF DANIEL MANUSCRIPTS FROM QUMRAN

1QDn^a (=Dn. 1:10–17; 2:2–6).

1QDn^b (=Dn. 3:22–30).

Both published by D. Barthélemy, *Discoveries in the Judean Desert*, 1 (OUP, 1955), pp. 150–152. 1QDn^a preserves the transition from Hebrew to Aramaic in 2:4.

Texts from Cave 4 are not yet published, but the following information about them is available :

4QDnᵃ (=Dn. 2 : 19–35).

4QDnᵇ preserves the transition from Aramaic to Hebrew (Dn. 7 : 28 – 8 : 1). Classified as Herodian, *i.e.* 30 BC or later, by F. M. Cross.[1]

4QDnᶜ Unpublished. Dated by F. M. Cross 100–50 BC.[2]

4QDnᵈ Unpublished.

6QDnᵃ (=Dn. 8 : 16, 17, 20–21; 10 : 8–16; 11 : 33–36, 38). Published by M. Baillet, J. T. Milik and R. de Vaux, *Discoveries in the Judean Desert,* 3 (OUP, 1962), pp. 114–116. The texts are dated *c.* AD 50.

XI. OTHER DOCUMENTS RELATING TO DANIEL

4QOrNab Prayer of Nabonidus.[3]

4QpsDnᵃ, ᵇ, ᶜ Aramaic documents, badly mutilated, representing one or more Daniel cycles of stories. They bear little relation to the canonical book.

4QFl The Florilegium of Eschatological Texts. Published by J. M. Allegro and A. A. Anderson, *Discoveries in the Judean Desert,* 5 (OUP, 1968), pp. 53–57. Quotations from Dn. 12 : 10 and 11 : 32 are introduced as 'written in the book of the prophet Daniel'.

---

[1] 'The Development of Jewish Scripts' in G. E. Wright (Ed.), *The Bible and the Ancient Near East,* p. 149. The semicursive script of this MS is reproduced along with other examples from Qumran.

[2] *Ibid.,* p. 178. *Cf.* F. M. Cross, *The Ancient Library of Qumran,* p. 33, in which he states that this MS is 'no more than half a century younger than the autograph of Daniel'.

[3] See the Additional Note, below, p. 116.

ANALYSIS

PART I : STORIES

I. PROLOGUE : THE SETTING (1 : 1–21)

II. THE NATIONS AND THE MOST HIGH GOD (2 : 1 – 7 :28)
  A. Nebuchadrezzar dreams of four kingdoms and of God's kingdom (2 : 1–49)
    B. Nebuchadrezzar the tyrant sees God's servants rescued (3 : 1–30)
      C. Judgment on Nebuchadrezzar (4 : 1–37)
      C¹. Judgment on Belshazzar (5 : 1–31)
    B¹. Darius the Mede sees Daniel rescued (6 : 1–28)

PART II : VISIONS

  A¹. Daniel has a vision of four kingdoms and of God's kingdom (7 : 1–28)

III. THE SECOND AND THIRD KINGDOMS IDENTIFIED (8 : 1–27)

IV. DANIEL'S PRAYER AND THE VISION OF THE SEVENTY 'WEEKS' (9 : 1–27)

V. VISION OF THE HEAVENLY MESSENGER AND HIS FINAL REVELATION (10 : 1 – 12 : 13)

COMMENTARY

PART I: STORIES

I. PROLOGUE: THE SETTING (1:1 – 21)

a. Historical introduction (1:1, 2)

The book opens with two verses which connect with world history. With characteristic brevity reference is made to the first ominous encounter between Nebuchadrezzar and the Davidic king of Jerusalem. All that the prophets had spoken indicated that this would not be the last of such encounters. Though on this occasion Jerusalem and its king had to give in to the superior might of the Babylonians, worse was to come in 597, when Jehoiachin surrendered and was deported, together with the cream of the population, and in 587, when the final destruction and deportation occurred (2 Ki. 24 : 10 – 25 : 21). When the evidence from Daniel is added to that of the historical books it becomes clear that the fall of Jerusalem was brought about in three stages, in 605, 597 and 587 BC, of which only the first is mentioned in Daniel, and only the second and third feature in the history.

The doubts to which this double tradition has given rise are referred to in the Introduction.[1] Though it has been usual to suspect the historicity of the Daniel information, there is no reason to do so in the light of the *Chronicles of Chaldean Kings* and of the so-called 'post dating' method of reckoning the years of a reign, current in Babylon at the time. The biblical editors did not attempt to synchronize dates, and the fact that the Babylonian way of reckoning remains in the text indicates that an ancient substratum underlies the chapter.

1. *Jehoiakim* ascended to the throne in Judea after the defeat and death of Josiah at Megiddo in 609 BC. According to Palestinian and Egyptian reckoning 605 would be the fourth year of the king (Je. 25 : 1, 9; 46 : 2), whereas in the Babylonian system it would be the *third year*. (See Introduction, p. 20.) Only here is it stated that Nebuchadrezzar

[1] See above, p. 19.

besieged Jerusalem (in 605 BC), and therefore the text has come under suspicion of inaccuracy, but in the absence of evidence either way one cannot be dogmatic. All that the text requires is that Nebuchadrezzar threatened Jerusalem, which, being a vassal of Egypt, came under the jurisdiction of Babylon when the Egyptian hold over Syro-Palestine was broken after the battle of Carchemish (2 Ki. 24:1; 2 Ch. 36:6). The spelling Nebuchad*r*ezzar, found in Ezekiel and used interchangeably with *n* in Jeremiah, takes account of the Babylonian original *Nabû-kudurri-uṣur*. The Hebrew spelling with *n* is followed by the Greek *Nabochodonosor*.[1]

2. Neither in this verse nor in 2 Chronicles 36:6 is it made absolutely clear that Jehoiakim was taken to Babylon. According to 2 Kings 24:6 he died in Judah, and the writer, implying that hostages as well as plunder would be taken, deals first with the Temple treasure because he is going to deal at greater length with the people, who are to be the chief characters in his book. From the outset the sovereignty of the Lord in history is asserted: *the Lord* (*'ᵃḏōnāy*) *gave* Judah's king into enemy hands. This name for God, a 'plural of majesty', designates Him the exalted one, responsible for all that happens to His people, and to be trusted even in disaster (Is. 43:2). It is not a long step from this conviction to Paul's 'prisoner for the Lord' (Eph. 4:1). *The land of Shinar* is a deliberate archaism, 'corrected' in the Greek to 'Babylon'. Shinar, site of the tower of Babel (Gn. 11:1–9; *cf.* 10:10), was synonymous with opposition to God; it was the place where wickedness was at home (Zc. 5:11) and uprightness could expect opposition. The phrase *to the house of his god* or *gods* (*'ᵉlōhîm*) is omitted in most of the Greek versions and may not have been in the original Hebrew. It looks like a case of dittography (repetition due to a copyist's slip), and the words are omitted from most modern versions, including JB, NEB. The effect of the repetition in RSV is to lay stress on the incongruity of the situation. Vessels dedicated to the true God were out of place in an idol shrine and it was only to be expected that in the providence of God they would in due course be restored, so vindicating

---

[1] P.-R. Berger demonstrates that writing with *n* is not improper for Hebrew (*Zeitschrift für Assyriologie*, 64, 1975, pp. 227–230). Contrast Montgomery (*ICC*, p. 118), who regards the spelling with *r* as correct, and Porteous (p. 26), who calls the spelling with *n* inaccurate and (p. 135) incorrect.

His authority.[1] Thus one theme of the book emerges. Mention of the Temple vessels also prepares the reader for Belshazzar's act of profanity in chapter 5.

b. The captives introduced (1:3–7)

The writer now explains how a few young men from the court in Jerusalem came to be in Babylon before the first deportation in 597 BC. A few choice hostages from the Judean court would weaken resources there, prove useful to the conqueror and reinforce Judah's vassal status.

3. The name *Ashpenaz* has not been satisfactorily explained. Perhaps it is an abbreviated or corrupted form of a Babylonian name, as Driver and others have suggested.[2] *Chief eunuch* translates *Rab-saris*, an Akkadian loan-word which RSV retains as a proper noun in 2 Kings 18:17 and Jeremiah 39:3, 13. This court official had responsibility for the education of the royal princes and for the well-being of the harem, but this did not exempt him from attending the king on campaigns. On this occasion he was expected to be able to spot future diplomats from among the royalty and *nobility (part^{e}mîm,* a Persian loan-word found also in Est. 1:3; 6:9).

4. Good looks, physical perfection and high intelligence were all to be combined in the men chosen for Nebuchadrezzar's court. It was assumed that they would already have had diplomatic training and have been proved to be capable of benefiting from the specialized education designed for them by the Babylonian king. In Hebrew usage the wisdom terms of this verse had ethical and religious overtones, for without wholehearted commitment to the Lord and obedience to His will there could be no wisdom (Jb. 28:28). *The letters and language of the Chaldeans.* Kaldu is referred to by Assyrian kings as the country inhabited by the Kaldai, independent tribes who lived by farming and fishing in the swampy land to the north of the Persian Gulf. They were Semitic people who migrated from the Syrian desert and 'in due course they mingled with the old-established city-dwelling Babylonians, and the late Babylonian language, used before Aramaic, is largely characterized by Aramaic syntax with Babylonian

[1] P. R. Ackroyd, 'The Temple Vessels—A Continuity Theme', in *Studies in the Religion of Ancient Israel* (Leiden, 1972), pp. 166–181. On Daniel, pp. 180, 181.
[2] *CB*, p. 4.

words'.[1] These Chaldeans championed national independence and finally overthrew Assyrian power when Nabopolassar, helped by the Medes, conquered Babylon in 612 BC. His son, Nebuchadrezzar II, belonged therefore to the Chaldean dynasty, and Chaldean was an appropriate term for the writer to use of this period when referring to the rulers of Babylon (*cf.* 5:30). It was because the Chaldeans were experts in magic lore that the term 'Chaldean' occurs alongside magicians, enchanters and sorcerers in Daniel 2:2.[2] This was the art for which they became famous and to which they gave their name. The accumulated literature included omens, magic incantations, prayers and hymns, myths and legends, scientific formulae for skills such as glass-making, mathematics and astrology.

To begin to study Babylonian literature was to enter a completely alien thought-world. 'According to the Sumerians and Babylonians two classes of persons inhabited the universe : the human race and the gods. Pre-eminence belonged to the gods, though they were not all equal. At the lower end of the divine scale came a host of minor deities and demons, while a trinity of great gods, Anu, Enlil, and Ea, stood at their head. A modern scholar will observe that many of these gods are personifications of parts or aspects of nature. The sun and moon gods are obvious examples.'[3] The writer of Daniel implies no objection to the study of a polytheistic literature in which magic, sorcery, charms and astrology played a prominent part, though these had long been banned in Israel (Dt. 18:10–12; *cf.* 1 Sa. 28:3ff.). These young men from Jerusalem's court needed to be secure in their knowledge of Yahweh to be able to study this literature objectively without allowing it to undermine their faith. Evidently the work of Jeremiah, Zephaniah and Habakkuk had not been in vain. In order to witness to their God in the Babylonian court they had to understand the cultural presuppositions of those around them, just as the Christian today must work hard at the reli-

---

[1] W. G. Lambert, 'The Babylonians and Chaldeans', *POTT*, p. 181.
[2] *Ibid.*, pp. 183, 184, 194. R. K. Harrison (*IOT*, p. 1113) draws attention to the double meaning of the word 'Chaldean' in Herodotus (*c.* 450 BC). For more detail see A. R. Millard, 'Daniel 1–6 and History', *EQ*, XLIX, 2, 1977, pp. 69–71.
[3] W. G. Lambert, *Babylonian Wisdom Literature* (Oxford, 1960), pp. 3, 4.

gions and cultures amongst which he lives, if different thought-worlds are ever to meet. Incidentally such openness to another culture was not a feature of orthodox Jewish faith at the Maccabean period. On the contrary, everything Greek was studiously avoided.

5. It was taken for granted that the monarch was responsible for the meals of his household (1 Ki. 4:7), but it was a special honour to be served the expensive menu of food and wine prepared for the king. The unusual term translated *rich food* (Heb. *paṭ baḡ*; *cf.* Gk. *potibazis*; 'dainties', RV mg.) is a Persian technical term derived from Old Persian and meaning honorific gifts from the royal table. It occurs in the Bible only here and in 11:26. The re-education of the hostages, no doubt in company with other representatives of newly conquered lands, was to equip them to *stand before the king,* a technical term for royal service (1 Ki. 10:8; the verb is translated 'serve' in verse 4. *Cf.* verse 19).

6, 7. The renaming of the foreigners was a matter of convenience rather than of ideology, and biblical characters from Joseph onwards (Gn. 41:45) accepted new names without fuss. All the same it is true that they forfeited names compounded with 'El' or 'Yah', and acquired Babylonian names some of which incorporated references to the deities of that land. Daniel's name *Belteshazzar* had until recently been explained as deriving from *Balâṭsu-uṣur,* 'May (a god) protect his life', though in 4:8 the author seemed to have shown himself to be ignorant of Babylonian names by implying that *Bel* was the name of Nebuchadrezzar's god. Recently an Assyriologist has suggested the alternative derivation *Bēlet-šar-uṣur,* 'lady, protect the king', 'Bēlet being a title for the wife of Marduk or Bēl, the patron of Babylon'.[1] According to this derivation there would be no discrepancy in 4:8. '*Shadrak* represents *šāduräku,* "I am very fearful (of God)"; *Meshach mēšāku* "I am of little account"; *Abed-nego* apparently an Aramaic form meaning "servant of the shining one", possibly involving word-play on an Akkadian name including the god Nabû.'

Thus in a skilful way the writer introduces those who are to feature in his book, and in particular *Daniel.* A king of this

---

[1] A. R. Millard, 'Daniel 1–6 and History', *EQ,* XLIX, 2, 1977, p. 72. He accepts this and the other three suggestions made by P.-R. Berger, *Zeitschrift für Assyriologie,* 64, 1975, pp. 224–234.

name appears in the Ugaritic texts of *c.* 1400 BC[1] and Ezekiel refers to a hero of patriarchal times, comparable to Noah and Job (Ezk. 14:14, 20; 28:3). Indeed it has been suggested that these three Daniels may all reflect one single figure, around whom different traditions had gathered. There are, however, good reasons for rejecting this viewpoint. For one thing the Ugaritic is spelt *dan'el* and Ezekiel's *dāni'ēl* as against *dāniyyē'l* in our text, but in the light of other variant spellings in Hebrew too much weight should not be put on this. More conclusive is the evident intention of the author to portray Daniel as a historical person who lived in the period of the Exile. Moreover the name was borne by other historical characters both before and after the Exile (1 Ch. 3:1; Ezr. 8:2; Ne. 10:6). There is, therefore, no reason to doubt his existence. Furthermore, it would have been no help to popularizing or authenticating the book if the author deliberately adopted the name Daniel, after the manner of later writers of apocalyptic, who used names such as Enoch, Moses and Solomon to commend their works. As Porteous points out, he was neither a patriarch nor a prophet, nor was he well known in Old Testament history. 'Daniel in fact seems to have acquired whatever authority he has from the book which bears his name.'[2]

c. To conform or not to conform? (1:8–21)

These godly men now have to decide how they will adjust to living in an environment unsympathetic to their religious convictions. Like everyone caught in cross-cultural change they had to think through the principles involved in their actions, and begin as they meant to go on.

8. Daniel accepts re-education and a new name, but makes his protest on the second of the three issues, that of food supplied from the royal table, though it is not immediately apparent why this should have defiled them. To say that the food had been offered to idols and was therefore to be shunned is to import a New Testament controversy into an Old Testament setting where the subject is not mentioned. True, the Babylonians did offer blood sacrifices to their gods, but they also offered every other kind of food and on this ground

---

[1] *DOTT*, pp. 124–128; *ANET*, pp. 149ff.
[2] Porteous, p. 18.

nothing could have been guaranteed to be ritually clean. Another suggested explanation is that in Babylon no distinction was made between clean and unclean animals, and therefore to eat the king's meat would have been to break the Levitical food laws (Lv. 3:17; 11:1–47). There was, for instance, no taboo on the pig, and pork was highly prized. Horse was also eaten freely.[1] Moreover the Law insisted that the blood was to be drained from the meat and was on no account to be eaten (Lv. 17:10–14). On both these counts it is possible to explain the scruples over meat dishes, but the text includes wine, against which there was no prohibition, except in the case of Rechabites and Nazirites, and there is no indication that Daniel and his friends were in either of those categories. Thus the Levitical food laws do not satisfactorily explain Daniel's resolve.

All food in Babylon or Assyria was ritually unclean (Ezk. 4:13; Ho. 9:3, 4) and from that there was no escape. The book itself provides the needed clue in 11:26, where the rare word *paṭ baḡ* recurs : 'Even those who eat his *rich food* shall be his undoing.' By eastern standards to share a meal was to commit oneself to friendship; it was of covenant significance (Gn. 31:54; Ex. 24:11; Ne. 8:9–12; *cf.* Mt. 26:26–28). Those who had thus committed themselves to allegiance accepted an obligation of loyalty to the king. It would seem that Daniel rejected this symbol of dependence on the king because he wished to be free to fulfil his primary obligations to the God he served. The defilement he feared was not so much a ritual as a moral defilement, arising from the subtle flattery of gifts and favours which entailed hidden implications of loyal support, however dubious the king's future policies might prove to be.

9. The reluctance of the sympathetic chief of the eunuchs to comply with the request is all the more understandable if Daniel's motive was to remain free from commitment to the will of the king. Nebuchadrezzar would certainly have interpreted the motive as treasonable and have held Ashpenaz guilty of complicity. But *God gave Daniel favour and compassion.* The active intervention of the Lord on behalf of His servants was in accord with Scripture (1 Ki. 8:50; Ps. 106:46) and

---

[1]H. W. F. Saggs, *The Greatness that was Babylon* (Sidgwick and Jackson, 1962), p. 176.

was proved in experience by the man of faith (*cf.* verses 2 and 17).

10. The assumption that rich food ensures the best of health went unquestioned in the mind of the eunuch, who was not going to risk his life by agreeing to any alteration of the king's orders. It is evident from the context that these foreign captives had their own quarters.

11–14. It was a lesser official who co-operated with them, *the steward* (Heb. *melṣar,* a word probably derived from Akkadian *maṣṣaru* and occurring only here in the Bible). With the connivance of the chief eunuch he evidently substituted his own meals for the royal delicacies and benefited from the exchange, a point which ensured the secret would be kept.

15, 16. The result of the ten-day experiment justified Daniel's confidence that their health would not suffer. Even a small act of self-discipline, taken out of loyalty to principle, sets God's servants in the line of His approval and blessing. In this way actions attest faith, and character is strengthened to face more difficult situations in the future.

17. The unseen hand of God directs the whole course of events (verses 2, 9) and gives not only physical health but also intellectual vigour to His faithful servants. Daniel's particular gift of understanding visions and dreams was appropriate to his need in a land where such was expected of wise men, and the God who was the source of all knowledge would also give discernment to distinguish the true from the false. Thus there was no need to fear that study of Babylonian or any other culture would result in conversion to an alien religion.

But more was at stake than their personal reputation or even their personal faith. As representatives of the only God they needed to prove in Babylon's highly competitive setting that the fear of the Lord is the beginning of wisdom. High intelligence and hard work alone did not account for their success, but their wisdom was God's gift (*cf.* Col. 1:9; 2:9, 10). The specific gift entrusted to Daniel was to make him not only a trusted adviser to Nebuchadrezzar but also a channel of revelation, as the next chapter begins to prove.

18–20. There is an element of hyperbole in Nebuchadrezzar's assessment of the abilities of the four men, but *ten times* is a common idiom (Gn. 31:41; Nu. 14:22; Ne. 4:12; and *cf.* 'seven times', Dn. 3:19). *Therefore they stood before* *the king.* Delighted with their performance, Nebuchadrezzar had them stand in his presence to serve him. Such an honour would not endear them to those whom they surpassed. *Magicians* (Heb. *ḥarṭummîm*) is used of the soothsayer priests of Egypt (*e.g.* Gn. 41 :8; Ex. 7 :11) and the word may be derived from an Egyptian original.[1] *Enchanters* (*'aššāp̄îm*) occurs only in Daniel; it comes from an Akkadian root and passed into Syriac, where it means 'snake charmer'.[2]

21. *And Daniel continued until the first year of King Cyrus,* that is, from 605 to 539. From the vantage-point of the writer, after the return from exile had taken place, it was possible to see that God had indeed purposed to restore His people to their land in accordance with Deuteronomy 30 :3–5 and Jeremiah's pronouncement of a seventy-year exile (Je. 25 :12). As at that time of severe political and cultural upheaval, so now : the Lord is in control and will in due course vindicate those who are loyal to Him because He must vindicate His own name.

II. THE NATIONS AND THE MOST HIGH GOD (2:1 – 7:28)

A. Nebuchadrezzar dreams of four kingdoms and of God's kingdom (2:1–49)

a. The forgotten dream (2:1–11)
In this chapter Nebuchadrezzar is no longer the one bestowing favours. Instead he appears as a frustrated human being, tantalized by his own forgetfulness, because he is convinced that the dream he can no longer remember is a significant one. The king's personal crisis gives Daniel the opportunity of ministry to him.

1. Nebuchadrezzar's *second year* would be that which began in March/April 603 BC. Hebrew usage, which reckoned fractions of a year as a full year, would have referred to this as the king's third year, and 'three years' (1 :5) would have been said to have been completed (*cf.* Mt. 12 :40). The biblical writers, however, rarely attempt to synchronize their refer-

---

[1] KB, p. 333.
[2] KB (p. 95) gives the meaning 'conjuror'.

ences to time.[1] What was troubling the king to cause him bad dreams and sleeplessness? According to an Akkadian saying, '[Wo]e and anxiety create (only bad) dreams'[2] (*cf.* Ec. 5:3). Each year in the early part of his reign Nebuchadrezzar's expeditionary force went to the extremities of the empire to ensure that subjugated lands paid their taxes. In 604 Ashkelon had put up stiff resistance and had had to be reduced to rubble; in 603 an extra large army, siege towers and heavy equipment are mentioned, and Babylonian troops were in the field for several months.[3] Such a show of prestige hid a fear of inadequacy : *his spirit was troubled.*

2, 3. The king would work out his anxiety on those specialists in psychic phenomena whom he housed and fed for just such an emergency as this. *Magicians . . . enchanters* : see the note on 1:20. *Sorcerers* (Heb. *mᵉkaššᵉp̂îm*; *cf.* Ex. 7:11; 22:18) were in certain periods resident in Israel (2 Ch. 33:6; Mal. 3:5), though their presence was condemned (Ex. 22:18; Dt. 18:10). This word comes only here in the lists of diviners in Daniel 1–5. 'The fourfold listing indicates the levy of the whole fraternity on this occasion.'[4] *Chaldeans* (*cf.* the note on 1:4) here denotes experts in magic lore, a non-Babylonian use

---

[1] Porteous sees a discrepancy between 1:5, 18 and 2:1 but says it 'need not be taken seriously, since the dates in this book do not imply a genuine historical interest' (p. 39). Another view is that, while chapter 2 is ancient, chapter 1 was written later as an introduction, and the redactor overlooked the contradiction. P. R. Davies (*JTS*, XXVII, 1976, p. 394) argues that the story of chapter 2 reached the redactor in an already literary form, but without verses 13–23, and thinks it likely that the date applied to a group of stories. The redactor would be responsible for the insertion of verses 13–23, which bring the story into accord with chapter 1, but not without some apparent inconsistencies. Westerners want to see all loose ends tied up, but this desire is probably misplaced in dealing with literature from the Ancient Near East.

[2] A. L. Oppenheim, 'The Interpretation of Dreams in the Ancient Near East', *Transactions of the American Philosophical Society,* Vol. 46, Part 3, 1956, p. 227.

[3] D. J. Wiseman, *Chronicles of Chaldean Kings (626–556 BC),* pp. 28, 29. A. K. Grayson, *Assyrian and Babylonian Chronicles,* pp. 100, 101. Wiseman informs me that in his forthcoming review of Grayson's *Chronicles* (to appear in *Bibliotheca Orientalis,* 1978) he says he thinks that there may be indications in the broken Babylonian Chronicle for 602 BC that it was in that year, rather than 605 BC, that prisoners (including perhaps Daniel and his companions) were taken to Babylon.

[4] *ICC,* p. 143.

of the term. Herodotus (*c.* 450 BC) used the word in this sense. 'The new slant to the word is easily explained as arising after the intrusion of the new Persian empire and religion, when "Chaldean" became a religious designation just as "Jew" became.'[1] These experts in dreams worked on the principle that dreams and their sequel followed an empirical law which, given sufficient data, could be established. The dream manuals, of which several examples have come to light,[2] consist accordingly of historical dreams and the events that followed them, arranged systematically for easy reference. Since these books had to try to cover every possible eventuality they became inordinately long; only the expert could find his way through them, and even he had to know the dream to begin with before he could search for the nearest possible parallel. The unreasonable demands of the king and the protests of the interpreters in verses 3–11 are in keeping with his character and the known facts concerning dream books.

4. With the reply of the 'Chaldeans' there is a language change in this verse from Hebrew to Aramaic, and the text continues in Aramaic as far as the end of chapter 7. Whereas AV, RV retain the indication of this change in the text, RSV, on the assumption that this was originally a marginal reference, relegates it again to the margin. This is the longest passage using Aramaic in the Old Testament, the others being Ezra 4:8 – 6:18; 7:12–26, and the gloss in Jeremiah 10:11.[3] *O king, live for ever!* Acclamations such as this, attributing life to the king, go back to time immemorial and reflect the association of the king both with the god and with the community. Opinions differ as to the ideology of the king in Israel, but David, for example, was so addressed by Bathsheba (1 Ki. 1:31; *cf.* verse 25), apparently according to court etiquette in Jerusalem.

5. There is every likelihood that Nebuchadrezzar had forgotten the details of the dreams that had been haunting him. 'Consciousness naturally resists anything unconscious and unknown',[4] but to be unable to recall the dream only added to his anxiety and therefore to his irritability. According to

---

[1] *ICC,* p. 73 footnote. *Cf.* R. D. Wilson, *The Book of Daniel,* Vol. 1, chapter 17, for evidence of uses of the term by the Greeks.

[2] A. L. Oppenheim, *op. cit.,* pp. 203ff.

[3] On the Aramaic of Daniel see Introduction, above, pp. 31–35.

[4] C. G. Jung (ed.), *Man and his Symbols* (Aldus Books, 1964), p. 31.

eastern superstition it was ominous not to be able to remember a dream : 'If a man cannot remember the dream he saw (it means) : his (personal) god is angry with him.'[1] Until the dream was both recalled and interpreted it hung over him as an evil dream, bothering and defiling him. *The word from me is sure* is the correct understanding of a Persian word misunderstood in AV, RV : 'the thing is gone from me,' that is, 'I have forgotten it.' The king is emphatically laying down the law. If these so-called specialists cannot solve his problem, there are plenty of better men where they came from, and he will have them mutilated and their homes ruined. There is evidence that such threats were not uncommonly carried out.[2]

6. The king also wanted to encourage initiative by offering incentives, hence his promised *gifts, rewards and great honour.* The word translated *rewards,* found in a similar context in 5 : 17, is rare and is probably a loan-word from Akkadian.[3]

8, 9. The king suspects that the interpreters of dreams are impostors who have secretly agreed to fob him off with mere words *till the times change,* until the crisis has passed and the king has forgotten the incident. If they can relate the dream this will authenticate their claim to be able to interpret it.

10, 11. Nebuchadrezzar is being entirely unreasonable. He may be the great and powerful monarch, but there are limits to what even he can demand. He had better address himself to *the gods* (or maybe God[4]), but they *dwell remote from mortal men* (NEB) and therefore do not disclose their secrets to mere human beings.

b. Daniel's response (2:12–24)

12. Nebuchadrezzar makes no attempt to disguise his rage. He will carry out his threats without delay and so teach his servants to respect his commands.

13–16. Why Daniel and his friends came to be ignorant of the decree, and how Daniel was able to have an audience with Nebuchadrezzar when he was under the threat of death, are

---

[1] Old Babylonian Omen Text (VAT 7525) of Berlin Museum (1:31–32). Quoted by A. L. Oppenheim, *op. cit.,* p. 237.

[2] See, for instance, *ICC,* p. 146, for several examples.

[3] KB, p. 1097. Contrast the older view that it was Persian; *cf. CB,* p. 21.

[4] Montgomery (*ICC,* p. 153) gives evidence for the possibility of a singular meaning in Aramaic outside the Old Testament and therefore in this context.

details which the story-teller's artistry omits. The name *Arioch* has given rise to scholarly debate as to its suitability in a Neo-Babylonian setting (*cf* Gn. 14 : 1, 9; Judith 1 : 6).[1]

Daniel's question is concerned with the hastiness rather than the severity[2] of the decree : *why has his majesty issued such a peremptory decree?* (NEB). He asks for time and promises he will give the interpretation.[3] The ability to keep calm under severe shock and pressure, to think quickly and exercise faith in a moment of crisis, these are aspects of *prudence and discretion* seen in Daniel here (14; *cf.* Phil. 4 : 7).

17, 18. In his dependence on God's mercy Daniel seeks out his like-minded companions to join him in prayer for a revelation of the contents of the dream, and at the end of his thanksgiving he acknowledges their help (23; *cf.* 2 Cor. 1 : 11). It is fitting that their Hebrew names should be used in this context of faith and prayer. The word for *mystery* (*rāz*)[4] is one of the nineteen or so words from Persian in the Aramaic of Daniel. In the context, what is needed is an answer to the 'problem', and this would appear to be the meaning here. There would have been no mystery apart from the fact that Nebuchadrezzar had forgotten his dream, and that Daniel had taken it upon himself to relate and interpret it. The name *God of heaven* is used frequently in texts of the post-exilic period (Ezr. 1 : 2; 6 : 10; 7 : 12, 21; Ne. 1 : 5; 2 : 4) but rarely in the pre-exilic period, when its likeness to *Ba'al Šamēn* (Phoenician 'Lord of heaven') made it unsuitable in Israel and Judah. There were many other names meaningful within Israel, but this was a fitting title for the true God in a country where

---

[1] Doubts raised by Sayce (*HDB*) were referred to by Driver (*CB*, p. 22); D. J. Wiseman, in a lecture 'The Period of the Exile', has suggested Ari-Ukki as a Babylonian form of name. On the accuracy with which Assyrian names were preserved in biblical Hebrew, see A. R. Millard, *JSS*, 21, 1976, pp. 1-4.

[2] *ICC*, p. 156.

[3] *Cf.* R. H. Charles, *A Critical and Exegetical Commentary on the Book of Daniel* (OUP, 1929), p. 35. Charles gives evidence for his view that the last clause of the verse is not a final clause (as in RSV) but represents the promise of Daniel, 'I will (it is my task to) show the king . . .', put into indirect speech.

[4] LXX and Theodotion translated *rāz* by *mystērion*, hence 'mystery' in English, though 'solution' would probably be more appropriate. At Qumran only the initiated understood a mystery (*rāz*) and could give its interpretation (*pᵉšar*). It is doubtful whether the words had this technical sense in Daniel.

astral worship was practised (*cf.* the insistence in Isaiah 40 – 55 that Yahweh is Creator of the earth and the heavens). The difficulty of knowing how to refer to the true God in a culture which has not hitherto acknowledged Him is still experienced by missionaries and Bible translators (*cf.* the name 'the living God', the source and sustainer of life, in 6 : 20).

19. Matters that were hidden from Babylon's wise men were *revealed to Daniel*. Where the former had been impotent (10), the God of heaven proved Himself able to reveal to His servants what they needed to know. *In a vision of the night* Daniel 'saw' what the king had seen in his dream and in addition realized what it meant. From the use of 'vision of the night' in Job 4 : 13 and 33 : 15 it seems that the recipient of the vision was in a deep sleep, but he was not said to be dreaming, perhaps because the imagery was arising not out of his own mind, but by God's direct intervention.

20–23. Relief found expression in a spontaneous hymn of thanksgiving to the only God who could so answer prayer, but there was also awe because that same God, unseen and infinitely great, had been directly in touch with him personally. This last thought lies behind the opening line of his hymn : *the name of God* is disclosed only by God Himself (*cf.* Ex. 6 : 3; Jdg. 13 : 17, 18) and represents what may be known of Him. Daniel has just seen something of His *wisdom* and *might* and has received from God a share of the divine attributes (23). God's might, explicitly to control the natural order and to govern human politics, anticipates the meaning of the dream, which the author has not yet disclosed. God's wisdom, likewise, is all-embracing (22), unlimited; but the emphasis throughout is on the fact that God makes His wisdom available : *he gives wisdom . . . and knowledge . . . ; he reveals . . . ; thou hast given . . . thou hast now made known to me . . . thou hast made known to us,* who together prayed for knowledge of the king's dream. *Wisdom to the wise* (21) means, not that only the wise receive the gift of extra wisdom, but that wherever there is wisdom it has been received as a gift from the only God who is its source. Accordingly there is emphasis in this psalm on the Giver. In lines 3–5 *he* is emphatic, and similarly *to thee* in line 6. This miraculous answer to prayer reminds Daniel of all he has heard of God's wonderful deeds in the past, and so he senses his continuity with those who have gone before him and praises the *God of my fathers* (23).

This little psalm is a model of thanksgiving. No word is merely repetitive; each of the first nine lines extolling God's greatness makes its contribution to the paean of praise, yet none is unrelated to Daniel's experience. The last four lines express his own amazement at the privilege of a share in God's *wisdom and strength* (better, 'might', as in verse 20; the same words are repeated in the Aramaic, so linking the end of the psalm with the beginning). The symmetry and beauty of the poetry make their own contribution to the praise of God.

24. It now remains to pass on to Arioch the good news that the executions will not need to take place, because Daniel can disclose and interpret the king's dream.

c. The dream and its meaning (2:25-45)

25. Arioch plays down Daniel's credentials and claims credit for himself in finding someone to meet the king's request.

26. The king's question implies incredulity, '*Are* you able . . . ?' Mention of the name *Belteshazzar* links this chapter with chapter 1:6, 7.

27, 28. Daniel's first concern is to disclaim any special power or qualification; *but there is a God in heaven* who is not only sufficiently great, but has also proved willing to make known the dream (*cf.* verse 11). Unlike Arioch, Daniel makes no mention of himself. God has made known the dream *to King Nebuchadnezzar*, and *what will be in the latter days*, or *at the end of this age* (NEB). The meaning of this phrase in the prophets is often quite general and refers not strictly to the end of the world, but rather to what will happen 'one day', a goal for history some time 'in the future' (*cf.* 10:14). Certainly it will not have meant more than that to Nebuchadrezzar,[1] and the parallel expressions in verse 29 bear this out.

29, 30. Before going to sleep the king had been thinking about the future and his dream had reflected his own thoughts, but God had also been speaking to the king through a dream which to some extent had a natural explanation.[2] It does not follow that, because some human explanation can be given,

[1] *Cf.* A. K. Grayson, *Babylonian Historical-Literary Texts*, p. 21, footnote: 'It must be emphasized that there is no suggestion in any Akkadian prophecy of a climactic end to world history.'
[2] See Additional Note, below, p. 96.

God has not been directly at work. Only now does Daniel mention himself, and then it is only to lay stress on the fact that what he is about to say was *revealed* to him expressly for the benefit of the king.

31–35. Nebuchadrezzar had dreamt he saw a huge statue standing before him. Aramaic *ṣᵉlem* means statue. and not idol. It was in human form, made of shining metal and *frightening,* with the numinous kind of terror conveyed in dreams. From its head of gold to its fragile feet of glazed china mixed with iron it represented a top-heavy figure, liable to topple to its ruin. To aid the process a stone, moved by a superhuman power, struck the statue at its feet, breaking first them and later every part of the statue into such small particles that the wind carried them away until nothing remained. The stone, however, grew into a mountain that filled the earth.

There can be little doubt that this dream reflected the fears of the Babylonian king, who had so recently come to the throne. 'People who have unrealistic ideas or too high an opinion of themselves, or who make grandiose plans out of proportion to their real capacities, have dreams of flying or falling. The dream compensates for the deficiencies of their personalities, and at the same time it warns them of the dangers in their present course.'[1] In his dream the statue stood for the king, with his huge empire that he could scarcely hold, and symbolized his inadequacy in the face of threats from breakaway factions. He feared he had over-reached himself and would fall. The stone which grew to fill the earth would have been a rival kingdom which supplanted his.[2]

36–38. In his interpretation Daniel was able to reassure Nebuchadrezzar. He was careful to address the king by his exalted titles, while at the same time declaring that he owed all his territory and authority over man and beast to the God

[1] C. G. Jung, *Man and his Symbols,* p. 50.
[2] P. R. Davies (*JTS*, XXVII, 1976, pp. 339, 340) argues that chapter 2 was originally an eschatological dream, and that Amēl-Marduk, Neriglissar and Nabonidus, the successors of Nebuchadrezzar, were represented by the silver, bronze and iron/clay. The fall of the statue is the fall of the dynasty, to be replaced in this Jewish story by a Jewish kingdom. 'If this interpretation is correct, we should ascribe the origin of the story of Dan. ii to the end of the exilic period, or possibly just after it.' Davies would attribute the interpretation of Daniel 2 to the Maccabean redactor.

of heaven who had given him these honours, and made him that *head of gold*. There is an element of flattery here, not only in the identification of Nebuchadrezzar with the most precious of the metals, but also in the statement that he rules over the whole inhabited world. Nevertheless his authority was a real authority, feared by all. The *sons of men* (*bᵉnê 'ᵃnāšā'*; cf. 7:13, where the singular 'son of man' raises many problems) are all human beings in general. His dominion includes the animal world (cf. Je. 27:6), and even 'the birds of the air' (Gn. 1:28).

39. Only after the time of Nebuchadrezzar will deterioration set in, when the gold will be replaced by silver and the silver by bronze,[1] but even so they will be world empires, not, in Daniel's explanation, successors to the Babylonian throne. Great as he is, Nebuchadrezzar is finite and will not live for ever.

40-43. Whereas the fourth kingdom of iron has greater strength than any previous kingdom, and *shatters* and *crushes* everything in its power, it proves to be a mixture and not solid metal. It has therefore an instrinsic weakness, for potter's clay and iron do not bond together. Unity is impossible and the kingdom is vulnerable because it is seeking to unite elements which will not coalesce. The *firmness* of this kingdom, represented by the iron, is emphasized, suggesting an enforced policy. This may be connected with the policy mentioned in verse 43, *they will mix with one another in marriage*; the last two words are literally 'by the seed of men' (*bizra' 'ᵃnāšā'*), an unusual expression, reminiscent of the prohibition to mix seed in the field (Lv. 19:19). Men devise schemes, but they are unsuccessful.

44, 45. By contrast the God of heaven will work out His sure purpose to set up a lasting kingdom *in the days of those kings*; the expression is vague, for no kings have been mentioned since Nebuchadrezzar, but it is natural to assume that the writer intends the kings of the last-mentioned kingdom. Whereas the world-kingdoms had been taken over by successive conquerors, none will take this kingdom by storm. The fact is rather that it will bring *all these kingdoms* to an end, but will itself endure for ever. Though the kingdoms have

---

[1] On the significance of these metals see *DNTT*, 2, 'Gold, silver, bronze, iron'. See also Introduction, above, section VII, Interpretation, and Commentary, below, pp. 161f.

appeared to be consecutive, there is a suggestion here that they could be contemporary, but this is part of the symbolism of the statue, which in the nature of the case represents all the kingdoms as falling at the same time. Some commentators have thought that the division of the legs and toes in the last kingdom should be interpreted, but again these are part of the symbolism of a human figure, which would not be complete without them. The writer does not mention the number ten, nor seem to attach any special importance to it, any more than he mentions the division of the body into two legs. Last to be mentioned is the stone, *cut . . . by no human hand* but divinely prepared and propelled to accomplish the divine plan. This development above all events in history was beyond human knowledge, but Nebuchadrezzar had been favoured by *a great God*, who had shown the future to him. Despite AV, RV, '*the* great God', there is no definite article in the Aramaic. Daniel lays stress on the certainty of the dream and its interpretation because he wants the king to face up to its immediate implications.

d. Nebuchadrezzar's gratitude (2:46–49)

This is just what Nebuchadrezzar did not do. He asked no questions either about the future or about Daniel's great God. Relieved that he was that head of gold and that his fears were groundless, he concerned himself with the present, and with the man who had met his need. Though he paid homage to Daniel and ordered *an offering* (*minḥâ*; specifically the word used for a grain offering in Ezr. 7 : 17), and *incense* to be offered to him, Nebuchadrezzar's intention may well have been to honour Daniel's God by honouring His servant (verse 47). All the same it would have been surprising if a writer of the Maccabean period had chosen to include this questionable act, or had allowed it to stand if he found it in his sources, considering that the struggle in 165 BC was against Antiochus Epiphanes, with his claims to be 'God manifest'. In such a situation it would have been unthinkable to give encouragement to the thought that any human being could receive worship.[1]

---

[1] The point is conceded by some modern commentators, *e.g.* J. Barr (*PCB²*, p. 594): 'Nebuchadnezzar here is not the pattern of godlessness, nor a symbol of Antiochus Epiphanes.' Presumably he is himself, then, the historical King Nebuchadrezzar, but maybe also a representative of Gentile powers humbled before Israel.

Lord of kings (47) is not a well-known ascription, but it occurs in the so-called Letter of Adon to Egypt, and dated in the early years of Nebuchadrezzar's reign.[1] It begins, 'To Lord of Kings, Pharaoh, thy servant Adon . . .'. It is interesting to have this contemporary evidence of the use of the title; later both Seleucids and Ptolemies are said to have borne it, but perhaps vocalized to mean 'Lord of kingdoms'. Despite the claim of Nebuchadrezzar that Daniel's God was superior to all others because He revealed the dream, the king is not committing himself to the notion of one true God, as Daniel no doubt realized. As a polytheist he can always add another to the deities he worships.

The king is as extravagant in the honours he bestows on Daniel as he had been in the punishments he threatened to mete out (verse 5). As ruler over the *province of Babylon* Daniel would hold office in the capital of the empire, and so keep closely in touch with the king; his promotion to *chief prefect over all the wise men of Babylon* would require his residence at court. Though from the king's point of view this office would be a logical reward for his success as an interpreter of dreams, from Daniel's point of view it could involve many questions of compromise, not to mention the objections of the professionals, who understandably operated a closed shop.[2] But the 'ultimate absurdity', as Montgomery calls this aspect of the story, need not be fiction; truth is often stranger than fiction, and the story-writer, who needs to have an eye to the acceptability of his tale, has to keep within the bounds of the probable, whereas the writer of history needs no such restriction. *Chief prefect* translates Aramaic *sᵉgan*, a loanword from the Assyrian dialect (Akkadian *šaknu*).

49. In typical eastern fashion Daniel seeks to put in a word for his friends, who had been associated with him in interpreting the dream (verse 47, 'your' and 'you' are plural), and succeeds in gaining for them also honour and high office; but whereas their spheres were in the country districts of the province, Daniel remained *at the king's court* (lit. 'in the gate of the king'), an idiom well attested in Near Eastern usage[3] and suggesting cabinet rank. The separation of their spheres

---

[1] W. D. McHardy in *DOTT*, pp. 251-255. He points out that the Aramaic word for 'lord', *mārē*, is found in 'Maranatha' (1 Cor. 16:22).
[2] Montgomery (*ICC*, p. 183) gives evidence for this.
[3] *ICC*, p. 184.

of work paves the way for the next chapter, in which Daniel does not feature.

Additional Note on Nebuchadrezzar's dream statue

Excavation of Nebuchadrezzar's Babylon by R. Koldewey between 1899 and 1917 unearthed the remains of impressive architecture but little in the way of sculpture, yet from the beginning of the third millennium BC the art of sculpture in the round was being developed in the Land of the Two Rivers. Limestone, alabaster and other types of stone were the basic materials for representations of gods and men, but the head of a bronze statue from Nineveh, dating from the Akkadian period (2371–2191), is proof of the highly-developed metal sculpture which as early as this had mastered hollow-casting and finest chasing.[1] Figures in composite metals are known from Syria and include a god modelled in bronze, with a headdress and head of gold and the body plated with silver.[2]

After about 1550 BC sculpture in the round was largely replaced by sculptured reliefs, which the Assyrians perfected, while in the Late Assyrian period (ninth century BC) so-called architectural sculpture developed. This was partly sculpture in the round and partly high relief. Giant blocks supporting walls and forming gateways were carved to represent animals and men.

When Nebuchadrezzar built his many shrines he revived the style used for shrines in the Sumero-Babylonian period, and in the process appears to have added to a collection of museum pieces found in the Central Citadel. These included statues of Puzur-Ishtar, governor of Mari at the beginning of the second millennium BC.[3] The statue of Marduk is known to have occupied an important place in the city of Babylon, for at the New Year the king had to grasp the hand of the god, but no such statues have been found in excavation, and 'must have been destroyed or stolen in ancient days',[4] though a representation of Marduk on a lapis lazuli cylinder was found

---

[1] Anton Moortgat, *The Art of Ancient Mesopotamia* (Phaidon Press, 1969), p. 51 and Plate 154.
[2] *ANEP*, p. 166, Nos. 481, 483, 484.
[3] André Parrot, *Babylon and the Old Testament* (SCM Press, 1958), pp. 28, 29.
[4] *Ibid.*, p. 54.

at Esagila.[1] It begins to become clear that statues were not lacking in the temples of Nebuchadrezzar's reign. Add the fact that it was not unusual for men to lie at the feet of a god in his temple in order to seek the guidance of an oracle, and the impression of a god towering above the sleeper was a predictable element in the subsequent dream.[2]

Lifelike as much of this sculpture was, the figure remained rigid and motionless, the artificial product of human handiwork, and as such the statue was a fitting symbol of man-made kingdoms. The stone, by contrast, was mobile, a 'living stone', which had within it the power to grow until it filled the earth. Montgomery, whose note[3] on the symbolism of the image and its interpretation is most comprehensive, says: 'In regard to the Image, . . . we discover, so far as our literary sources go, an entirely original piece of symbolism.'[4] Delcor, on the other hand, states that in the history of religions the world is represented by a great statue, an idea particularly familiar to the Egyptian astrologers.[5]

The series of metals unconnected with any statue is certainly found in literature outside the Bible, the earliest and best-known example being Hesiod's *Works and Days*, which probably comes from a period slightly later than Homer. In view of the special interest of this work for comparison with Daniel, an assessment of it by A. R. Burn may be found helpful: 'Hesiod also, in the *Works and Days*, has a theory of human history. He knows that he lives in the Iron Age, and he finds it bad. Old poems told him that before it there had been a Bronze Age, when iron was unknown. . . . Then, seeing that in the course of human degeneration the baser metal had replaced the nobler one, either Hesiod or a predecessor had the bright idea of extrapolating a Golden and a Silver Age before the Bronze.'[6] Hesiod inserted an Age of Heroes between the Bronze and the Iron Ages, so arriving at five ages between the time of man's innocence and his own day: gold, silver, bronze, the age of heroes, iron. (Other references to a four-

---

[1] Parrot (*ibid.*, p. 55) illustrates this.
[2] A. L. Oppenheim, *The Interpretation of Dreams*, pp. 189, 190.
[3] *ICC*, pp. 185-192.
[4] *Ibid.*, p. 186.
[5] Delcor, p. 79. He makes reference to Festugière, *La Révélation d'Hermès Trismégiste*.
[6] A. R. Burn, *The Pelican History of Greece* (Penguin Books, 1966), p. 76.

kingdom sequence are given in the Introduction, above, p. 55.)

It will be observed that, in contrast to the writer of Daniel, Hesiod is looking back over history, and has no interest in the future, whereas in Daniel the golden age is the present, and the starting-point for a forward glimpse into the future. 'The series begins from the exile of the Jews and leads to the kingdom of their God; it is not a scheme of universal history but an eschatological scheme with a particular starting-point.'[1]

Parallels have also been drawn between the four periods of Daniel's image and the Parsee notion that history from the time of Zoroaster is a period of a thousand years, divided into four periods represented by gold, silver, steel and a substance mixed with clay. Yet the *Dinkart*, from which this information is drawn, is a work of the ninth century AD,[2] and the *Avesta*, which contains the preaching of Zarathustra and the teaching of Zoroastrian religion, is from the third or fourth century AD. Chronological uncertainty as to the origin of these ideas makes it impossible to assert dogmatically that there was Persian influence behind Daniel 2.[3] In any case the metals were not identical, and Daniel does not have four world-periods, but world-kingdoms. Barr sums it up well : 'The idea of the division of the world's existence into periods is a common one. But, in conformity with the Israelite interest in history, the periods are not succeeding legendary conditions of humanity (Hesiod) or successive cosmological states of created things (Iranian religion); they are historical periods of imperial domination.'[4]

As for the interpretation of these periods, only the identification of Nebuchadrezzar with the head of gold is made at this point in the book. Not until nearly forty years had passed did Daniel have visions of his own which supplemented this dream of Nebuchadrezzar's, and revealed further indications of future empires. Consideration of the whole subject of interpretation of the kingdoms will be dealt with in connection with chapters 7 – 12 (see especially p. 161 and *cf.* the Introduction, above, section VII, Interpretation).

[1] J. Barr, *PCB²*, p. 594.

[2] See Introduction, above, p. 48; also J. Dresden, 'Avesta', *IDB*, I, p. 322, and N. Smart, *The Religious Experience of Mankind,* p. 303.

[3] For the view that the Persian books are more likely to be dependent on the Bible, see J. H. Moulton, *HDB⁴*, 'Zoroastrianism'.

[4] *PCB²*, p. 549.

B. Nebuchadrezzar the tyrant sees God's servants rescued (3:1–30)

'King Nebuchadrezzar made an image of gold' and 'set it up'. These words form a refrain through the first half of the chapter (verses 1–18). The image was intended to be worshipped, but the writer does not call it a god. The fact that all peoples, nations and languages were to fall down and worship it suggests that Nebuchadrezzar intended to unite his kingdom under one religion. It may even be that the image represented himself. Having been told that he was the head of gold, what more natural than to capitalize on the fact and to make the whole image of gold? Like the smaller statues that have survived, it was no doubt made of some less precious material and plated with gold.

The size of the image and its shape are both remarkable. In height it vied with the date-palms that still grow in the plains of Iraq to approximately the height of this image (90 feet), and it was almost as slender, at nine feet in width. It must have been more like an obelisk than a statue, and stylized if it resembled a human being at all. The writer, however, is not interested in such details, but rather in the ideology it stands for and to which he cannot subscribe. The incident represents the conflict between worship of the true God and the humanistic use of religion to boost the power of the rulers of this world.[1] It is characteristic of idolatry that the idol is at the worshipper's disposal to achieve his ends. Nebuchadrezzar can see no reason but insubordination for refusal to worship as requested and therefore he does not hesitate to prescribe a brutal punishment in the furnace. Furnaces in Babylon were connected with the firing of bricks (*cf.* Gn. 11 :3), which were widely used in the absence of stone. The

[1] In the recent history of Ghana the President allowed a slightly more than life-size statue of himself to be erected in front of Parliament House, Accra. He 'could tolerate no disunity in Ghana, which he shaped into a monolithic republic under the complete control of his party and dominated by his own personality as President (1960)' (J. D. Fage, *A Short History of Africa,* Penguin Africa Library, 1962, pp. 251f.). An inscription on the side bore the words, 'Seek ye first the political kingdom and all other things shall be added unto you.' The statue was religiously controversial from the beginning and was destroyed after the bloodless coup of 1966. *Cf.* Africa Survey, No. 50, October 1975, p. 46. I am indebted to Dr Myrtle S. Langley for drawing my attention to these details.

fuel was charcoal which, given the needed draught, produced the high temperatures required at the brick-kiln and at the ironsmith's forge (Is. 44 : 12). Some large brick-kilns have been excavated outside Babylon.

The majority of commentators regard this chapter as a kind of allegory rather than as a historical event. Every aspect of the story has in turn been called in question, but evidence has been produced to establish the realism of its features, strange as they are to the modern western reader. If an obelisk ninety feet in height be regarded as improbable, the colossus of Rhodes was higher (70 cubits as opposed to 60). As for the overlaying of images with gold, not only have some examples of this gold-plating been found, but the practice is referred to in Isaiah (40 : 19; 41 : 7) and Jeremiah (10 : 4), and in the writings of Herodotus.[1]

Death by burning at the hands of Nebuchadrezzar is recorded in Jeremiah 29 : 22, and a directive of the ruler Rīm Sin (1750 BC) of Larsa, 'Because they threw a young slave into an oven, throw ye a slave into a furnace,'[2] proves that the idea did not originate with Nebuchadrezzar. Thus there is nothing improbable about the story until it comes to the miraculous intervention by which the lives of the three men were saved and a fourth accompanied them in the furnace. Not surprisingly, popular Jewish legends based on this chapter developed in connection with other worthies. S. R. Driver quotes a story of Abraham who, for refusing to worship Nimrod's gods, was cast by him into a furnace of fire and miraculously delivered,[3] but these provide no evidence for a legendary background to the chapter.

When all has been said, the reader is left to come to terms with the statement of faith of the three men, 'Our God whom

[1] Herodotus i. 183, and quoted by Montgomery (*ICC*, p. 193). Herodotus is referring, however, to the Babylon of his day, under the Persians.

[2] John B. Alexander, 'New Light on the Fiery Furnace', *JBL*, 69, 1950, pp. 375f.; Emil G. Kraeling, *Rand McNally Bible Atlas* (Collins, 1956), p. 323. Alexander concludes: 'Now while the parallel is not exact, in the decree of Rīm-Sin as in that of Nebuchadrezzar, a human being is thrown into a furnace apparently as a form of punishment. It may be mere coincidence that the author of Daniel 3 has described a method of punishment actually used by a Babylonian king some 1200 years earlier, but it may be that this practice persisted to much later times and is correctly reflected in the book of Daniel.'

[3] *CB*, p. 35. See also his footnote for references to similar stories.

we serve is able to deliver us from the burning fiery furnace' (verse 17). It is worth noting that they had to endure the ordeal of being thrown into the fire, but nevertheless their lives were spared. There is no suggestion here or elsewhere in Scripture that the believer will be cushioned against trouble and suffering except by the presence of the Lord with him in it (Is. 43 :2; Jn. 12 :26).

a. Nebuchadrezzar's golden image unites the empire (3:1-7)

1. *Sixty cubits ... six cubits.* The Sumero-Akkadian number system was mainly sexagesimal, as opposed to the decimal system rigidly adhered to in Egypt. The use of a measuring-reed six cubits long (Ezk. 40 :5) reflects the same Babylonian influence.[1] *The plain of Dura.* This plain would have been named after a city, but *Dura,* which means 'walled place', is an abbreviation of a longer name compounded with Dur-, such as Duru sha-karrabi, a suburb of Babylon.[2] Other suggestions have been made, and, while certainty is impossible, Kraeling's theory is attractive because it would bring the ceremony within easy reach of Babylon, as the story requires.

2, 3. The long list of notables assembled for the dedication of the image grades them according to status. *Satraps* is a transliteration of the Greek word which, in turn, represents a Median original.[3] The word means 'protector' and it was used in the Persian empire for a governor of a province. *Prefects* (Aram. *sᵉgan*) and *governors* (Aram. *peḥāh*) are Semitic words of Assyrian origin, often used in the Old Testament, mostly in texts relating to the exilic and post-exilic periods. *Counsellors* (*'ᵃdargāzar*) is a word of Persian origin and is unique to Daniel in extant Aramaic literature. Of the remaining terms those translated *justices* (Persian *dᵉṯābar*) and *magistrates* (Aram. *tiptāy*) occur so far only in Daniel and in Aramaic documents of the sixth and fifth centuries.

[1] Further information will be found in *IDB*, 3, 'Number', p. 561. It is interesting that the sexagesimal system survives in our divisions of time, the degrees of a circle, the dozen and the gross.
[2] E. G. Kraeling, *Rand McNally Bible Atlas*, p. 322.
[3] 'The title *khshathrapanva* is Median, and the organization was a development of the provincial governorships initiated by the Assyrians' (D. J. Wiseman, 'Some historical problems in the book of Daniel', *Notes on Some Problems in the Book of Daniel*, p. 14. He refers in a footnote to R. N. Frye, *Iranica Antiqua*, IV, 1964, p. 74).

It was usual to hold a ceremony of *dedication*, and the local colour in this chapter is correct.[1]

3. The exact repetition of the list of officials and of the musical instruments may reflect a Semitic style of rhetoric, but the writer succeeds in achieving a satirical effect which may not have been unintentional. Here are all the great ones of the empire falling flat on their faces before a lifeless obelisk at the sound of a musical medley, controlled by the baton of King Nebuchadrezzar. Greek translators, preferring brevity, omitted the repetitions of the lists but sacrificed the satire and with it the subtle comment of the writer.

4. First the *herald* (*kārôz*; once thought to be a word of Greek origin but now thought to be from Old Persian[2]) takes the stage and issues the ultimatum.

5, 6. The fanfare is to sound from a collection of both wind and stringed instruments. Of the six instruments named here, only the first, *horn*, occurs also in the Hebrew of the Old Testament (Aram. *qarnā'*, Heb. *qeren*). *Pipe* (Aram. *mašrôqîta*) is difficult to identify for lack of evidence, the only clue being a possible connection with the Hebrew *šāraq*, 'to hiss', hence 'whistle'. *Lyre* (Aram. *qayt̠erōs*) is either a loan-word from the Greek *kithara*, or together with the Greek it is borrowed from a common ancestor. *Trigon* (Aram. *sabbekā*, but with a different initial *ś* in verses 7, 10 and 15) also seems to be a foreign word of unknown source. The translation *trigon* is arrived at from the Greek word used to translate it in the Septuagint, *sambukē*, which means a triangular harp. *Harp* (Aram. *pesantêrîn*) is generally agreed to be another stringed instrument of triangular shape, the Greek *psaltērion*. The last word in the list (Aram. *sûmpōneyâ*), *bagpipe* (RSV), may not be a musical instrument at all, but may rather signify 'in unison'. Alternatively it has been argued that a percussion instrument may be intended.[3]

---

[1] Morris Jastrow, *Die Religion Babyloniens und Assyriens*, I (1905), pp. 375ff.; B. Meissner, *Babylonien und Assyrien*, I (1920), p. 71, quoted by Montgomery (*ICC*, p. 197) to draw a parallel between the list of five classes of officials invited by Sargon on a similar occasion and those in this verse.

[2] KB, p. 1087.

[3] For detail on this and other terms here used see T. C. Mitchell and R. Joyce, 'The Musical Instruments in Nebuchadrezzar's Orchestra', *Notes on Some Problems in the Book of Daniel*, pp. 19–27, and P. W. Coxon, *Transactions of Glasgow University Oriental*

In view of the tentative state of present knowledge of these words it is precarious to base any theory of the date of the book on the evidence of these instruments.[1]

6. The punishment for anyone foolish enough to refuse to comply is to *be cast into a burning fiery furnace*. The adjectives appear redundant, and it may be that the expression has not been fully understood. This may be a way of expressing the superlative or perhaps 'fiery furnace' is a technical term.[2] The *furnace* (Aram. *'attûn*) would have been enclosed, for the person was to be thrown into the interior of it (Aram. *gô'*), and the technology of raising the heat by forcing a draught requires it.[3]

7. The original reads literally, 'As soon as they were hearing they were falling down.' There was total and immediate response. The king had achieved the unity he sought.

b. Three Jews protest (3:8–18)

Apart from the work of informers, Nebuchadrezzar would never have known that the three men he had promoted were paying no heed to him. That it should be leaders in the home province who were defying him would be an added provocation. How Daniel evaded the issue is not explained.

8. *Maliciously accused* translates the picturesque expression 'eat the pieces of flesh torn off from someone's body' and so 'to slander'.[4]

12. The accusers are well aware of the circumstances in

Society, 25, 1973–74 (1976), pp. 24–40: 'Greek Loan-Words and alleged Greek Loan Translations in the Book of Daniel'.

[1] See Introduction, above, p. 33.

[2] D. J. Wiseman has pointed out that the same problem occurs in connection with 'fiery flying serpents' (Is. 14:29; 30:6); *cf.* his article in *Tyndale Bulletin*, 23, 1972, pp. 108–110.

[3] It is difficult to envisage what the furnace is likely to have looked like, for, despite excavations, proper drawings and dimensions are rarely available. There is, however, a significant diagram in R. J. Forbes, *Studies in Ancient Technology*, VI, 1958, p. 67, representing an ancient Mesopotamian pottery-kiln of Nippur, *c.* 2000 BC. It resembles a railway tunnel blocked at one end but with an entrance at the other. Uprights at frequent intervals support the dome and serve as ventilation shafts also. Charcoal provides the heat, and it is estimated that the temperature would have been 900–1000°C. The suggestion that the furnace was an open surface pool of gas or oil set alight, such as may be seen today in the Near East, *e.g.* at Kirkuk, does not satisfy the requirements of the text.

[4] KB, p. 1121, *qrṣ*.

which these Jews were appointed to office and they resent the king's promotion of foreigners over their heads. Now is their opportunity to gain the favour of the king by revealing treachery.

13–15. Justice demanded that the three men should not be condemned on hearsay alone and therefore, despite his furious rage, Nebuchadrezzar gave them opportunity to recant. It was imperative that the great king should not lose face before the magnificent array of international delegates, and he defied any god to deliver them from the hands of his Babylonian Majesty. This shows human pride taken to its logical conclusion, saying 'thou shalt have no other god but me'.

16–18. There is nothing the three can say in their own defence. They are technically guilty, but they have also been misrepresented. All they can do is to cast themselves on their God whom the king has defied. They do not doubt the power of their God to deliver them from the king's furnace, but they have no right to presume that He will do so. If He does not, they are ready to take the consequences rather than compromise on such a contrived issue. *If it be so* represents an approximate meaning of an idiom which has puzzled translators from ancient times.[1] Taken literally it was theologically unacceptable : 'The early translators were well aware that *'îṭai* [be] denoted existence but they recognized the dangerous implications of a literal rendering . . . ("If our God exists . . .") with its even more portentous corollary . . . ("but if not . . .") in the next verse.'[2] The marginal reading in RV and RSV, which has been adopted in JB, NEB and is preferred by Montgomery and Porteous, takes *'îṭ ai* to be a particle with the effect of making emphasis. This gives the sense : 'If our God whom we serve is able to deliver us from the fiery burning furnace and from your hand, O king, he will save (us); but if not . . .' (Montgomery). Coxon argues that this is the sense of the Aramaic and, by drawing a parallel from Akkadian usage and by a study of the use of the word in biblical Aramaic, he answers objections which have been raised to this translation. The construction is found in Daniel in direct speech and in dramatic situations, where the break with normal syntactical

[1] P. W. Coxon ('Daniel III 17: A Linguistic and Theological Problem, *VT*, XXVI, 1976, pp. 400–405) summarizes the renderings of representative translators of this phrase from LXX onwards.
[2] *Ibid.*, p. 401.

sequence injects 'a realistic note into the dialogue' (so 3 :12, 'pay no heed').[1]

The parallel between the phrasing of Nebuchadrezzar's proposition in verse 15 and the response in verse 17, pointed out in the same article, is important. 'If you are ready' . . . 'but if not' is matched by a corresponding conditional sentence and open choice of action. That these men will not be involved in idolatry is a fixed point. That their God has power to save them is even more sure, hence the emphatic particle, but they will not presume to know whether in this instance He will intervene, hence the 'if'; but they are prepared to stake their lives on the One whom they serve.

c. Deliverance in the furnace (3:19–30)

19–23. The predictable fury of the king at this challenge to his authority provokes him into issuing urgent orders. *Heated seven times more* is not to be understood literally. The writer is using a proverbial expression (*cf.* Pr. 24 :16; 26 :16).

Picked troops were ordered to bind the three condemned men, to prevent them from struggling and so possibly evading their punishment. The standard English translations of the various garments named conjure up the picture of three Elizabethan courtiers. Incongruous as this is, the ancient translators were equally puzzled, as the variety of interpretations proves.[2] This points to some long lapse of time between the date of the original, from which the translators were working, and their own day. Granted that the occasion demanded court attire, it is inconceivable that even specialized vocabulary should not have been within the capacity of an official translator if he lived within fifty years of the writer; yet LXX, which would be the earliest of the versions, made the best sense it could but reduced three words to two in the process. JB probably gets as close to the meaning as any with 'cloak, hose and headgear'.

[1] *Ibid.,* p. 408. *Cf.* his conclusion (p. 409): 'Linguistically and theologically the verses as they stand in the Masoretic text are unobjectionable.'

[2] Montgomery (*ICC,* p. 211), 'Since for each of these three terms every category of gear for head, body and legs has been adduced (*e.g.,* the EVV and margins), the possible permutations are many.' See his long and detailed discussion of the vocabulary. See also S. A. Cook, 'The Articles of Dress in Dan. III, 21', *Journal of Philology,* 26, 1899, pp. 306–313, to which Montgomery refers.

The king, impatiently giving orders, watched as his hench-men became the victims of the newly-stoked fire, while carry-ing out their duty.

It is at this point in the text that Greek versions include a long addition : a prayer, a prose description of their deliver-ance and a hymn, commonly known as the Benedicite, sup-posedly sung by the three men, or by Azariah alone (according to Theodotion), from the furnace. Evidence from Qumran has shown conclusively that these additions were not part of the original.[1]

24–26. Instead of three men bound, Nebuchadrezzar sees *four men loose*. The fourth is *like a son of the gods*[2] or 'god-like', despite his apparent humanity, and it dawns on the king that there *is* a God who can deliver out of his hand. The three men are free to make their way to him out of the furnace at his command.

27–30. Impressed by the absence of any sign of burning, the king is forced to acknowledge that their God has delivered them and brought Nebuchadrezzar's decree to nothing. Though he can make decrees that are binding on the world, his power is far from absolute. He has left out of his reckoning *the Most High God* (verse 26), whose power he proceeds to acknowledge in the decree of verse 29. This title for God is often found in the mouth of non-Jews (Gn. 14 : 19; Nu. 24 : 16; Is. 14 : 14). There is nothing unlikely in the edict, which does no more than declare legal in the empire the religion of the Jews. *Yielded up their bodies.* Theodotion adds 'to the fire', a reading used by Paul in 1 Corinthians 13 : 3. *Promoted* (30) really means 'to cause to prosper'; *cf.* JB, 'Then the king showered favours on' the three men.

---

[1] Montgomery (*ICC*, pp. 8, 9) summarizes the discussion of this topic up to 1929. On the Daniel portions from Qumran, see J. T. Milik, *Ten Years of Discovery in the Wilderness of Judea* (London, 1959), p. 28 and F. M. Cross, *RB*, 63, 1956, p. 58: 'The portion preserved in 1QD*b* includes the place where LXX incorporates the Prayer of Azariah and the Song of the Three Hebrews, but like the Massoretic text it lacks these additions. The variations between the text of the fragments from Cave 1 and the M.T. are insignificant; the fragments from the other caves also resemble the M.T. apart from a few variants related to the *Vorlage* of the LXX.'

[2] Montgomery (*ICC*, p. 214) produces evidence to show that this term and its parallel 'angel' in verse 28 are entirely genuine to Aramaic paganism. 'The Son of God' (AV), implying a pre-incarnation appear-ance of Christ, is probably not correct here.

C. Judgment on Nebuchadrezzar (4:1–37)

This fourth and final incident from the life of Nebuchadrezzar belongs to the period when his great building projects had been completed (verse 30). The king tells the story against himself to explain how he came to capitulate to the God of the captives he had brought from Judea. A mysterious dream which alarmed the king and mystified his expert interpreters was related to Daniel (4–18); after some hesitation Daniel told the king what it meant (19–27). Twelve months later the king was suddenly taken ill with a strange mental illness which eventually left him when he 'lifted up his eyes to heaven'. In glad response he gave thanks to the Most High God and published his experiences (28–37). Thus not only kingdoms but individual kings are shown to be under the control of Daniel's God, who has afflicted the king because He desires to show mercy to him.

The chapter has been described as an edict, but it makes no law; perhaps it would be better to think of it as a confession made in a kind of open letter. In the original it has a poetic quality which is faithfully conveyed by JB and NEB, though they do not choose the identical passages to put into poetic form. Evidently the work of a skilled writer has gone into the phrasing of the text. It may have been a deliberate ploy to transpose verses 19–33 into the third person, for, as Montgomery notes, the same phenomenon appears in the book of Tobit (3 : 7 to the end), and he puts it down to an unconscious dramatic sense in the writer : 'The account of the king's madness is told in the third person, for of that he would not have been a sane witness.'[1]

A note in the margin of our English versions draws attention to the fact that verses 1–3 are attached to chapter 3 in the Aramaic, but this does not reflect ancient tradition. When the chapter divisions of the Latin Bible were made in the thirteenth century they were taken over from the Vulgate and used also in the MT and Greek versions, but it is generally agreed that these verses properly belong to this chapter. That being so the main divisions of the chapter reveal a literary structure A B B A. The king begins and ends with an ascription of praise to the Most High (1–3; 34–37), while the main story divides into two parts : i. Nebuchadrezzar's narration of his dream (4–18) and ii. its interpretation and fulfilment (19–33).

[1] *ICC*, p. 223.

Important as it may be to recognize literary forms, the modern reader is often preoccupied with the credibility of this chapter. That a king should issue in his own name an edict or statement drawn up by someone else does not worry us, because the same applies in affairs of state today. That he should use the biblical phraseology found in verses 3 and 37 requires only that someone well versed in the Scriptures drafted the statement. What does seem to most commentators unlikely is that a Babylonian king should become a believer in the God of the Jews.[1] The official annals, it is true, make no reference either to the king's illness or to his conversion, but information concerning his last thirty years is in any case slight. Even if the available Babylonian Chronicles did include the later part of Nebuchadrezzar's reign, it is unlikely that such an incident would be recorded. As it happens they end with the eleventh year of his reign, 594 BC, and resume only briefly in that of Nabopolassar. No contemporary source of information has come to light, therefore, and, as is so often the case, the biblical narrative stands as a lone witness, unless the 'Prayer of Nabonidus' refers to the same event.[2]

Later references to the illness of Nebuchadrezzar towards the end of his reign are found (i) in the writings of Eusebius of Caesarea (c. AD 265–339). He quotes Abydenus (c. second century BC), who, on the authority of Megasthenes (c. 300 BC), relates a Babylonian tradition that from the roof of his palace, being possessed by some god or other, he cried out : 'O Babylonians, I, Nebuchadrezzar, announce to you beforehand the coming misfortune. . . . A Persian mule will come, having your own deities as his allies, and will bring slavery.'[3] The king goes on to describe the animal-like existence to which he would condemn the conqueror of his land, and 'having uttered this prophecy, he forthwith disappeared'. It is hard to know how much importance to attach to this fourth-hand information. (ii) Slightly earlier is that of Josephus (AD 37-post 100) who, on the authority of Berossus (fourth century BC), first corrects a false impression that an Assyrian queen was responsible for

[1] *E.g.* Montgomery (*ICC*, p. 222): 'As an edict the document is historically absurd; it has no similar in the history of royal conversions nor in ancient imperial edicts.'

[2] See Additional Note, below, p. 116.

[3] *Praeparatio Evangelica* in J. P. Migne, *Patrologia Graeca*, XXI, 762 A. English translation: E. H. Gifford, *Eusebii Praeparatio Evangelica* (Oxford, 1903).

building Babylon by asserting that its builder was Nebuchad-rezzar. After referring to the same passage in Megasthenes as Eusebius knew he added, 'Nabuchodonosor, after he had begun to build the forementioned wall, fell sick and departed this life when he had reigned forty-three years'.[1] There is then some late evidence for the king's illness, and even for its psychological nature, not long before his death. Nor could Nabonidus have been intended, because he reigned only seventeen years. The mention of possession by a god, fore-telling from the roof of his palace, and prediction concerning the Persian, Cyrus, all point to a tradition in keeping with the narrative in Daniel.

The illness referred to, known as lycanthropy, is well attested in pre-scientific times,[2] but is not referred to today under that name. Dr M. G. Barker, a consultant psychiatrist, writes : 'As far as Nebuchadrezzar's illness is concerned, the features are of a fairly acute onset of insanity, with the appar-ent delusional idea that he was an animal. The length of time that he was unwell is not clear, but he also seems to have had a spontaneous remission and returned to sanity and changed his way of life and outlook subsequently. This kind of history is much more typical of a depressive illness with relatively acute onset, delusional beliefs of a morbid nature and, in the days before drugs and E.C.T., most such illnesses had a spontaneous remission within a period of one, two and, occasionally, more years. The person who recovered would recover complete insight, as did Nebuchadrezzar, apparently.' Dr Barker goes on to cite two patients in his own clinical experience whose illness took the form of thinking they were changing into animals and who responded to treatment. 'The reason why this particular manifestation of depression is so rare is because of the increased sophistication of people since the seventeenth century and this bizarre way of the mind

[1] *Against Apion* i. 20.
[2] See the older commentaries, *e.g. ICC*, pp. 220–222. I am indebted to Dr Montagu G. Barker for the following reference : 'Lycanthropy, a condition frequently mentioned in earlier times and often linked with hydrophobia in which sufferers were believed to imitate dogs and wolves. Its decline into oblivion in the seventeenth century was due partly to a more widespread recognition of the symptoms of mental illness, and partly to better community care which prevented the insane from walking abroad' (Richard Hunter and Ida Macalpine, *Three Hundred Years of Psychiatry, 1535–1860* (Oxford, 1963), p. 168).

acting out its guilt and feelings is no longer necessary, as people will accept depression and distress more readily.'[1]

It follows that the evidence of this chapter can be taken as a serious description of a recognizable illness. Nebuchadrezzar was evidently aware of some degree of guilt which worked itself out, first in the dream and then in delusions.

a. Address and ascription of greatness to the Most High God (4:1-3)

In the accepted style of ancient letter-writing the author names himself and those whom he is addressing. As 'king of all the earth' Nebuchadrezzar is in a unique position of advantage from which to commend to all the nations of the earth the blessing he has received from the Most High, whose kingdom is not only greater in extent than his own, but endures through all generations. He has arrived at this conviction as the result of his experience of *signs and wonders,* events explicable only in terms of divine intervention, and it is of these that he intends to write. There is nothing in the poetry of verse 3, despite reminiscences of the language of the Psalms, that absolutely demands knowledge of the Scriptures. Marduk in the Babylonian Epic of Creation was thought of in similar terms :

'For unspecified time shall thy word stand inviolate,
    To promote and abase lie both in thy power.'[2]

The greeting, *Peace be multiplied to you!* (*cf.* 6 :25; lit. 'your peace be multiplied'), was in use internationally.

b. The disturbing dream (4:4-18)

4-7. It was while the king was basking in contentment at the thought of all his achievements that his peace of mind was shattered by this dream. Contrast the ambitions and fears which lay behind his dream in chapter 2. Again the king summons his experts. The last-named in verse, 7, *astrologers* (*gāzᵉrayyā'*) did not appear in the list in chapter 2. The word evidently puzzled the early translators,[3] but it has turned up

---

[1] Dr Montagu G. Barker in a personal communication.
[2] Epic of Creation IV. 7, 8. Translation of J. V. Kinnier Wilson, *DOTT,* p. 8. On the other hand E. J. Young (*The Prophecy of Daniel* (Eerdmans, 1949), p. 98) is inclined to the view of C. F. Keil that the edict was probably prepared under the influence of Daniel.
[3] LXX omits verses 6-9; Theodotion merely transliterates, presumably because he did not know the term. The root verb means 'to cut', hence 'those who divine from the entrails of an animal by consulting

in the Prayer of Nabonidus, where it is translated 'magician' by J. T. Milik and 'diviner' in the more recent version.[1] On such scant evidence the meaning of the word is necessarily tentative. Whatever their methods, none of these experts satisfied the king. Either they were impotent or, if they realized the meaning of the dream, they were lacking in courage.

LXX inserts a date at the beginning of this section (verse 4, LXX 4:1). 'In LXX, despite some omissions, this chapter is a quarter as long again as in the Massoretic text' (JB mg.).

8, 9. Daniel was in a class apart, operating not as one of a group but as a free individual whose superiority stemmed from that of the God he worshipped. When all others failed, the king was prepared to consult Daniel, in whom was *the spirit of the holy gods* (*'elāhîn*). Since Hebrew *'elōhîm* (pl.) is used for the true God, the question arises whether Nebuchadrezzar is acknowledging the Spirit of God as the source of Daniel's wisdom (*cf.* RSV mg. 'Or *Spirit of the holy God*'). Against this, note (i) the plural adjective. Usually any adjectival attribute to *'elōhîm*, when it means the true God, is singular (*cf.* Ne. 8:6; Ps. 7:10 (Heb. 9)). A possible exception is Joshua 24:19. (ii) Nebuchadrezzar uses the singular in the same sentence to refer to his own patron god. Clearly he does not worship Daniel's God. (iii) The queen (5:11) and Belshazzar (5:14) use the same expression, which suggests that it was a current idiom. Daniel was 'very spiritual'.

10–16. The tree is such a frequent subject in literature of all countries that to say the writer is borrowing from Ezekiel[2] is gratuitous. More to the point are references to trees in documents from Mesopotamia[3] on the ground that dreams are sometimes prompted by ideas imported into the mind by reading, conversation or event. Anthropologists claim that the tree is a not unusual dream symbol, representing the growth and development of psychic life.[4]

---

the liver' (KB). Evidently the word was no longer current when the Greek translations were made, or perhaps there were regional vocabulary differences.

[1] See Additional Note, below, p. 118.
[2] So, *e.g.*, Lacocque, p. 67; *ICC*, p. 228; *TBC*, p. 149.
[3] G. Widengren, *The Tree of Life in Ancient Near Eastern Religion* (Uppsala, 1951); Mircea Eliade, *Traité d'Histoire des Religions* (Paris, 1959), pp. 99–101.
[4] Joseph I. Henderson, in C. G. Jung (ed.), *Man and his Symbols*, p. 153; M.–L. von Franz, *ibid.*, p. 162.

Nebuchadrezzar was at the height of his powers, established and proud of his achievements as the head of a world empire; accordingly the tree he saw in his dream was of cosmic proportions, towering to heaven (*cf.* Gn. 11:4) and providing food and shelter for all the nations of the earth. His psyche felt secure and at ease. His ambitions had been achieved. But the dream had a second part. The tree was to be felled by order of *a watcher, a holy one,* who *came down from heaven* (13). The idea of heavenly beings whose task it is to keep watch seems to have originated in Babylon (Ezk. 1:17, 18; Zc. 1:10; 4:10), though T. Francis Glasson finds them in Hesiod.[1] This 'watcher', like the Lord he serves, 'neither slumbers nor sleeps' (Ps. 121:4) and has power to make decrees and carry them out in order to bring home to men the fact that the Most High rules in human affairs (verse 17). If the idea behind the term is pagan in origin, as commentators suggest, that is in keeping with the present context, though it is also true that Nebuchadrezzar equates them with 'holy ones' of heavenly origin, whatever he may have meant by these terms. In later pseudepigraphic books, such as Jubilees and in some of the Qumran literature, the term reappears, but in the sense of rebellious angels. After the tree has been felled the stump is to be preserved and protected, though too little is known of tree culture in the Ancient Near East for the practice of placing metal bands round the stumps of trees to be verifiable or its purpose explained. Within the symbolism of the dream this metal band prevents removal and so reassures the dreamer. The wording begins to make the interpretation plain : the tree stump is human, yet destined to revert to an animal existence, watered by dew like the grass which it shares with the beasts. Indeed he exchanges his human *mind,* or intelligence (lit. 'heart'), for that of a beast, but for a limited period, *seven times* (LXX 'seven years'). The word '*iddānîn* is not specifically 'years' but can signify 'seasons'. It is the word 'time' in 2:8 and 3:5. Its duration is uncertain, and this is intentional.

[1] T. F. Glasson, *Greek Influence in Jewish Eschatology* (London, 1961), p. 69. R. H. Charles (*Apocrypha and Pseudepigrapha,* II, p. 188), commenting on the occurrence of the word 'watchers' in 1 Enoch 1:5 (he reckoned 1 Enoch 1–5 to have been written in the first century BC), says the name first occurs in Daniel. He implies that Daniel was written earlier. 1 Enoch 1–36 is now reckoned third or early second century BC (see below, p. 153 and Additional Note on 'Son of man' (p. 148).

17. The purpose of this illness is made plain: it is to bring low one who has forgotten his human dependence on *the Most High,* whose prerogative it is to decide who is to receive the right to rule. The angel, in keeping with the teaching of Scripture as a whole, announces that God exalts *the lowliest of men* (*cf.* 1 Sa. 2 :8; Ps. 113 :7, 8; Lk. 1 :52).

b¹. Daniel's interpretation and its fulfilment (4:19–33)

It is in this section that Nebuchadrezzar ceases to speak in the first person, as though he were no longer capable of speaking for himself.

19–22. Understandably *dumbfounded* and *dismayed* (NEB) at the embarrassing message he had to give, Daniel delayed to speak until encouraged by the king to do so. There is a suggestion of warmth in the relationship between the two men in this chapter (*cf.* verse 9). An ominous note is sounded by the ascription of the dream to the enemies of the king (19); but by repeating the favourable details of the dream (20, 21) and coming to the point, *it is you, O king* (22), while he could speak of greatness, strength and dominion, Daniel tempered the fearful impact of his message.

23–27. The decree of 'a watcher' and 'a holy one' (17) becomes in Daniel's recapitulation *a decree of the Most High* (24), thus bypassing the intermediaries. The felling of the tree points to the isolation of Nebuchadrezzar from human society. Unlike the maniac of Mark 5 :1–20, he would be peaceful enough, sharing the pasture of the cattle. *Till you know that the Most High rules the kingdom of men* (25). Ultimately Nebuchadrezzar's kingdom is the kingdom of God, and the king has only to acknowledge that fact to regain his sanity and his throne; so it would appear that he is, after all, in control of his fate. As metal bands protected the tree stump, so the throne of the king would remain inviolate and sure for him, once he knew that *Heaven rules* (26). 'Heaven' as a synonym for God is unknown elsewhere in the Old Testament, though it is found in the books of the Maccabees (*e.g.* 1 Macc. 3 :18, 19, 50; 2 Macc. 7 :11; 8 :20) and in the New Testament, most obviously in the phrase 'kingdom of heaven', Matthew's counterpart to 'kingdom of God' in the other Synoptic Gospels.

Daniel exhorts the king to avert the tragedy by acting immediately on his advice, and here he resembles the classical prophets (*e.g.* Am. 5 :15) in that there is a contingent element in his prophecy : *Break off your sins by practising righteousness* (27). Here is no passive determinism. On the contrary the writer urges an incentive to a change of life-style. It is not that by good deeds the king can save himself, but that by changing his way of life the king will be demonstrating his acceptance of the truth of Daniel's words (*cf.* Acts 26:20). *Mercy to the oppressed* draws attention to injustices in the state which it was within the king's power to put right. *Righteousness* (*ṣiḏᵉqâ*) is translated by LXX as 'almsgiving', and the verb *break off* (*pᵉruq*) as 'redeem'. Thus understood, this verse appeared to support a doctrine of merit earned by good works, and became a centre of controversy at the time of the Reformation. The root meaning of the verb is clearly seen in such contexts as Genesis 27:40, 'you shall break his yoke from your neck' and Exodus 32:2, 'Break off the golden rings' (RV). Accordingly the meaning is 'break with the old habits' and 'do what is right', a command which has meaning even without special revelation. The translation 'almsgiving' reflects the viewpoint current when the LXX translators were at work,[1] and is plain in the Sermon on the Mount, where 'do . . . righteousness' (Mt. 6:1, RV) is expounded in terms of almsgiving, prayer and fasting. Exactly what ideals the Babylonian king would have had we cannot know, but it evidently took more than warning and exhortation to move him to action.

28-30. Twelve months later Nebuchadrezzar, true to type,[2] was admiring the city which was the culmination of his life's work, and it was an achievement to be proud of by human standards.[3] Labourers on the project might have been excused, however, for regarding with some cynicism the king's claim to have built the city, and oppression did nothing to increase the glory of his majesty.

[1] The date of the LXX translation of Daniel cannot be made with any certainty, but 'righteousness' appears as 'almsgiving' in the book of Tobit 12:9; 14:11.

[2] Montgomery (*ICC,* p. 243) comments, 'The setting of the scene and the king's self-complaisance in his glorious Babylon are strikingly true to history.' He refers to Nebuchadrezzar's words as recorded on the Grotefend Cylinder; *cf.* C. D. Gray in R. F. Harper, *Assyrian and Babylonian Literature* (1904), pp. 147–150.

[3] A plan of Nebuchadrezzar's Babylon is given in *NBD*, p. 119. For more detail of excavations see *IBD*, 1, pp. 335–338. See also A. Parrot, *Babylon and the Old Testament*, pp. 23–67. The original excavation reports in German were published in *Wissenschaftliche Veröffentlichungen der Deutschen Orient Gesellschaft.*

31-33. By ignoring all warning Nebuchadrezzar brought disaster upon himself. His own boasting was interrupted by a voice from heaven, understood to be that of God (*cf. the Most High,* 32), addressed to the king by name. The words of Daniel's warning are repeated but with the preface *the king-dom has departed from you.* Jewish legend relates that during the period of the king's madness state officials took Amēl-Marduk and made him king in his father's place. However, Nebuchadrezzar returned and subsequently threw his son into prison for life, holding him responsible for this act of infidelity. Even after Nebuchadrezzar's death, so the story goes, it was only when the corpse had been dragged through the streets that Amēl-Marduk would ascend the throne.[1] In the light of the discovery of the Prayer of Nabonidus and its possible implications for this chapter[2] doubt has been cast on the value of this legendary material, a slightly different version of which was referred to by Jerome.[3] Yet it is important to take account of such evidence as there is for a period which is not well documented.

The pathetic condition of the erstwhile king, dishevelled and unkempt among the animals, brings to an end the account in the third person.

a¹. Thanksgiving for recovery (4:34-37)

Restored to his right mind, Nebuchadrezzar takes over the narrative, with the simple explanation *I, Nebuchadnezzar, lifted my eyes to heaven.* That he was able to do so proves that he was still human and capable of response to God, despite his derangement. The one who, 'grown and become strong' (22), had no use for the Most High is now 'the lowliest of men' (17). Thus suffering has a kindly role here (*cf.* Jn. 11:4), and enables the king to appreciate how frail he is. Having learnt his lesson he is restored to health and to his throne.

34, 35. The song of praise, reminiscent of Psalms 145:13; 115:3; Isaiah 40:17; 14:27, is not so incongruous as might at first sight appear. *Him who lives for ever* merely applied absolutely to God the courtly ascription to the human king in

---

[1] R. H. Sack, *Amēl-Marduk 562-560 BC* (*Alter Orient und Altes Testament,* 4, 1972), p. 26.

[2] See Additional Note, below, p. 117.

[3] Quoted by Ginsberg, who in turn is quoted by R. H. Sack, *op. cit.,* p. 26.

2 :4. In the Prayer of Nabonidus the moon god Sin is addressed as 'Lord of gods . . . king of kings, lord of lords . . . with the fear of thy great divinity, heaven and earth are filled . . . without thee who can accomplish anything?'[1] The devotees of false gods were not devoid of suitable vocabulary for worship, but Nebuchadrezzar's psalm is no formality. He has felt his impotence even to question the intention of this God, and is duly reverential. Moreover he recognizes that there is a heavenly kingdom transcending his own, and claiming his allegiance.

It is important to note the connection here between the exercise of faith and the return of reason. While he was full of his own importance Nebuchadrezzar's world revolved round himself. It did not strike him how unrealistic this was until he was brought low by illness. Sanity begins with a realistic self-appraisal.

36, 37. How deeply the lesson went is open to question, for the characteristic self-centred language reappears. Habitual thought-patterns of a lifetime are not easily changed. In saying *I . . . honour the King of heaven* Nebuchadrezzar was using a form of address which comes only here in the Bible. As a synonym for God the word 'heaven' occurs as a catch-word in this chapter (verses 13, 20, 26, 34, 37). This impersonal reference to God keeps Him at a distance, and this last word of Nebuchadrezzar in the book, while formally acknowledging the power and justice of God, appears to fall short of penitence and true faith. What these stories vividly illustrate is the providential ordering of the events of human lives, not only of believers but of unbelievers also; God does not leave Himself without witness, but desires all men to come to a knowledge of the truth (1 Tim. 2 :4).

Additional Note on the Prayer of Nabonidus

Among the many thousands of documents from Cave IV at Qumran, one which J. T. Milik first published became known as 'The Prayer of Nabonidus'. It is a small document in Aramaic which reads, 'The words of the prayer made by Nabonidus, king of [Assyria and of Ba]bylon, [the great] king, [when he was smitten] with a malignant disease, by the decree

[1] C. J. Gadd, 'The Harran Inscription of Nabonidus' in *Anatolian Studies,* VIII, 1958, p. 61.

of the [Most High God in the town of] Teima. "I was smitten [with a malignant disease] for a period of seven years, and became unlike [men. But when I had confessed my sins] and faults, God vouchsafed me a magician. He was a Jew from among [those exiled in Babylon]. He gave his explanation, and wrote an order that honour and [great glory] should be given to the Name of the [Most High God. And thus he wrote: While] you were smitten with a [malignant] disease [in the town of] Teima [by decree of the Most High God], you prayed for seven years [to gods] of silver and gold, [of bronze, iron], wood, stone and clay. . . ." [1] It is assumed that the story would continue to relate how the Jewish 'magician' (the same word as *gāz^{e}rayyā'* in 4:7 (Aram. 4:4)) exhorted the king to seek the God of the Jews, and that the king found healing.

Long before this text came to light there had been conjectures that this story of Nebuchadrezzar's illness might originally have been told of the lesser-known king, Nabonidus.[2] The king's name (Aram. *nbny*) in the Cave 4 text is taken to be an abbreviated form of Nabonidus, the name of the last king of Babylon. The expected spelling would be *nbnd*, which 'having possibly become corrupted to *nbkd* . . . was then regarded as an abbreviation of Nebuchadnezzar'.[3] The number seven occurs in Daniel 4:16. Teima is known to have been the residence of Nabonidus for ten years of his reign, and the general similarity between the Prayer and Daniel 4 has given rise to the opinion that the Qumran text represents an older and more accurate version of the story. Traditions about Nabonidus, it is argued, became attached to the more famous name Nebuchadrezzar, presumably after the story was brought to Palestine.

Nevertheless there are significant differences, and there is no sign of literary dependence.[4] For this reason an independent

---

[1] The translation is from J. T. Milik, *Ten Years of Discovery in the Wilderness of Judea*, pp. 36, 37. Bracketed conjectures to complete the sense of the damaged text vary slightly in other versions.

[2] See, *e.g., ICC*, pp. 221f. Herodotus knew only the name Labynetos for both Nebuchadrezzar (Labynetos I) and Nabonidus (Labynetos II).

[3] F. F. Bruce, 'The Book of Daniel and the Qumran Community' in *Neotestamentica et Semitica*, p. 224.

[4] Louis F. Hartman, 'The Great Tree and Nabuchodonosor's Madness' in John L. McKenzie (ed.), *The Bible in Current Catholic Thought* (Herder and Herder, 1962), pp. 78–82.

but more conservative line of orally-transmitted material from Babylon is suggested. The fact that it arrived in Qumran after the book of Daniel was completed suggests to D. N. Freedman that members of the sect had brought it from Babylon at a relatively recent time. The Daniel stories he thinks to have preserved essentially Babylonian traditions (apart from the name), which had already assumed their present form in the pre-Palestinian period and were incorporated as a unit by the author of Daniel.[1]

A recent edition of the text[2] dates the script as coming from a document written at the beginning of the Christian era, 'but the writing itself might be some centuries older. The language of 4QOrNab corresponds significantly with that of Daniel'. Despite the lateness of the script as compared with some of the fragments of Daniel, the account is reckoned to represent an earlier stage in the tradition history of Daniel 4. Part of the evidence is that the seer, though said to be a Jew, was not yet identified with Daniel.

The new translation given in this edition is more in line with Daniel 4 than that of Milik given above. In some cases this involves a different understanding of the decipherable text, so that 'unlike [men]' becomes instead 'like the animals', and 'He gave his explanation' is taken as an imperative, 'Make a proclamation', in accordance with which 'you were smitten' becomes 'I was smitten'. The disease, translated here 'malignant boils', remains quite different from the malady described in Daniel 4.

Commenting on the work of J. T. Milik and R. Meyer in this connection, J. C. H. Lebram draws attention to the poverty of our information about the period.[3] It is tempting to speculate, but until more evidence comes to light it is impossible to evaluate these theories, and meanwhile the text of Daniel has not been proved incorrect. There the name is clearly Nebuchadrezzar, and it remains a conjecture that the text became corrupted; his illness was different from that of Nabonidus, which was strictly 'a burning' or inflammation, and he was in Babylon, not Teima.

[1] 'The Prayer of Nabonidus', *BASOR,* 145, 1957, pp. 31f.

[2] B. Jongeling, C. J. Labuschagne, A. S. van der Woude, *Aramaic Texts from Qumran* (Leiden, 1976), pp. 123ff.

[3] J. C. H. Lebram, 'Perspektiven der Gegenwartigen Danielforschung', *JSJ,* V, 1975, p. 12.

C¹. Judgment on Belshazzar (5:1–31)

Without any explanation or indication of date the narrative leaps from the reign of Nebuchadrezzar to the very end of the Babylonian empire, the night on which its last ruler was killed and the city fell to the Medes and Persians. Chapters 5 and 6 are one continuous narrative in which the profligate Belshazzar contrasts with the well-meaning but outwitted Darius. Thus three monarchs are shown with their different responses to the living God. None of them is deliberately persecuting the people of God in the way that Antiochus Epiphanes was to do centuries later; persecution is not the point, though in chapters 3 and 6 godly men did suffer. The episodes chosen demonstrate that the world's great empires, and the kings who represent them, are all subject to the God of the exiles from Judah, who made Himself known outside the land of promise as well as within it.

The historicity of Belshazzar is argued in the Introduction.[1] Despite the references to him which have appeared in Babylonian documents, little is known of the man apart from the derogatory information of this chapter. With the armies of a conqueror pressing at the capital this deputy ruler took refuge in an orgy of wine. Throwing off all restraint and defying the accepted sanctions, he sent for the sacred cups and bowls which had been plundered years before from the Jerusalem temple (Dn. 1:2), so that he and his guests could use them at the banquet. Mysterious writing on the wall struck terror in the place of revelry, and Daniel alone was able to expound the significance of the cryptic words. The chapter ends dramatically with the death of Belshazzar and the fall of the Neo-Babylonian empire.

It is not easy to reconstruct the events surrounding the fall of Babylon. The so-called Nabonidus Chronicle[2] is incomplete, but it tells of the return of Nabonidus to Babylon to perform the new year festival. The date is missing, but 'seventeenth year' is conjectured, for the armies of Cyrus were closing in. The month Tashritu (the seventh month) is named in connection with the attack of Cyrus on the Babylonian army at Opis on the Tigris and the revolt of the city and its massacre. 'The 15th day Sippar was seized without battle. Nabonidus fled.

[1] See above, pp. 21–23.
[2] *ANET*, pp. 305f.

The 16th day Gobryas the governor of Gutium and the army of Cyrus entered Babylon without battle.' Presumably this was the event referred to in Daniel 5 :30, though it was during the next month that Cyrus entered the city in person (2 November 539).

Seen in the light of this background Belshazzar's banquet was sheer bravado, the last fling of a terrified ruler unsuccessfully attempting to drown his fears. Little wonder that panic seized him and made a fool of him as soon as the unexpected happened. The fact that his father abandoned the capital and left him to face the enemy arouses a certain amount of sympathy for this weak and sacrilegious prince.

a. The writing on the wall (5:1–12)

1–4. The extravagance of the feast described here is not without parallels (*cf.* Esther 1 and references to Persian drinking habits[1]). The word *thousand* is no doubt to be taken as a round figure giving the approximate number of guests, before whom Belshazzar *drank wine* at the high table after the meal. *When he tasted the wine* refers at face-value to the banqueting ritual which marked the start of wine-drinking, but some commentators have taken these words as a reference to the influence of the wine upon him, and they may be right, for superstition alone would normally guard a man from putting sacred vessels to a common use. The inclusion of *wives* and *concubines* at such a feast differs from Esther 1 :9–12. Their civilizing influence in the circumstances would be limited (*cf.* 1 Esdras 4 :29–32). *Then they brought in the golden and silver vessels.* The RSV translators have supplied the words 'and silver' from the early versions, thus completing the sense from verse 2. Though the versions could represent a more exact original, the author may have preferred to avoid exact repetition.

5–9. It is significant that only the king is said to have seen *the fingers of a man's hand* writing *on the plaster of the wall . . . , opposite the lampstand.* The circumstantial detail suggests the testimony of an eyewitness, in this case the king himself. The excavation of the palace has uncovered beyond

---

[1] Carey A. Moore, 'Archaeology and the Book of Esther', *BA,* 38, Sept.–Dec. 1975. Several classical allusions to such feasts are given by Montgomery (*ICC,* p. 250).

three impressive courtyards a large room (52m by 17m) which has become known as the Throne Room. 'Inside the throne room, and facing the doorway, a recessed niche in the wall probably indicates where the king's throne stood.'[1] One wall was 'adorned with a design in blue enamelled bricks', but the others were covered with white plaster.

The *lampstand (nebraštâ)*, spoken of as though it were the only one in the huge hall, may have been unusual, for the word is not otherwise known. In its light the king saw the hand moving as it wrote. Immediately he was seized with symptoms of extreme fear, ludicrous to those ignorant of the vision which had caused them. In a state of collapse the king *cried aloud* for help. By appropriating the sacred treasures he had brought upon himself a divine response, a word written for him alone, which was a privilege he did not appreciate.

On the principle that wealth will buy anything, Belshazzar offers his reward in terms which would have appealed to him: right to wear the royal *purple,* a gold chain of office and the status of *third ruler in the kingdom.* 'Third' may be intended literally, but it has been pointed out that the term may indicate an army rank.[2] The helplessness of *the enchanters, the Chaldeans, and the astrologers* (see notes on 2:2 and 4:7), and therefore of the king, forms a stark contrast with the brash confidences of verses 1–4, and the mirth came to a sudden end.

10–12. The identity of *the queen* is of interest; she is evidently not Belshazzar's queen, for his wives and concubines were present at the feast and this lady was not. She was at court in the reign of Nebuchadrezzar and her memory appears to go back to the early days of his reign. The mother of Nabonidus is known to have been a powerful personality, who hints at having obtained the throne for her son, whose paternity is not mentioned,[3] but she seems to be ruled out because the Nabonidus Chronicle records the death of the king's mother

[1] A. Parrot, *Babylon and the Old Testament,* pp. 39f.
[2] J. V. Kinnier Wilson, *The Nimrud Wine Lists,* p. 7. See also the Introduction, above, p. 22, footnote 2.
[3] C. J. Gadd, 'The Harran Inscription of Nabonidus', *Anatolian Studies,* VIII, 1958, pp. 35–92. Her name is Adda-guppi, 'votaress of the gods of Sin, Nergal, Nuska and Sadarmunna, my deities'. See also *ANET*[3], pp. 560–563. She makes no mention of her husband in any of her inscriptions.

in the ninth year of his reign.[1] This queen is most likely to have been the wife of Nabonidus and mother of Belshazzar.

On this occasion the queen mother took the liberty of entering the king's presence unbidden (*cf.* Est. 4:11); so unlikely did this seem to LXX translators that they began this verse 'The king called the queen on account of the mystery'. But the political emergency, not to mention the personal plight of the king, would override protocol. Her welcome suggestion that there was someone who could help gave hope. Here was information to act upon, even if it was a last resort. Belshazzar was unlikely to appreciate the elderly Daniel, hence the testimonial of the queen, couched in the formalized language of 4:8, 9 (*cf.* 1:17). Daniel had testified that the source of his knowledge was God alone (2:28).

b. Daniel's interpretation (5:13-31)

13-16. On being presented to the king Daniel hears what others have said about him, what is being asked of him and the reward he can expect if he is able to meet the challenge.

17-23. Daniel begins by dissociating himself from any thought of reward. This was in line with prophetic consciousness that the needed word of wisdom came from the Lord, and that it could not be bought at any price (Nu. 22:18; Mi. 3:5). On the contrary it was fitting that Belshazzar, like Naaman before him (2 Ki. 5:16), should acknowledge his debt to the true God and not delude himself into thinking that he could discharge that debt with rewards, or purchase his release from disaster.

Belshazzar had made mention of 'the king my father' (verse 13). Daniel proceeds to fill in the picture of the dealings of the

---

[1] *ANET*, p. 306. She was born in 650 BC and lived to the ripe old age of 104. The influence in Judah of the queen mother is well attested (2 Ki. 24:15) and there is evidence that in Persia 'she might properly hold the title of queen' (*ICC*, p. 258). Those who think Nabonidus is the person intended instead of Nebuchadrezzar in this chapter point out that the queen's frequent references to 'your father' would be explained if she was the wife of Nabonidus (*cf.* F. M. Cross, *BASOR*, 145, 1957, p. 32). Also the transition between chapters 4 and 5 would be less abrupt. It has already been argued, however, that there is no good reason for substituting Nabonidus for Nebuchadrezzar, and certainly Nebuchadrezzar is intended in verse 13. For the use of 'father' in connection with kingship see the Introduction, above, p. 22. The constant reference to Nebuchadrezzar as father of the king seems to betray a fear of rejection as illegitimate.

Most High God with Nebuchadrezzar his 'father', in order to demonstrate that, great as he was, he owed his empire to the Most High God who had given it to him. The attributes of verse 18 are in Scripture ascribed to the Lord (1 Ch. 29:11; Rev. 5:13) and not to men, but if men appropriated them they needed to learn that they were subject to a higher authority. This lesson Nebuchadrezzar had learnt when he was driven from among *men* (21; *bᵉnê ʾᵃnāšāʾ*, lit. 'sons of men', that is, human kind) to live like a beast. Belshazzar had not learnt the lesson of history and was in all the greater danger than his father because he had deliberately defied *the Lord* (Aram. *mārēʾ* : see note on 2:47) *of heaven* (23) by profaning what had been dedicated to Him, worshipping lifeless gods, and giving not even a passing nod to the God to whom he owed his very existence. He has had many successors. Against the background of wilful rejection of truth he could have known, Belshazzar hears the meaning of the handwriting.

24-31. Daniel's first point is that the hand which wrote was sent from the Creator God with a message expressly for the king. Only now is the wording of the writing disclosed, and its meaning given.

The three terms, *Mene, Tekel* and *Parsin* (the 'u' of *Upharsin* of AV, RV is 'and') were meaningful to readers of Hebrew and Aramaic and did not represent some strange tongue, as they do for most modern readers. For the king the difficulty was not to give the 'dictionary definition' of the terms, but to see what significance they had for him.

It is nevertheless a fact that scholars have had the added task of identifying the words and their original connotation. This is not made easier by the oriental love of word-play, so that one cryptogram can convey a world of meaning. The suggestion that these words were the names of weights was made at the end of the last century by Clermont-Ganneau[1] and has since been substantiated. An account of the way understanding unfolded is given by Emil Kraeling.[2] The early view was that *parsin* meant 'portions', but in 1878 the discovery in the British Museum of a weight bearing the inscription *prš* led to investigation of the late Hebrew *prš*. It means 'half' anything. *Tekel* was thought to be the Aramaic equivalent

---

[1] *Journal Asiatique*, Juillet–Aout 1886, pp. 36ff. Reprinted in *Recueil d'Archéologie Orientale*, i, 1888, pp. 136ff.
[2] 'The Writing on the Wall', *JBL*, 63, 1944, pp. 11ff.

of 'shekel' and *mene* would be 'mina'. C. C. Torrey rejected this theory; but in 1923 the spelling 'tekel' turned up in an Assuan papyrus[1], and S. M. Paul and W. G. Dever, in a useful section on weights and measures, include a table arranged according to the Mesopotamian system, showing the ratios of measures of weight.[2] The mina is well known (1 Ki. 10:17; Ezr. 2:69; Ne. 7:71, 72). So obvious were these words to Jewish expositors that they postulated that the words were written vertically from left to right to form an anagram. Read horizontally they would be unintelligible; but the significance, as opposed to the meaning of the words, was sufficiently obscure without such a device.

Here then was the king, confronted with three words indicating measures of weight, mina, shekel, half (as it might be 'ton, hundredweight, quarter'), and claiming to have seen a magical hand writing them! In view of the effects of much wine the appearance of a hand is not difficult to account for, and it was suggested many years ago that 'the words *Mene, Tekel, Parsin* are just what would be suitable to a steward's room, which may have communicated with the banqueting hall. . . . Some serving man may have left the door into the banqueting hall open so that the words caught the king's eye at a moment when his conscience was struggling with his clouded brain, and the lights of the candlestick may have contributed to produce the awful effect. Nevertheless, it was a message from God, though produced, as Divine messages usually are, by natural means'.[3] The suggestion accounts for the facts recorded, and in no way detracts from the truth of verse 24.

The *interpretation* (*pešar*) which follows is based not on these nouns but on verbs associated with them. Daniel's skill consisted in drawing the connection between the sign given and the doom which he knew to be imminent. Such solving of riddles (*cf.* verse 12) is reminiscent of the 'wisdom' of much earlier days (Jdg. 14:14; Pr. 23:29, 30), with which it has in common the ability to see clearly the outcome of a given way of life. *Mene* is explained as the past participle of a verb *menē'*,

[1] A. Cowley (ed.), *Aramaic Papyri of the Fifth Century B.C.*, 10, 5.
[2] S. M. Paul and W. G. Dever, *Biblical Archaeology* (Keter Publishing House, Jerusalem, 1973), p. 179. See also *NBD*, pp. 1320f.
[3] Margaret D. Gibson, 'Belshazzar's Feast', *ET*, XXIII, 1911–1912, p. 181.

'numbered' or *mᵉnâ,* 'appointed', a verb used in 2:49 and 3:12. Similarity of sound conveys the double idea that a destiny shapes his end and that his 'days are numbered'. *Tekel* (Heb. *šeqel*) is taken in its verbal form to mean 'weighed' or 'assessed'. The idea is present in 1 Samuel 2:3, 'by him [the Lord] actions are weighed' (*cf.* Jb. 31:6). Like the men whom the psalmist had in mind (Ps. 62:9), Belshazzar fails to tip the balance and reveals his lack of solid worth on God's scales. *Pêrēs* (*Parsin* is plural) is literally 'part', hence 'half-mina', and the verbal form means 'shared'; Belshazzar's kingdom is to be shared out between the Medes and *Persians* (*Pārās*). This extended play on the word did not require mention of the Medes, but they are coupled with the Persians here and in the following chapter as joint conquerors of the Neo-Babylonian empire. As a matter of history Cyrus headed up the Medo-Persian empire when he conquered Babylon in 539 BC.

The promise of reward was implemented and Daniel was decked in the insignia of his new status and proclaimed 'third ruler', but the honour was short-lived. *That very night* the end came, not only for the king but for the Babylonian empire. The new ruler would appoint his own cabinet. The name *Darius the Mede* is unknown to history apart from this book.[1] The inclusion of the information, *being about sixty-two years old,* implies the existence of a particular person and not just a vague memory.

This chapter illustrates the involvement of king and kingdom in one destiny. Belshazzar's blatant disrespect for the Most High God was all of a piece with the national character, indeed with our human condition, as it is depicted in Psalm 90. Though human days are numbered (verse 10), few number them for themselves and 'get a heart of wisdom' (verse 12). Belshazzar in this chapter presents a vivid picture of the fool, the practising atheist, who at the end can only brazen it out with the help of alcohol which blots out the stark reality.

Looked at from another point of view, the chapter contains a shrewd comment on power politics. 'The whole chapter is an instructive symbolic assessment of the perils and limits, the sources and responsibilities, of power in human affairs.'[2]

[1] For discussion of his identity, see the Introduction, above, pp. 23–28.
[2] Paul Lehmann, *The Transfiguration of Politics* (SCM Press, 1975), p. 311, footnote.

Leadership was lacking and a change of government was overdue. There can be little doubt that in this case it was a change for the better.

B¹. Darius the Mede sees Daniel rescued (6:1–28)

Despite the change of government Daniel continued to enjoy favour. This is the point of interest connecting the two chapters. The Persian empire, which incorporated that of the Medes, a vast area forming an arc to the north of the Babylonian territories, extended eventually to Asia Minor, Libya and Egypt to the west, and to the Indus river and the Aral Sea to the east. It was the largest empire the world had yet seen, hence the urgent need for an efficient organization from the very beginning. The division of the whole kingdom into satrapies is known from Esther 8:9, where the number given is 127, but that belongs some fifty years later than the fall of Babylon. Strictly the text speaks only of the appointment of satraps (see note on 3:2), and above the satraps were three overseers, of whom Daniel was one. When it seemed that Daniel was set for promotion his jealous peers schemed to bring about his death, but they were thwarted in their plot.

Similarities between this chapter and chapter 3 include not only the general theme of God's deliverance from certain death but also structure, style and vocabulary. There is the same use of repetition effectively employed so that, for example, the thrice-repeated refrain 'the law of the Medes and the Persians, which cannot be revoked' anticipates the irony of verse 26, where the new decree effectively negates the object of the original decree of verse 7. There is also a certain overlap in vocabulary between the two chapters, illustrated by the word 'satrap' just cited, by *dāṭ*, 'decree' (3:29; 6:5 'law') and by the idiom 'make a decree' (3:10, 29; 6:26).

So far as subject-matter is concerned, however, there are important differences. Daniel, hitherto prosperous, is now in his old age subjected to trial as his friends had been but, as Driver points out, 'it is not a question of a positive sin which he will not commit, but of a positive duty which he will not omit'.[1] Merely by continuing a lifelong habit of worship he is contravening the law of the land. His miraculous deliverance,

[1] *CB*, p. 71.

like that of the three friends in chapter 3, is not, of course, the experience of all who are loyal to God in persecution (*cf.* Acts 12 :2 and 11), but examples still occur in times of severe trial, especially perhaps in churches newly born in a pagan environment.

The modern man who is accustomed to seeing lions only in the zoo finds the very idea of a king keeping lions somewhat fantastic, though an increasing number of safari parks, even in the western world, have brought lions back into the natural scene. In the ancient Near East the sport of kings was lion-hunting, as works of art from Egypt to Mesopotamia prove [1] (*cf.* Ezk. 19 :6, 8, 9). The pit in which the lions were kept provided a trouble-free method of disposing of undesirable members of society in Roman as well as Persian times.

That Daniel escaped from the mouth of the lions is the point of the story (Heb. 11 :33), just as the miraculous escape of the righteous from their persecutors is the point of the books of Judith, Tobit, Susanna, Bel and the Dragon in the Apocrypha, and of the Wisdom of Aḥikar.[2] The period of persecution was only just beginning for God's people in the sixth century BC and deliverances from death had a symbolic significance beyond the actual event. As G. J. Wenham points out,[3] a book of old, authentic stories would have provided comfort to sufferers of later generations far more convincingly than a book of new parables (*cf.* Heb. 11, especially verses 33, 34).

a. The plot (6:1–9)

1–5. *Darius* the Mede, who was, as we have argued,[4] none other than Cyrus the Persian, using what may well have been his enthronement name during the first year of his reign,[5] contrasts in character with Belshazzar. The way in which he is portrayed is in keeping with what is known of Cyrus from

---

[1] Yigael Yadin, *The Art of Warfare in Biblical Lands* (Weidenfeld and Nicolson, 1963), pp. 214, 215, 300, 380.
[2] See Introduction, above, p. 49.
[3] *Themelios*, 2.2, 1977, p. 51.
[4] See Introduction, above, pp. 26–28.
[5] The name Darius is used only in connection with the first year (5:31; 9:1; 11:1). Tiglath Pileser III (745–727 BC) ruled as king of Babylon from 729 as Pul; his son Shalmaneser V ruled in Babylon under the name Ululai. It was far from uncommon to adopt more than one name.

Ezra 1 and the Cyrus Cylinder.[1] His intention in appointing overseers of his civil service is that *the king might suffer no loss,* that is, in territory due to uprisings, or in taxation due to graft. The danger was ever present (*cf.* Ezr. 4:13, relating to the next century) and a senior person known to be impervious to corruption (verse 4) would be an obvious candidate for extra responsibility. In obedience to the law of the land Daniel was above reproach, but if the law of his God conflicted with the law of the land, opportunity might arise to make accusation against him. The writer is not claiming that Daniel was sinless, but only that he was law-abiding, and that his first allegiance was to his God.

6–9. The suggestion made to the king was calculated to boost his ego and give expression to his new authority. Such evidence of allegiance on the part of his civil servants would be wholly welcome; if it implied that he was semi-divine this too would play its part in establishing him as king (*cf.* 3:7), and even if it did encroach on private, personal religious devotion, the period of the edict was limited and no possible harm could be envisaged. The inexperienced king could hardly have been expected to realize that some ulterior motive prompted this show of loyalty, or, if he was suspicious (for the verb 'came by agreement' is a little weak; collusion and conspiracy are implied), he could think of no ground for concern. He therefore signed the document which made him god-king for thirty days, according to the law of *the Medes and the Persians* (linked unmistakably as one kingdom), *which cannot be revoked*. The assumption that Persian law could not be altered is made in Esther 1:19 and 8:8, and Montgomery cites an incident in the reign of Darius III (336–331 BC) when that king put to death a man he knew to be innocent : 'immediately he repented and blamed himself, as having greatly erred; but it was not possible to undo what was done by royal authority.'[2] There is reason therefore to take seriously the immutability of laws passed by the Medo-Persian regime.

b. Daniel accused (6:10–18)

10. As soon as the document had been signed Daniel knew that he had been framed. If the possibility occurred to him that he could change his prayer routine, or pray without ap-

[1] *ANET*, p. 315.
[2] *ICC*, p. 270. The quotation is from Diodorus Siculus xvii.30.

pearing to do so, it was dismissed as out of the question. He steadily continued his lifelong habit of regular prayer, as his accusers expected he would. Had he taken evasive action no doubt some other plot would have been laid against him, and by saving his own skin he would have betrayed the God whom he had served for some seventy years. Nothing would have been gained and he would have lost the opportunity to prove the faithfulness of his God.

Verse 10 supplies welcome evidence concerning prayer habits during the later biblical period. *Windows . . . open toward Jerusalem* is a literal understanding of Solomon's petition, 'when he comes and prays toward this house, hear thou' (1 Ki. 8:41–43; *cf.* 2 Ch. 6:34). The fact that Jerusalem was in ruins called forth faith that it would again be restored because the God who had set His name on the city was the continuing, unchanging God, in control of history (Ps. 106:44–47; Lam. 3:31–33). Prayer towards Jerusalem is mentioned also in later Greek books: Tobit 3:11; 1 Esdras 4:58. *He got down upon his knees,* prostrating himself in worship (*cf.* 1 Ki. 8:54; Ezr. 9:5; Ps. 95:6; Lk. 22:41; but *cf.* also Gn. 18:22; Ps. 106:23; Je. 18:20; Mt. 6:5; Lk. 18:11). There is evidence for both standing and kneeling in prayer. *Three times a day* may take literally Psalm 55:17, 18, where David in a time of danger also testifies to the value of set habits of prayer. This verse became axiomatic for the rabbis, though they attributed the institution of the practice to Moses.[1]

In the east windows are small and high, as a protection against heat and robbers respectively; there was often a wooden lattice-work in place of glass, so letting in any breeze, but obscuring the view of prying eyes.

11. Apart from deliberate intent (*came by agreement*; *cf.* verse 6), Daniel's prayer would have gone unnoticed. This was intrusion into personal liberty such as is not unknown today in some situations, usually under the cover of some political or quasi-political issue.

12–14. Having rehearsed the terms of the law they wished to invoke, and heard the king repeat that it could not be repealed, the deputation accused Daniel of blatant law-breaking. The distress of the king, who had become trapped by his own legislation, reveals the dilemma of a ruler who wishes to

[1] G. F. Moore, *Judaism,* II (Cambridge, 1946), pp. 218, 220.

pursue liberal policies, but who is under pressure from his court, and therefore less than free, although he seems to have all power. 'Did you not sign?' (12), 'you have signed' (13), 'the king establishes' (15). Absolute power could not achieve the release of Daniel because of the greater power of united public opinion. This is an altogether different dilemma from those which faced Nebuchadrezzar or Belshazzar, and presents another aspect of the limitations of a human ruler (*cf.* Mk. 15 : 15). There is also more than a side-glance at laws which become absolute and are rigidly enforced, with resulting injustice to individual citizens.

15. The tyrants would not permit the king to play for time. The sentence had to be carried out that very day (again the same verb, *came by agreement*).

16-18. Pressure made the king give in. He commanded and the sentence he least wanted to pass was carried out, but not without a prayer that Daniel's God would deliver him. It is this prayer above all that makes this chapter different from all that has gone before, because an 'outsider', a king of the nations, is exercising faith, however dimly, in Daniel's God, and it is in the interests of fostering that faith that evidence of God's power can be expected. No prayer of Daniel is recorded, but he is less concerned for himself and his safety than is the king, who spent a sleepless night and refused both food and *diversions* (the exact meaning of *daḥᵃwān* is not known).

The text implies that the lion-pit had two entrances, a ramp down which the animals would enter, and a hole in the roof by which the food would normally be fed to them. Whether Daniel was thrown in from the top or from the side, there would be only one way out unless someone let down a rope. It was probably to prevent such a rescue that *a stone was brought . . . and the king sealed it with his own signet and with the signet of his lords* (17). In this way neither party could act independently of the other, and the possibility of surreptitious intervention was ruled out (*cf.* Mt. 27 :66).

c. Daniel's deliverance (6:19-28)

19-23. Sunrise saw the king making his way anxiously (rather than *in haste,* though that is also implied) to the lion-pit. In his question he speaks of *the living God* of Daniel, who had probably used the name (*cf.* Dt. 5 :26; Jos. 3 :10; Je. 10 :10; *etc.*). The reply of Daniel proves that his God is indeed living, and has been able to deliver him. The implication that God *is* and that He rewards those who trust Him is the most important discovery Darius could make. While Daniel claims that he has been spared because he was *blameless* (22), that is, innocent of the charge against him, the narrator claims it was *because he had trusted in his God* (23). Both are true. Daniel was *taken up out of the den,* much in the same way as Jeremiah (Je. 38 : 11-13), and was found to be entirely unharmed. If we ask how this miracle could be (*cf.* Heb. 11 :33), a clue is found in the prophetic literature (Is. 11 :6; 65 :25; Ho. 2 :18) and in the intention at creation that man should have dominion over the beasts. 'Part of the glory of the coming regeneration when the king comes back, will be that nature and the lower orders of creation will once again be subject to man redeemed and saved to sin no more.'[1] In the man of God the powers of the world to come have broken in, in anticipation of what will be when the king comes to reign.

24. Retribution fell on those who had falsely accused Daniel, and on their wives and families. This is recorded as a fact, without either approval or disapproval. The solidarity of the family when punishment was inflicted is attested in Persian times by Herodotus (iii.119). Mass executions under the Nazis have proved the extent to which rulers will go in attempting to achieve their sadistic aims, and in this knowledge the tragic dénouement is less absurd than Montgomery thought.[2] If the story is taken at its face-value, and not interpreted as the work of a second-century Jew, the action of the king is entirely understandable. He did not know the prophetic teaching that every man was to die for his own sin (Je. 31 :29, 30; Ezk. 18), but acted according to the accepted standards in Persian society (*cf.* the massacre in Est. 9, demanded by the Jews but authorized by the Persian king Ahasuerus).

25-28. The decree recalls that of Nebuchadrezzar (3 :29), but whereas his was couched negatively to punish any word against the God of the three men, here awe of Him is positively commanded throughout the empire. The ascription is rightly given poetic form in the more recent translations. As for its content, it sums up what Darius learnt of God from the experience. He repeats the name *'the living God'* (*cf.* verse 20);

---

[1] James Philip, *By the rivers of Babylon* (Didasko Press, Aberdeen, 1972), p. 18.
[2] *ICC,* p. 278.

enduring for ever picks up the thought expressed in the conventional address to the human king, 'live for ever', but asserts that there is a God of whom it is true; *his kingdom* is conceived not so much territorially as dynamically, for His rule overrides the agitations of men and accomplishes His will. Deliverance in this one instance is seen as proof of God's reign of righteousness, fundamental to the whole of history; *enduring for ever, ... to the end.*

The chapter ends with an enigmatic note connecting the reign of Darius with that of Cyrus. We have argued in the Introduction[1] that the word *and* here and often in the book, as for example 7:1, has the force of 'namely', or 'that is', so being used explicatively. The writer is explaining that the two names belong to the same person, and that the reader needs to note the fact (*cf.* 1:21; 10:1). 'The whole of 6:28 could be taken as the explanation of the introduction of a ruler's name otherwise unknown to the reader.'[2]

Survey of Part I

The time-span covered by these six chapters is from 605 BC, the year when Nebuchadrezzar became king of Babylon, to 539/538 BC, the first year of the Persian empire. Incidents selected from three reigns depict the confrontation between polytheistic rulers and the one true God as represented by His servants at the foreign courts. The significance of these stories is not unanimously agreed.

Porteous expresses a widely-held point of view : 'As we now have these stories ... they are intended by the author of the book to illustrate the qualities of loyalty and endurance which the crisis of the second century B.C. called for.'[3] In all these chapters then we are intended to sense the shadow of Antiochus IV, Epiphanes, imposing Greek ways of life on the Jews within their own city and district, and legislating against the practice of their covenant religion. Now in view of the

---

[1] See above, pp. 26f.

[2] D. J. Wiseman, *Notes on Some Problems in the Book of Daniel*, p. 12, footnote. He argues (p. 13) that Cyrus, who in inscriptions uses 'King of Anshan', 'King of Persia', 'King of Babylonia' or 'King of the lands', did not use 'King of Media' in view of the unity of the Aryan Medo-Persian coalition under his rule.

[3] Porteous, p. 16.

fact that the stories originated under alien regimes, it is to be inferred that they will have some bearing on the conduct of God's people under such circumstances at any time, including the Maccabean period, but scholars have been sensing that there are factors in these stories inappropriate to the witness of Jews during the crisis of the mid-second century BC.

Chapter 1 raises a cultural problem : how far should a loyal Jew accept the alien culture of a conqueror? The second-century Maccabees rejected the language, literature and customs of the Greeks, whereas Daniel and his friends accepted and adapted to all three, taking a stand only on the matter of gifts from the royal table. In the Nebuchadrezzar stories the addition of Qumran evidence to the cycle of Daniel literature has tended to convince scholars that Daniel 4 was formulated before the second century and should perhaps be seen in connection with Isaiah 2 :9ff.[1] The gradual capitulation of Nebuchadrezzar before the God of his captives, and the favour shown by Darius toward Daniel, make it hard to see that they easily pointed to the tyrant Antiochus. Belshazzar might seem to symbolize him, and yet chapter 5 is considered by Montgomery to be far more ancient than the second century BC.[2] Recently M. Delcor has expressed the opinion that this story circulated independently in the Persian period or at the beginning of the Greek period between 400 and 300 BC.[3] Lacocque, on the ground that the chapter bears witness to reminiscences of the fall of the Babylonian empire, agrees that its origin is older than the second century, but thinks it was modernized by the redactor in order to make it applicable to Antiochus.[4] Against the last point Montgomery's argument has weight, 'Belshazzar is not the type of the arrogant despot Antiochus Epiphanes; he does not appear as the destroyer of the Jewish religion, only as the typical profligate and frivolous monarch.'[5]

In the light of this uncertainty, what are the alternative possibilities? A fresh look at these selected stories from court life at Babylon is overdue. The characters ring true and yet the stories have not been written as character studies, nor are

---

[1] So Lacocque, p. 66.
[2] *ICC*, p. 249, where he cites J. Meinhold, G. Behrmann and D. S. Margoliouth in support.
[3] Delcor, p. 132.
[4] Lacocque, p. 77.
[5] *ICC*, p. 249.

the famous people the main interest of the writer. Many of the circumstantial details, once suspect on historical grounds, have now been proved authentic, but the writer is not mainly a historian. The unprejudiced reader notices that Daniel and his friends are not the persecuted victims of tyrant rulers in any of these narratives; when trouble comes it is the jealousy of disappointed rivals that brings them into conflict with the monarch (chapters 2 and 6). In other incidents Daniel proves to be of unusual service to the ruler who responds with honours and rewards, and grows fond of this gifted but un-compromising adviser. It was this devotion to principles that kept Daniel apart from his contemporaries (1 :8; 2 :18; 4 :7, 8; 5 :11). A man in touch with the living God was best left alone until his help became the only remaining resort; to receive the moral insights he brought was too humbling an experience to be welcome.

The dramatic interest in these stories consists precisely in the fact that Daniel and his friends represent the followers of the living God at the courts of the most powerful rulers the world had yet seen. Not since the sojourn in Egypt had such a confrontation taken place, but, whereas Joseph and his relatives had voluntarily remained in Egypt, Nebuchadrezzar had conquered Judah and, according to the understanding of that time, might have thought his gods superior to that of any conquered nation. In that respect the Babylon experience was new, and raised new questions for believing exiles. The writer of this book believes he has the answers to those questions. In every chapter his emphasis is on the superior might of the Most High God. Nebuchadrezzar did not have the decisive word in international affairs, for it was the Lord who gave Jerusalem into his hand (1 :2), and in Babylon God gave His loyal followers a favourable reception (1 :9) and equipped them with needed knowledge and insight (1 :17).

When the first great test came it was to the God of heaven that these men appealed for help (2 :18) and to whom Daniel gave the credit for the interpretation of the dream (2 :28). The central theme of chapter 3 is the ability of 'our God whom we serve' to deliver His servants out of the hand of the king of Babylon (3 :17, 18), and in chapter 4 the dramatic intervention of the God of heaven in the life of that same king is calcu-lated to bring even Nebuchadrezzar to the sanity of realistic self-appraisal and submission to the only God. In the presence of Belshazzar Daniel insists that the Most High God rules in the kingdoms of men (5:21), a fact which Belshazzar is at that moment facing along with his own guilt. The Most High God was giving him opportunity to repent on the last night of his life. Darius is different from either of the two previous kings, in that he is favourably disposed to Daniel from the start, and would have saved him from death if he could have changed his own decree. What the earthly emperor was unable to accomplish, the living God achieved; He shut the mouths of the lions and delivered His servant from death (Heb. 11:33).

The poems incorporated into the stories support the view that the writer's concern was the greatness of his God, for every one of them, whether in the mouth of Daniel (as in 2:20-23) or spoken by one of the kings of the nations (4:3, 34, 35; 6:26, 27) is a hymn of wonder at the evidence of God's rule in earth and heaven. Though many a psalm had taken up this theme, never before had there been an opportunity to witness in such alien circumstances the triumph of God over powerful international regimes. It follows that there can never be an emperor so mighty that he is not under the control of the only God; not only will his end come when God sees fit, but meanwhile he will serve God's purposes, and if he persists in his arrogance he will be brought up short by God's intervention (4:28; 5:30).

In the first part of his book the writer presents the situations out of which his theology has grown, and the lessons are plain for all to see. But from the very fact that his God is in control of time and circumstances in heaven as well as earth, any experience of His deeds, whenever it may have occurred, is valid for all time and even for eternity (6:26). It is on this firm theological understanding that the revelations of the second part of the book are made.

PART II: VISIONS

The four visions which make up the second part of the book are recorded in chronological order, just as the stories of part one are in historical sequence; there is, however, an overlap between the two parts. Chapters 7 and 8, in the first and third years of Belshazzar, belong chronologically between chapters 4 and 5; chapter 9 on our reckoning (see note on 9:1) takes place at approximately the same time as the events of chapter 6, and the last vision (chapters 10–12) is the latest date recorded in the book. The grouping of the material into two parts is thus seen to be deliberate. The change in subject-matter is immediately apparent. Whereas in previous chapters incidents are recorded in story form using mostly the third person, now Daniel relates experiences which purport to have come to him personally as dream visions. In the nature of the case these are unverifiable; historical questions no longer arise, not at least in the same form as they arose in chapters 1–6. Instead the reader is confronted by mysterious symbols, allusions, enigmatic phrases and numbers, which have baffled interpreters through the ages and have given rise to many different schemes of interpretation.

In the light of such difficulties there are two dangers at least which threaten the reader. On the one hand he may decide to omit these chapters from his study, preferring to confine himself to safer, more familiar parts of Scripture. On the other hand he may become over-absorbed in working out his own theory of their significance and become unbalanced in the amount of attention he gives to them at the expense of other parts of Scripture. The attempt will be made in expounding these visions to show that they are not without their connections with the rest of the Old Testament, and that it is these connections which provide the original material out of which the visions have grown. That does not mean that the possibility of foreign borrowing is ruled out; on the contrary, the book itself tells how thoroughly the young captives studied the literature and especially the wisdom of the Chaldeans (1:4). These acquired literary skills may well provide some of the symbolism and literary forms, but the books in which these men had been instructed from childhood were the formulating influence giving the direction to their thinking, and the same would be true of the editor/writer, whose theology plays so controlling a part in chapters 1–6.

A¹. Daniel has a vision of four kingdoms and of God's kingdom (7:1–28)

Though chapter 7 opens the second part of the book, it has affinities with what has gone before in two obvious respects. It is still in Aramaic, and from the language point of view continues the narrative of 2:4 – 6:28. It also has much in common, from the point of view of subject-matter, with chapter 2, so much so that it is impossible to interpret the one without reference to the other, as we shall see. Looked at in relation to the Aramaic section this chapter constitutes the climax, and it is the high point in relation to the whole book; subsequent chapters treat only part of the picture and concentrate on some particular aspect of it.

The vision is of four great beasts which come up out of the sea; three bear some resemblance to known animals, but the fourth is grotesque, sprouting ten horns, one of which is singled out for special mention. At that point Daniel perceives the throne-room of heaven and the awesome splendour of 'the Ancient of Days', seated to execute judgment on the beasts, whose kingdom was given to 'one like a son of man'. 'One of those who stood there' answered the questions Daniel raised, but mysteries remain, and the vision which so deeply disturbed Daniel continues to concern us, 'upon whom the end of the ages has come' (1 Cor. 10:11).

Despite the welter of interpretations there is one thing above all that the chapter is proclaiming quite unambiguously : the Most High is the reigning king in heaven and earth. There is an opposition to His rule, formidable in appearance and powerful, but all the time the Most High is in control, even when His opponents seem most successful (7:26). Therefore those who are allied with Him triumph also. No wonder the chapter has been called 'the centre of gravity of the whole book', and 'one of the summits of scripture'.[1]

Once convinced of the truth this chapter is proclaiming, the reader is in possession of the key to history. The international

[1] Lacocque, p. 98.

scene is not after all out of hand, for it is in God's hand, and individual lives find their meaning in relation to His kingdom. Those who pray sincerely 'Thy kingdom come' lose themselves in His great cause and in the process find their own identity (Mk. 8:35; 10:45).

a. The vision (7:1–14)

1. *The first year of Belshazzar* would be 552/551 BC, over fifty years since Daniel's deportation to Babylon. God does not reveal all His truths at once, even to the wise, but reserves much for age and experience. *A dream and visions of his head* may be another example of the special use of 'and' beloved by this writer (*cf.* note on 6:28). The Aramaic says 'Daniel *saw* a dream, even visions of his head' and we discern the writer's wish to convey that this was no ordinary dream. Daniel *wrote down the dream*, so that others could have knowledge of it, *and told the sum of the matter*. That sentence is a good example of the wordy style of the book; *cf.* NIV, 'He wrote down the substance of his dream'.

2. *Daniel said*. These words end the editorial introduction, and the rest of the book, apart from 10:1, is presented as a huge extract from Daniel's memoirs. Most commentators regard this as a literary device and take it that the writer proceeds to compose allegories in which to convey his message. We shall treat them as direct revelations from God to Daniel.

I saw in my vision by night is similar to Zechariah 1:8, and *the four winds of heaven* to Zechariah 2:6; 6:5 (cf. Dn. 8:8; 11:4). Here is a symbolic number which promises not to cause problems of interpretation. The four compass-points register every possible wind-direction, and as a working hypothesis we might take four to symbolize completeness, 'the whole earth' in this context. *The great sea*, whipped up by the winds, is the 'substance' of the vision; Daniel saw a limitless ocean, not an inland sea. To the Hebrews the sea was both dangerous and mysterious, a restless element (Is. 57:20) but not beyond the Lord's power to tame (Ps. 107:23–29). The nations were like the sea (Is. 17:12, 13).

3. In eagerness to identify the beasts it is important not to miss the emotional reactions these fierce symbols arouse. 'Signals and signs operate almost entirely at the rational and conscious level to convey compressed meanings which are known to the participants. Symbols proliferate meanings and

associations in the unconscious mind and feelings.'[1] The reader is meant to register terror before these fearsome beasts, especially in view of their supernatural features, and not regard them merely as signs, satisfactorily interpreted by reason alone. Moreover animals, normal, hybrid and mythical, depicting gods, cities and nations, though a common sight in Babylon, were repulsive to the exiles who lived by the law of Moses. These beasts, which Daniel saw, *came up out of the sea*, perhaps thrown up in its turmoil.

4. The first creature, combining the majesty of the *lion* with the power of the *eagle* (Aram. *neŝar*[2]), suggests dominion and strength. The lion and the eagle are both used by Jeremiah in a description of Nebuchadrezzar (Je. 49 : 19-22), and the plucking off of wings and being made to stand up like a man are reminiscent of chapter 4, where the proud, self-sufficient king is made to realize his weakness (*cf.* Ps. 49 :20).[3]

5. The second beast, *like a bear*, is almost as formidable as the first. The brown Syrian bear may weigh up to 250 kilos and has a voracious appetite, as this verse implies. *It was raised up on one side*, in the act of rising in order to pounce on more prey. *Three ribs* represent the victim of a previous hunt which has not satisfied its appetite.

6. *Another, like a leopard*, the most dangerous of the beasts of prey, is known for its sudden, unexpected attacks, and *with four wings of a bird on its back* attention is on its swiftness of movement (Hab. 1 :8). *And the beast had four heads.* If the

---

[1] Max Gluckman, *Politics, Law and Ritual in Tribal Society* (Oxford, 1965), p. 252. Quoted by Myrtle S. Langley, *Ritual Change among the Nandi: A Study of Change in Life-Crisis Rituals 1923–1973* (unpublished Ph.D. thesis, University of Bristol, 1976), p. 305.

[2] The lion of Babylon is illustrated by A. Parrot, *Babylon and the Old Testament,* facing p. 65. Zoologists of ancient times did not distinguish between the eagle and the vulture. In modern times eight species of eagle and four of vulture are found in Palestine. 'Most passages in which the word *nesher* occurs speak of the beauty and majesty of a bird of prey, which can most adequately be attributed to the eagle. This is also true of the passages from the book of Daniel (*neshar*).' *Fauna and Flora of the Bible: Helps for Translators,* XI (United Bible Societies, London, 1972), p. 84. Contrast Driver (*CB,* p. 81), quoting H. B. Tristram, *Natural History of the Bible,* pp. 172ff., where the griffon-vulture or great vulture is said to be the bird in question.

[3] For the view that the four beasts derive from the signs of the zodiac see A. Caquot, 'Les quatre bêtes et le fils d'homme', *Semitica,* XVII, 1967, pp. 35-71.

interpretation of 'four' suggested above is valid, this beast is looking in all directions for prey, *i.e.* empire. *And dominion was given to it*. Like the other two beasts it is subject to an unnamed higher power. It does not achieve dominion by its own abilities.

7, 8. If the other beasts were the most powerful and savage known to man, there is even worse to come, *a fourth beast, terrible and dreadful and exceedingly strong*. Its *great iron teeth* may correspond to the fourth layer of the image in chapter 2, but whereas there the image is static, here there is action of the most ruthless kind. *It had ten horns* : the horns of an animal represent its strength in self-defence or attack (Zc. 1 : 18–21). Ten horns, five times the natural two, represent pictorially the extraordinary power of this beast. And yet there is still another horn to come, and though it is *a little one* it succeeds in uprooting three of the first horns, so arrogating their power to itself. Its *eyes like the eyes of a man* give the clue that a human ruler is symbolized by the little horn, and by the other symbolic animals. If 'the eyes of a man' suggest powers of observation and intelligence, *a mouth speaking great things* has ominous overtones (Ps. 12 :3, 4; *cf.* Rev. 13 :5, 6).

Though the vision continues without a break it is convenient to survey the chapter so far in order to come to some tentative assessment of its meaning. World-rulers, glimpsed through the thin veil of imagery, all inspire terror, the more so as history progresses, for the worst is reserved for the end. Moreover the vision takes place in the night, when the darkness highlights fear and imagination is at its most vivid. If commentators are right in interpreting the great sea as a reference to the mythi-cal abyss of Babylonian literature, and home of all kinds of monsters,[1] little is added to the intensity of the emotional reaction, though the contention that we are in the realm of primitive fears is reinforced.

The writer was not encouraged to see in history evolutionary progress, but rather the reverse. Modern technological pro-gress in no way invalidates this judgment, for it is international justice, peace and human contentment and fulfilment that are in mind, and in these realms it would be hard to argue that there has been progress.

---

[1] See, *e.g.*, the discussion in Porteous, pp. 99ff. On their origin, the various theories are summed up by A. Caquot, 'Sur les quatre bêtes de Daniel', *Semitica*, V, 1955, pp. 6ff.

The juxtaposition of four winds and four beasts (verses 2, 3) raises the question whether the symbolism of four applies to both concepts. Are the four beasts meant to represent between them world-dominating figures of all time as four winds represent all possible directions? If so, this would not rule out the possibility of specific identities of some or all of the kings; they could still be representative figures.[1]

9, 10. The scene and character change is complete and instantaneous. *Thrones were placed* but only one was occupied, and the seer's attention is riveted by that one, the only one that mattered. He is seeing heaven. The balanced poetry conveys the order and beauty which surround the divine judge as opposed to the chaos of the sea and its beasts.

One that was ancient of days, or 'elderly', is an unusual expression; it appears in Enoch 47:3 as 'the Head of days', suggesting that he is the source of time,[2] but that is a later interpretation. RSV may be right in avoiding capital letters on the grounds that at first the seer does not grasp the significance of the scene, and sees only an old man, seated on a throne. Unlike Ezekiel (Ezk. 1:4–25) he is totally unprepared for a vision of God. The dazzling whiteness of both robes and hair[3] would be suggestive of purity (Ps. 51:7), and as he discerned the fiery nature of the throne and its wheels the likeness to Ezekiel's vision would convince him that he was glimpsing heaven itself (Ezk. 1:26–29), and the Lord's chariot-throne, from which streamed a river of fire. The thought is not original to Daniel. From the burning bush (Ex. 3:3) to Malachi's judgment by fire (Mal. 4:1) fire frequently depicts God's presence, or is pictured as going before Him to prepare for His coming (Pss. 50:3; 97:3). It is fitting that innumerable servants should wait on the supreme judge. *A thousand thousands* is entirely parallel with *ten thousand times ten thousand,* so proving that the numbers are not meant to be taken literally. The description builds up to the climax: judgment is about to begin, the court is seated, the written evidence produced, for God has His books (Ex. 32:32; Ps. 56:8; Mal. 3:16) prepared for that day.

---

[1] *Cf.* Introduction, above, p. 61, and Commentary, pp. 92f.

[2] Liddell and Scott, *Greek Lexicon, kephalē.* C. K. Barrett, *The First Epistle to the Corinthians* (Black, 1968), p. 248.

[3] The translation here should in all probability be 'the hair of his head was like lamb's wool'. M. Sokoloff, *JBL,* 95.2, 1976, pp. 277-279.

11, 12. The description of heaven finished, the writer reverts to prose as he turns again to the beasts. His attention is attracted by the *great words* coming from the little horn, which he had temporarily forgotten (*cf.* verse 8). Suddenly, *as I looked, the beast was slain.* No more needs to be said about the little horn or any of the other horns, for they have been destroyed with the fourth beast whose body is consumed in the fire (*cf.* verse 10). The dramatic turn of events proves beyond doubt the sovereignty of the heavenly judge.

As for the rest of the beasts. It is a little surprising that the three kingdoms first mentioned still survive. Two points are clear : (i) whoever the original beasts stood for, their kingdoms continue to have a recognizable identity, and (ii) history has not yet come to an end, despite the intervention of God's judgment, though *a season and a time* implies a limited future.

13. Now that the scene of the vision changes again to depict heavenly events, prose gives place to poetry. This verse has been the subject of more scholarly papers than any other in the book, so indicating its centrality, not only for Daniel but for the New Testament also. Yet the only indication that an important disclosure is to be made is the introductory phrase, *I saw in the night visions,* which is longer than the previous introductions, *e.g.* verse 9. Otherwise the scenes appear in one and the same sequence : heaven and earth are closely linked.

With the clouds of heaven is reminiscent of the Sinai covenant, for in the Exodus narrative the glory of the Lord appeared in the cloud (Ex. 16 : 10; and in the covenant inauguration, 19 : 9). A concordance will reveal how frequent is the reference to clouds in connection with the presence of the Lord, not only in the Pentateuch but throughout the Old Testament poetry and prophetic literature.[1] The reader should therefore be taken by surprise to see in such a setting *one like a son of man* (Aram. *bar ʾᵉnāš*, which is idiomatic for 'a man', hence NEB, 'one like a man'). The same construction occurs in 5 : 31, ' a son of . . . years'. The effect of the idiom is to intensify the quality in question, so that 'son of man' lays stress on the humanity of the person (Ps. 146 : 3). Yet he is only *like* a human being, just as the beasts were 'like' a lion or a bear.

---

[1] See also L. Sabourin, 'The Biblical Cloud', *Biblical Theology Bulletin,* IV, 1974, pp. 290–311, esp. p. 304: 'In connection with Daniel 7:13 it is observed that the coming with clouds is an exclusively divine attribute.'

Ezekiel was equally unwilling to commit himself in describing his vision (Ezk. 1 :4ff.) and made use of such words as 'appearance', 'form', 'likeness'; but a distinction needs to be made between the inadequacy of language to describe God (Ezk. 1 :26–28; Dn. 7 :13) and the likeness of the beasts earlier in chapter 7. The beasts turn out to be representative of certain human beings; the one who comes with the clouds is like a human being in the sense that He is what every human being should be if he is true to type, that is, one who is made in the image of God (Gn. 1 :26, 27).

And he came to the Ancient of Days (cf. comment on verse 12). RSV now uses capital letters, to imply the certainty of His divine identity, the great God presiding at the investiture of the one like a man, who is first *presented before him.*

14. To this man *was given dominion (cf.* Gn. 1 :26) *and glory and kingdom.* This second allusion to Genesis 1 indicates an enlarged status for the human race, greater than that which it received at the first, in the person of the representative 'man'. All peoples, nations and languages, instead of worshipping a lifeless statue (3 :4, 5), will serve this man. The fact that the kingdoms of the beasts were not 'for ever' sharpens the contrast between them and the new ruler of the earth, for it is all joy that His kingdom is to be everlasting and never pass away. Mystery remains, however, and the question of the psalmist arises, 'What is man . . . and the son of man?' (Ps. 8 :4) to be given such power and authority. The vision ends on this breath-taking note.[1]

b. The interpretation (7:15–28)

15. The personal cost of receiving divine revelations is never underestimated in the Old Testament (*cf.* Je. 4 :19; Ezk. 3 :15; Zc. 9 :1; 12 :1, AV, RV), and the book of Daniel insists here and in subsequent chapters (8 :27; 10 :1, 10, 11, 15, 18) on the anxiety and psychological turmoil involved in receiving, even at God's hand, understanding of the future course of history. *My spirit within me was anxious.* The words 'within me' translate two Aramaic words which caused a problem even for the early translators.[2] Now in the Genesis Apocryphon from

---

[1] Further discussion of 'son of man' may be found in the Additional Note, below, pp. 148–154.

[2] JB footnote to this verse reads: 'Two incomprehensible Aramaic words are omitted here as in LXX and Vulg.'

Qumran the expression occurs with the meaning 'within its *sheath*' (*nidâna*'; cf. 1 Ch. 21 : 27 where the same word occurs in a Hebrew text).[1] The word is Persian, and the idiom reflects a vivid metaphor which had dropped out of use or had never been known by the Greek and Latin translators. Modern EVV avoid the metaphor, *e.g.* NIV, 'I, Daniel, was troubled in spirit.' For *the visions of my head* NIV has 'the visions that passed through my mind'.

16, 17. The visionary situation continues, for Daniel is able to approach *one of those who stood there, i.e.* one of the thousands of retainers waiting at court to be of service (7 : 10), and to ask for the meaning of what he has seen. The explanation is tantalizingly brief : *These four great beasts are four kings*; and yet later (verse 23) 'king' becomes 'kingdom'. 'It is noteworthy that the concepts of king and kingdom are indissolubly bound the one to the other, for there is no kingdom without a king and vice versa of king without a kingdom.'[2] The interpreter is made aware of the fluidity of thought which can move easily between an individual and a collective idea, and will take note that rigidity of interpretation is out of place here. These kings *shall arise out of the earth*, whereas in the vision they are expressly said to come up out of the sea (7 : 3). A figurative meaning is indicated and such a use of the word in Isaiah 57 : 20 conjures up a picture of flotsam and jetsam, agitated by the ceaseless tossing of the waves. There may also be a memory of Isaiah 17 : 13, 'the nations roar like the roaring of many waters', but only until the Lord rebukes them. Turbulent international relations are well depicted by the restless sea.

18. The astonishing second part of the interpretation takes up the theme of the kingdom, which in the vision was given to one like a son of man (14) but now is said to be received by *the saints of the Most High*, who *possess the kingdom for ever, for ever and ever*. The main questions raised in the immense literature on the subject run parallel with those on Son of man and are referred to in the Additional Note.[3] They concern

---

[1] B. Jongeling, C. J. Labuschagne, A. S. van der Woude, *Aramaic Texts from Qumran*, Genesis Apocryphon, Col. II. 10. The expression also occurs in the MS published by Shelomo Morag, *The Book of Daniel, A Babylonian-Yemenite Manuscript*, XI, XII.

[2] Delcor, p. 157.

[3] See below, pp. 148–154.

mainly the identity of these *saints* or 'holy ones' (Aram. *qaddîšê*), for angels are so described in 4:17, and the enduring nature of the kingdom given to them might appear to support 'heavenly beings'. On the other hand the title is parallel with 'one like a man', and in verse 27 the wording becomes 'the people of the saints of the Most High'. *Most High* is plural in form here and in verses 22, 25b, 27. Lacocque is of the opinion that these holy ones participate in the Most High and are divinized.[1] Heaton thinks the writer wished to symbolize 'a special group nearer to the ideal of "a kingdom of priests, a holy nation" (Ex. 19:6), than the rank and file of Judaism'. Driver and Montgomery think of the plural as a plural of majesty, a Hebraic idiom interchangeable with the singular (as in 25a).

19, 20. Daniel's interest was less in the glorious future kingdom than in the terrible fourth beast whose rule must precede it.

21, 22. The dream continues even while the question about the fourth beast is being asked, and those who had seemed so exalted (18) are now overcome, and referred to merely as *saints* (lit. 'holy ones'), as though some doubt were now raised as to their relationship to the Most High. The defeat of the saints receives fuller treatment in 8:24, but here it is mentioned only in order to give the firm assurance that their downfall will be brief because their God will intervene. *Judgment was given for the saints of the Most High*, that is, in their favour and not 'to the saints' (AV, RV), an idea which does not belong to the sense here (though see 1 Cor. 6:2). Ultimately *the saints received the kingdom*.

23. The standard translations differ as to whether verses 23–27 should be considered as poetry. RSV and JB write them in poetic lines; NEB, NIV retain prose. In either case the style is studied; there are alliterations (the three verbs in 23d, 23e have the same two initial letters in the original, and though this is a grammatical prefix the threefold repetition is forceful); even in English the recurrence of the same word several times within a few lines (fourth, ten, kingdom, kings, times) and the same idea in different words ('kingdom, dominion, greatness', verse 27) build up an emphatic assurance of divine control

---

[1] Lacocque, p. 114. Accordingly he translates 'les Saints-Très-Altiers', but in this he goes beyond the general tenor of Scripture.

over events, from the most dreaded suffering history can bring to the triumph of right in a world-wide kingdom.

The *fourth kingdom* is *different* from preceding ones, not so much in kind as in intensity. Beast-like, it will *devour the whole earth*; the bear was to devour much flesh, but this one is to devour all. *Trample down, break to pieces* : both verbs imply wanton destruction.

24. This total demolition is the policy of the *ten kings*, and not only of the eleventh. This empire as a whole is destructive. The ten kings seem to rule simultaneously each with his own territory, and *another shall arise after them*, a usurper, who *shall be different from the former ones* in a way which will be explained (25), but whose territory is gained at the expense of *three kings*. There is dissension within the empire.

25. Four characteristics of his rule are given : (i) blasphemy, (ii) long-drawn-out persecution (*wear out,* as a garment, implies this), (iii) a new table of religious festivals[1] (so suppressing Israel's holy days), and (iv) a new morality; the outcome will be the subjugation of God's people. Of these the third and fourth indicate an intention which is not necessarily allowed to be carried out, but the people are *given into his hand*. A greater than he is in control, and whereas this last king thought to change the times, a greater than he has decreed the *time, two times, and half a time*. The expected progression, one, two, three is cut off arbitrarily but decisively.

26, 27. The veil between heaven and earth's kingdom is drawn back. The heavenly court decrees that *his dominion shall be taken away*, and he whose rule has been destructive will in turn see his dominion totally destroyed. *The people of the saints of the Most High*, having passed through trial, now triumph. Individual kingdoms remain, but all are subordinated to the one everlasting kingdom where right prevails. Verse 27, the interpretation of verse 14, implies an identification between the people of the saints and one like a son of man, and thus has to feature in any attempt to arrive at the meaning of these titles.[2]

[1] J. T. Milik, *Ten Years of Discovery in the Wilderness of Judea,* p. 111: 'In civil life . . . from the Persian period onwards the lunisolar calendar (of Babylonian origin) was employed. It can be imagined that at some time an attempt was made to introduce this calendar . . . into the Temple as well.'

[2] See Additional Note, below, pp. 150.

28. The conclusion marks not only the end of the angel's interpretation but also the account of the whole incident. *I kept the matter in my mind* does not sound like the end of a book, though there are those who are of the opinion that the original book, in Aramaic, ended with this verse.[1]

If we allow the book to be its own interpreter we can now look back to chapter 2 and compare it with chapter 7, to see whether it is possible to identify any of the features they have in common. The great image was composed of four metals, and from the sea there arose four beasts. Chapter 2 is dated in the Babylonian period and so is chapter 7. The former ends with a kingdom set up by the God of heaven (2:44) and so does the latter, though chapter 7 does not specifically say who sets up this kingdom, but is concerned rather with the people who receive it.

The one identification made in chapter 2 is the head of gold. This is Nebuchadrezzar (2:37, 38). Accordingly we may test out whether the lion may also represent Nebuchadrezzar. Already in the comments on 7:4 reference has been made to Jeremiah 49:19-22, where that king is compared to a lion and an eagle, and to chapter 4 where he is stripped of his power. The indications are that this first beast symbolizes Nebuchadrezzar and the Babylonian empire of which he was the representative. No specific identification is given in chapter 7, but there is in 2:39 the information that the empires follow one another. The writer is clear that the empire which followed that of Babylon was the Medo-Persian (6:8, 12, 15), and therefore the bear is likely to symbolize the Persian empire, as we more readily call it. In that case the third would be the Greek,[2] and presumably the fourth, the Roman, but there will be more to help us in the next chapter.

---

[1] A. Lenglet, 'La Structure Littéraire de Daniel 2-7', *Biblica*, 53, 1972, pp. 169-190 and Heaton, p. 190. By contrast, Jeffery, *IB*, p. 468 and Porteous, p. 117, see the verse as forward-looking.

[2] The Greeks were already coming into conflict with the powers to the east during the Neo-Babylonian period. In 556 BC Neriglissar of Babylon confronted the Lydians, and Nabonidus (or Nebuchadrezzar, for the name Labynetos was used for both; see p. 117, footnote 2, above) acted as intermediary between the Persians and the emerging power to the west.

Additional Note: Son of man

The Christian reader, familiar with the use Jesus makes of the words 'Son of man', understandably identifies this concept in Daniel 7:13 with Jesus without necessarily suspecting the wealth of meaning it contains, or the distinctions that need to be drawn between this and other concepts. The aim of this note is to provide a pointer to the significance of the phrase in Daniel, and its influence in later literature.

Linguistically the Hebrew terms *'āḏām* and *'enôš*, together with their Aramaic equivalents, are collective for mankind, and any individual human being is a 'son of man', *ben 'āḏām*. This is the way Ezekiel is addressed (*e.g.* Ezk. 2:1, 3, 6, 8; 3:1, and so throughout the book); the effect of avoiding his name and calling him 'mortal man' (TEV) is to draw attention to Ezekiel's humanity over against God's might. That this is the essential meaning is borne out by parallel wording in Hebrew poetry. An obvious example, which incidentally also shows that these two words for man are interchangeable (*cf.* Is. 51:12), is Psalm 8:4 (Heb. 5): 'What is man (*'enôš*) that thou art mindful of him, and the son of man (*ben 'āḏām*) that thou dost care for him?' Often there is a contrast between the great Creator and creaturely man, as in Numbers 23:19 and Psalm 146:3, 4. Man (*'āḏām*) needs to recall that he is made from earth (*'aḏāmâ*), and so in a context like this 'son of man' is a corrective to human self-confidence. The writer of Daniel uses the term with this 'earthy' sense in 8:17. At the same time there is also a dignity proper to man; he was made in God's image, and God reveals Himself to a son of man (Ezk. 2:1).

In Daniel 7:13, however, the visionary setting introduces new elements. The seer has been lifted above the earth and is able to discern amid the clouds of heaven the judgment-throne of God. In these unfamiliar surroundings he could commit himself only to saying that the one he saw was *like* a son of man, just as the first three animals had been like their earthly counterparts. Whereas dominion had been exercised by beasts, the last of which was the epitome of destructive terror, dominion was now given to one like a mortal man. In view of the fact that the beasts stood for world-rulers who reckoned to be human, we may tentatively adopt the view that the writer is passing judgment on their inhumanity and is proclaiming that the day is coming when the reins of government will be for ever in the hands of a man worthy of the name : man as God, at creation, intended him to be. But were there overtones of ancient creation-myths to be detected in this imagery?

For several decades following the publication by George Smith in 1876 of the Babylonian Epic of Creation, interest in Near Eastern mythology was considerable. In 1895 H. Gunkel published his book *Schöpfung und Chaos in Urzeit und Endzeit* (Creation and chaos at the beginning and end of time) which popularized his mythological interpretation of much biblical literature, especially books like Genesis, Job, Psalms and Daniel. In 1900 N. Schmidt was applying the Marduk myth to the 'manlike being' of Daniel 7:13, and around the same time attempts were made to derive the concept from Iranian folk-lore, while somewhat later Egyptian, Jewish and Gnostic sources were explored.[1] In the light of subsequent reflection there is a growing consensus among scholars that Near Eastern mythologies do not help to explain the use of the term in Daniel, and that they are not the source of it either. Colpe deals with Near Eastern sources under the heading 'untenable hypotheses' and J. Jeremias endorses his assessment: 'A thorough examination of the comparative material has shown that these hypotheses stand on very slim foundations. In particular the derivation of the title from the Iranian Gayomart has been rejected by the Iranists.'[2] M. D. Hooker in her section on Daniel argues that the Old Testament is the source of the concept,[3] a conclusion which brings us back to the term as it is used in Daniel. She would therefore agree that there is no need to go further back than the Old Testament for light on its use in the Gospels.

The setting of Daniel 7 is judgment. Indeed it could be a response to the assertions and prayers on that subject in Psalm 9 : 'The Lord sits enthroned for ever, he has established his throne for judgment' (7); 'The Lord has made himself known, he has executed judgment' (16); 'Arise, O Lord! . . . Let the nations be judged before thee!' (19). The dazzling appearance

[1] A full bibliography may be found in *TDNT*, VIII, pp. 408–415. The writer, C. Colpe, rejects Near Eastern origins but postulates a Canaanite source for the term.

[2] J. Jeremias, *New Testament Theology*, I (SCM Press, 1971), p. 268. Of Colpe's Canaanite derivation he says, 'In view of the enormous lapse between the texts from Ras Shamra and the book of Daniel this is hardly conceivable.'

[3] M. D. Hooker, *The Son of Man in Mark* (SPCK, 1967), pp. 17–20.

of the judge, His fiery throne and His myriad attendants inspire awe, and the opening of the record-books dread, and yet, presented before the divine judge, is 'one like a man'. Although he is not explicitly said to be given the task of judging, this is implicit in the rule committed to him. Judgment then is committed to one who seems to share humanity and therefore to know from experience the odds against mankind.

Everything in chapter 7 is on a world-wide scale, the empires of the beasts, the judgment, and the nations that worship and serve the one like mortal man. All distinctions of race and colour and nationality are stripped away and one apparently human figure represents the whole human race. Derived from one, all are summed up in one, and the original goal 'have dominion' (Gn. 1 :28) is fulfilled in the one like a son of man who is given a kingdom that shall not be destroyed (14). Though the kingdom theme predominates in the second poetic oracle (23–27), nowhere is the king mentioned.

Totally unexpected then is the interpretation given in verse 18 (*cf.* 27) where the saints of the Most High are said to receive the kingdom and possess it 'for ever, for ever and ever'. Who are these saints or 'holy ones', that the kingdom given to the one like a son of man is received and possessed by them? One possibility is that the term 'son of man' is a collective way of referring to the saints of the Most High, in which case the terms are virtually equivalent. In support of this position is the parallelism between verses 14 and 18/27. The passage would be proclaiming the creation of a community of those committed to a life of discipleship, who would thus fulfil the role first intended for man. But this would not be achieved without suffering because 'this horn made war with the saints, and prevailed over them' (21). Triumph is promised, but not this side of the grave. Despite assertions to the contrary, this is not a reference to the expected transfer of power to the hitherto humbled people of Israel, for the term is 'son of man' and not 'son of Israel/Jacob'.[1] That is not to say that afflicted Jews would not rightly see themselves as included; the Qumran community certainly thought of themselves sharing in the inheri-

[1] G. Vermes, *Jesus the Jew* (Collins, 1973) would disagree. 'In the mind of the biblical narrator this phrase, "one like *a son of man*", refers collectively to "the saints of the Most High", interpreted as the Israelites persecuted by Antiochus Epiphanes' (p. 169).

tance of the saints (1QS 11 :7f.), but the concept is far wider, embracing all mankind.

A second possibility is to see the one like a son of man as *representative* of the saints of the Most High. In verse 13 he appears to be an individual figure; the Old Testament priest, among others, had a representative role (Ex. 19 :6; *cf.* Ex. 28 :1), so the idea was familiar, and Jews of a later period thought of the Son of man in Daniel 7 :13f. as an individual figure.[1] Equally representative but closer to the context of Daniel 7 is the figure of the king, implicit in that he is given a kingdom, though the one who bestows it is ultimately the king *par excellence*. Psalm 80, addressed to the Shepherd of Israel who is enthroned on the cherubim, is a prayer for the vine Israel, now ravaged by enemies. Hope is set upon 'the son whom thou hast reared for thyself' (15, RSV mg.), 'the man of thy right hand' (17), that is, in the place of honour and rule (Ps. 110 :1), 'the *son of man* whom thou hast made strong for thyself'. On the ground of the parallelism it is possible to argue that 'son of man' was a circumlocution for 'king'. By avoiding the word the Messianic overtones for Israel were avoided, and a wider kingship was implied, embracing all men who acknowledged the authority of this son of man.

Whether collective or representative, the term implies the creation of a community, a kingdom, which will undergo a period of intense suffering as a result of the despotic cruelty of the fourth beast. Like the Servant of the Lord (Is. 52 :13 – 53 :12) and the enigmatic shepherd figure of Zechariah 9 – 14, the saints of the Most High, associated with the one like a son of man, must suffer.

One further point of view must be mentioned, namely that the saints of the Most High are angelic beings, and the one like a son of man the leader of the angelic host.[2] This is contended on the ground that (i) 'holy ones', when used as a noun

---

[1] O. Cullmann, *The Christology of the New Testament* (SCM Press, 1959), p. 140. G. Vermes (*op. cit.*, p. 176) concludes that one like a *son of man* in Dn. 7:13, 'though not individual and Messianic in origin, acquired in the course of time a definite Messianic association'.

[2] Some of those who represent this view are John J. Collins, 'The Son of Man and the Saints of the Most High in the Book of Daniel', *JBL*, 93, 1974, pp. 50–66; L. Dequecker, 'The "Saints of the Most High" in Qumran and Daniel', *Oudtestamentische Studien*, XVIII, 1973, pp. 108–187; M. Noth, *The Laws in the Pentateuch and Other Studies* (Oliver and Boyd, 1966), pp. 215–228.

in the Hebrew Bible, usually refers to angels, not men; (ii) that the one like a son of man in Daniel 7 : 13 is a superhuman figure, and therefore those associated with him in 7 : 18 must also be superhuman; (iii) the word translated 'people' ('*am*) in 7 : 27 can mean 'host', so giving the sense 'people associated with the holy ones of the Most High'. Michael, Israel's guardian angel (10 : 13, 21; 12 : 1) and other figures who come alongside Daniel (8 : 15; 10 : 18) are thus accounted for, and it is argued that texts from Qumran support the angelic interpretation.

Each of these arguments has been countered. Vern Poythress[1] shows that the support for '*am* meaning angelic host is exceedingly precarious, and that the great weight of Old Testament witness supports the view that Israel is the holy people. On the other hand the meaning 'angels' occurs (Jb. 15 : 15; Ps. 89 : 5, 7; Dn. 8 : 13), and Poythress thinks that Daniel may not have been able to tell which of the two meanings was intended, for all those he saw looked like men. G. Vermes thinks that the identification with angels is basically irrelevant. He dismisses this and the theory of a mythological background because 'in the actual Daniel narrative no knowledge of such a conjectural prehistory is shown or presumed'.[2] Apparently decisive against the angelic view is the suffering and defeat implied in 7 : 21, 25.

The bridge between Daniel 7 and the use of 'Son of man' by Jesus has been the goal of much study, on the assumption that literature of the intervening period would reveal a development connecting the two. It has been customary to use for this purpose apocalyptic books of early Judaism, and in particular the Similitudes or Parables of Enoch (1 Enoch 37 – 71), which on the authority of R. H. Charles have long been accepted as a pre-Christian Jewish apocalypse. Other such books which bear on 'son of man', the Apocalypse of Ezra and the Testament of Abraham, are post-Christian and therefore, though they bear witness to the development of thought concerning 'son of man', they cannot provide background to Jesus' use of the term. It now appears likely that these relevant chapters of 1 Enoch are also post-Christian, for they do not appear at all in fragments from Qumran, whereas every other

---

[1] *VT*, XXVI. 2, 1976, pp. 208–213.
[2] G. Vermes, *Jesus the Jew*, pp. 169, 170.

chapter of the book except the Book of the Parables is represented.[1]

A new turn to the argument has been presented by T. F. Glasson, and taken up by Black in his article. It is based on 1 Enoch 14 :8–25, Enoch's description of his throne vision, which Glasson takes to be pre-Maccabean in authorship and date, and source material for the writer of Daniel 7.[2] According to Milik this chapter, which is preserved in two substantial fragments at Qumran, belongs to an even older source than 1 Enoch 1 – 36, about the middle of the third century BC. In view of the fact that 1 Enoch 71, in which Enoch is designated 'son of man', is based on 1 Enoch 14, it is argued that the author of Daniel is more dependent on 1 Enoch than the other way round. Whether or not this evidence proves acceptable, the fact is that the Similitudes of Enoch must be excluded from the argument when connecting-links between Daniel and Jesus are being sought. Indeed no evidence remains on which to construct such a link.

The possibility that no such link existed is borne out by the fact that, with the exception of John 12 :34, 'Son of man' is found in the Gospels only on the lips of Jesus. Others found the term mystifying (Jn. 8 :28; *cf.* 8 :53; 9 :36; 12 :34) or maybe so general as to tell them nothing. G. Vermes argues that it was frequently a self-designation in a situation requiring reserve and modesty, but also used in contexts of humiliation and death.[3] True, the words occur in sayings connected with Jesus' suffering, death and perfecting (notably Mk. 10 :45; but *cf.* Mk. 14 :21; Lk. 9 :44; *etc.*). In other sayings Jesus is speaking of coming in His kingdom to judge mankind (Mt. 16 :27, 28; 19 :28; Jn. 5 :27). Undoubted references to Daniel are Mark 13 :26; 14 :62 and parallels, and Matthew 19 :28, which

---

[1] J. T. Milik, *The Books of Enoch: Aramaic Fragments of Qumran Cave* 4, edited by J. T. Milik with the collaboration of Matthew Black (OUP, 1976), and quoted by M. Black, 'The "Parables" of Enoch (1 Enoch 37–71) and the "Son of Man" ', *ET*, LXXXVIII.1, 1976, pp. 5–8.

[2] T. F. Glasson, *The Second Advent: The Origins of the New Testament Doctrine* (London, 1963); and 'Son of Man Imagery: Enoch XIV and Daniel 7', *NTS*, 23, 1976, pp. 82–90.

[3] G. Vermes, *op. cit.*, pp. 167, 168. The literature he quotes belongs to the second century AD because that is all that is available, and comes from Galilee. J. Jeremias (*New Testament Theology*, I, p. 261 footnote) rejects the conclusion of Vermes on this point, though he agrees the term could include the speaker.

look forward to the manifestation of the glory of the Son of man, the gathering of God's people and their public vindication, for they will rule together with Jesus. Thus in the Gospels 'Son of man' implies majesty, as in Daniel 7. In Revelation the son of man is not only king but also judge (14:14), and in 1:13 the one like a son of man is characterized by the description of the divine messenger in Daniel 10:5, who is usually assumed to be an angel. The son of man is not only king but God, though, as is characteristic of apocalyptic style, this is conveyed in veiled terms. Perhaps, therefore, it would be wise to guard against too rigid an interpretation and allow for fluidity of meaning.

It is no exaggeration to say that no other concept in the Old Testament, not even the Servant of the Lord, has elicited a more prolific literature.[1] Of all the figures used in the Old Testament to designate the coming deliverer; king, priest, branch, servant, seed—none is more profound than 'Son of man'. Here there is a vision of man as he was intended to be, perfectly embodying all his potential in obedience to his Creator. 'Son of man' is also a term of glory, both in Daniel 7 and in Jesus' use of the term, but 'the epiphany of the glory of the Son of man will be to those who have been proved by suffering'.[2]

III. THE SECOND AND THIRD KINGDOMS IDENTIFIED (8:1–27)

Chapter 2, with its image in four metals, spanned history from the period of the Babylonian exile to the setting up of God's kingdom, when all nations and peoples would acknowledge and serve Him. Elsewhere in the book only in chapter 7 is so broad a canvas presented, and there is much to be said for looking upon the six chapters in Aramaic (2–7) as the nucleus of the book,[3] of which chapter 7 is the climax. In chapter 8 the narrower scope is indicated by the fact that only two animals appear in the vision, which is located in Susa, the ancient capital of Elam, destined to become one of the great cities of the Persian empire (Ne. 1:1). Though the vision is

[1] For the most recent bibliography see *DNTT*, article 'Son'.
[2] J. Jeremias, *New Testament Theology*, I, p. 275.
[3] See Introduction, vi. Structure, above, p. 60. 8:1 resumes in Hebrew.

dated in the Babylonian period, Babylon is no longer taken into account.

For the first time since 2:38 the writer interprets his symbols. The ram with the two horns represents the kingdom of the Medes and Persians (20). Thus, if the book is allowed to be its own interpreter, there is no question of the writer having been mistaken in his history to the extent of thinking that there was a separate Median kingdom, as many commentators assert. The he-goat is the king of Greece (21) or the empire of Greece. It is the horns which represent particular kings, insofar as they are specified. This vision goes no further than the Greek empire.[1] Its bold ruler who dares to defy the Prince of princes will mysteriously 'be broken', but at that point the revelation ceases, and though it concerns 'the time of the end', what is referred to is 'the restoration of the sanctuary' (verse 14). No mention is made of the setting up of God's kingdom (2:44; 7:27). For some reason the writer puts the spotlight on the Greek period, and in particular on one despotic ruler who rises from one section of the divided empire. This concentration is to become even more detailed in chapter 11.

a. The vision of the ram and he-goat (8:1–8)

1. *The third year of the reign of King Belshazzar* would be 550/549 BC, a significant year in which Cyrus broke free from his allegiance to Astyages the Mede and established the joint state of the Medes and Persians. The one whose right hand the Lord had grasped (Is. 45:1) was already unwittingly fulfilling his God-appointed role in history and some of the exiles in Babylon no doubt recognized the fact. *After that which appeared to me at the first* is not a redundant statement, but points out that the content of this vision is dependent on that of chapter 7.

2. The fourfold *I saw* conveys something of the involvement of the seer's consciousness as he orientated himself first to the fact that he was receiving a vision, then to his geographical surroundings and finally to the particular image presented to his gaze. *Susa the capital*, or *'fortress'* (Heb. *bîrâ*), implies strong fortifications. It is the word used regularly in apposition to Susa in Esther and in Nehemiah 1:1, and it describes the Temple ('palace') in Jerusalem in 1 Chronicles 29:1, 19. The river *Ulai* (Gk. *'Eulaios*) was originally the name of a canal

[1] For a tabulated presentation of the kingdoms, see below, p. 161.

on which Susa was built, though in the time of Alexander it was the name of the Abi-diz waterway to the east of Susa, down which he sailed his fleet.[1] *Cf.* NIV, 'the Ulai canal'.

3, 4. *A ram . . . It had two horns.* The male of the flock represented for Ezekiel oppressive rulers (Ezk. 34 : 17; 39 : 18; *cf.* Je. 51 :40; Zc. 10 :3). According to the interpretation (21) the two horns represented kings of Media and Persia, the larger being the dominant Persian who was already master of Media. The rapid progress of Cyrus during the ten years 549–539 suggested a ram goring every beast that withstood him. By thrusting westward and northward into Asia Minor he bypassed Babylon, only to capture it later and take lands to the south-west and south-east. The writer is passing judgment in noting that *he did as he pleased and magnified himself.* Nearly two hundred years of history and political aggrandisement, such as the world had not before seen, are summed up in this verse.

5–8. The ram from the east, encountering *a he-goat . . . from the west,* found more than a match for his strength and speed and met his end. 'He-goats of the earth' is an expression used in Isaiah 14 :9, (prosaically translated in RSV 'leaders'), but the speed and scope of this next empire-builder, identified in history as Alexander the Great (21), make the goat an appropriate symbol. The irresistible power of the one *conspicuous horn* broke the two horns of the ram, but the goat's horn was in turn broken. The sight and sound of horns breaking off typifies the brittle nature of political might, especially as the goat had his great horn broken *when he was strong* (8). The audio-visual impact of the vision has continuing relevance : great power, resulting in self-importance, invites a great reversal (Lk. 1 :52).

The continuing vision shows *four conspicuous horns* replacing the one broken horn; four kings between them take over the empire of their predecessor, who had laid claim to the face of the whole earth (5), and rule each his allotted portion. Prominent they may have been, but they are passed over without comment.

b. A little horn (8:9–14)
The conflict between power and greater power develops now into a trial of strength between a man and God Himself.

[1] J. J. Finkelstein, 'Ulai and its topography', *JNES*, 21, 1962, pp. 89f.

9. The insignificant origin of the one who took so much upon himself is made plain; yet he succeeded in making conquests in more than one direction and so *grew exceedingly great . . . It grew great* (10). The scorn of the writer is skilfully conveyed. *Toward the glorious land* (lit. 'the beauty') : the full expression 'the beautiful land' occurs in 11 :41 (*cf.* Je. 3 :19; Ezk. 20 :6, 15). The land of God's promise could not but be most beautiful, especially to those exiled from it.

10. *The host of heaven* are the stars (Dt. 17 :3), which were all too often the object of Israel's worship (Je. 8 :2; Zp. 1 :5), though their God was 'Lord of hosts', who called them all by name (Is. 40 :26). The little horn, in reaching for the stars, is claiming equality with God. But earlier kings had nursed similar ambitions (Is. 14 :13) and stars could refer in a secondary sense to earthly monarchs (Is. 24 :21); *some of the host of the stars* are therefore rival kings who suffered a cruel fate at the march of this upstart (*cf.* Rev. 12 :4).

11. *It magnified itself, even up to the Prince of the host.* Note the progression, 'magnified himself' (4), 'magnified himself exceedingly' (8), until pride showed its ultimate goal in defying the Prince of both stars and monarchs, their Creator and God. This defiance took the form of a sacrilegious attack on the Temple such as had taken place once already under Nebuchadrezzar. *The continual burnt offering* (Heb. *tāmîḏ*) : 'the continual' is a technical term referring to the daily sacrifices, morning and evening, prescribed in Exodus 29 :38–42. By the one word the whole sacrificial system is implied. *The place of his sanctuary was overthrown* represents a fair translation of the writer's enigmatic style, with its ambiguous pronouns and prepositions. The word 'place' (*māḵôm*) is reserved for God's abode (*cf.* 1 Ki. 8 :30, 'heaven thy dwelling place'; 2 Ch. 6 :2, the Temple). An attack on the place set aside for worship of God is tantamount to an attack on God Himself.

12. The obscurity of the first part of this verse is noted in the margin of RSV, and has puzzled translators from early times. The grammar is difficult and the sense hard to establish. *The host was given over to it* (Heb. 'a host' or army) seems to mean that the horn gained military support[1] *against* (rather

---

[1] Many commentators hold that the host in verses 10 and 12 refers to Israel, mainly on the evidence of Dn. 12:3, but also because it makes good sense in 8:13. The question is whether Israel is envisaged as 'heavenly' (verse 10).

than *together with*) the daily sacrifices *through transgression*, on account of the transgression of God's people. By a slight change of pointing and by redividing the consonants it is possible to translate 'hosts he delivered up', but then a verb needs to be supplied : ['It rose up against] the continual burnt offering . . .'[1]

Truth (God's truth, that is) *was cast down to the ground* or, as we might say, 'dragged in the mud', and yet the horn not only went on with his plans but *prospered*.

13. In his vision the seer overheard the dialogue of two holy ones (see note on 4 : 10) asking not why this should be, which calls in question God's moral ordering of events, but *how long* (*cf.* Ps. 6 : 3; Is. 6 : 11; Zc. 1 : 12), which presupposes that God is limiting the triumph of evil. The rest of the verse summarizes what has gone before, though the trampling of *host* as well as sanctuary seems to add a further detail.

14. *And he said to him* is logical, and follows the ancient versions, but the Hebrew 'to me' may be the original. The seer was asking the same question. The answer is given in terms of the evening and morning sacrifices which would never be offered (verse 11 : *cf.* Gn. 1 : 5) and by dividing this number by two the number of days can be arrived at, namely 1,150, during which the sanctuary will be desecrated. This is less than three and a half years (*cf.* 7 : 25), a relatively short time, after which *the sanctuary shall be restored*, or 'vindicated' (Montgomery).

c. An interpreter explains the visions (8:15–27)

15–18. If Daniel returned to consciousness at all he was soon back in a visionary state and saw before him a man-like figure, who was being addressed by a human voice as *Gabriel,* 'God has shown himself strong'. In the Old Testament only in the book of Daniel are angels named (*cf.* Michael, 10 : 13) but in 1 Enoch 9 : 1; 20 : 1–8, dated in the pre-Maccabean period[2], Raphael, Uriel, Raguel, Saraqqel and Remiel were angels, each with a particular sphere of work.

The approach of Gabriel caused Daniel to fall down in fear, as Ezekiel had done in his visions (Ezk. 1 : 28; 3 : 23; 44 : 4), and the address to Daniel as *son of man*, human as opposed to

[1] See C. G. Ozanne, 'Three Textual Problems in Daniel', *JTS*, XVI, 1965, pp. 445f.
[2] *Cf.* p. 152, above.

divine, is a further link with Ezekiel. *The vision is for the time of the end* needs to be interpreted in connection with prophetic use of 'the end', for it does not necessarily mean the end of all things, but may refer to the question asked in verse 13; verse 19 supports this interpretation. Ezekiel, quoting Amos 8 :2, had used the word 'end' in 7 :2, 3. For the Northern Kingdom at the time of Amos the end was brought about by Assyrian invasion and captivity; for Judah the end was the sack of Jerusalem by the Babylonian armies (*cf.* Ezk. 21 :25, 29; 35 :5). In each case the end meant the end of rebellion against God, because He intervened in judgment. The same sense applies in Daniel 8 (*cf.* 9 :26). As in the annunciation to Mary (Lk. 1 :28–30), Gabriel was bringing good news.

The inappropriateness of *deep sleep* for the reception of an angelic message seems to be insisted upon (*cf.* 10 :9; Rev. 1 :17). The recipient must not only be awake but standing ready to obey orders (*cf.* Ezk. 2 : 1–3).

19. *The indignation* is the sentence of God which must eventually fall on those who rebel against Him and fail to repent. His own people were not exempt (Is. 10 :5–11), but neither were the nations (Je. 10 :10). Here the question was how long God would allow His earthly sanctuary to be trampled on (*cf.* 1 Macc. 1:54), and Daniel could be sure there was a time appointed for the end.

20, 21. The specific identification of the two beasts provides the writer's own understanding of the sequence of future events. He envisages one Medo-Persian empire followed by a Greek empire, inaugurated by one powerful king, *the great horn,* who in the event was Alexander the Great. The *he-goat* (lit. 'hairy he-goat', *haṣṣāp̄îr haśśā'îr* : note the assonance) had a horn *between his eyes,* that is, on the front of his head.

22. The horn, broken at the height of success (8), was replaced by *four others,* less powerful than the first. The death of Alexander in 323 BC, only ten years after the collapse of the Persian empire, followed by an extended struggle for power, is well-known history (*cf.* 1 Macc. 1 : 1–10). His kingdom was divided into four parts, but only one of these is relevant to the vision, namely the eastern area with its capital at Antioch, which was to include Judea in the second century BC.

23, 24. It was in 175 BC that Antiochus IV began his infamous reign, and in 169 he first entered the Temple. This foreshortening of history is usual in apocalyptic writings, where the aim is not to recount future events in detail but to select what is significant, even if this involves omitting over a hundred years of history, as in this instance. *When the transgressors have reached their full measure* (so MT). All the ancient versions understood 'transgressions', which presupposes no change in the consonantal text but only a different vowel pointing; *cf.* NEB, 'when their sin is at its height'. This reading is probably to be preferred. God in His mercy refrains from judgment until the measure of sin is such as to make it inevitable (Gn. 15 : 16; 1 Thes. 2 : 16).

The salient features of this character-sketch present a description which could apply to more than one political leader known from the history books. *Bold* (*'az*) is close in sound to the word for 'goat' (*'ēz*, verses 5, 8) and means both 'hard' and 'insolent'. *One who understands riddles* uses the Hebrew equivalent of the word 'riddles' in 5 : 12. Intellectually gifted, this ruler will have a great capacity for good or evil; his power will achieve his ends at the price of human lives, including *the people of the saints* (*'am qᵉdošîm*; *cf.* 7 : 25 and see the Additional Note, above, pp. 150–152), and by attacking God's people he will be defying God Himself (Zc. 2 : 8).

25, 26. To cruelty and scorn of God are added *cunning* and *deceit* combined with a great opinion of himself. JB takes up the metrical form :

'Such will be his resourcefulness of mind

that his treacherous activities will succeed.

He will grow arrogant of heart,

take many unawares and destroy them.'

He shall even rise up against the Prince of princes (*cf.* 10 : 20; 12 : 1), more directly this time than through his people, but the extremity of his daring is the occasion of his downfall. The statement *he shall be broken* is as decisive as it is brief and his downfall will not be the result of human scheming. That much is clear, but there is no interpretation given of the number of evenings and mornings (*cf.* 14) which formed the climax of the vision. The point of interest was not 'the future' as such, but the vindication of God's sovereignty by the restoration of His sanctuary. In the third year of Belshazzar Jerusalem was still a ruin, and hopes of return and rebuilding could not yet be implemented; but the vision referred to, a later destruction and restoration, hence the need to *seal up the vision,* for it had no immediate application. The verb here (*sātam*) has the idea of making unrecognizable to the enemy access-points and wells; applied to a book it is not strictly 'seal' but rather 'guard from use' and therefore from misuse (*cf.* 12 : 3).

27. There is a price to be paid in physical terms for spiritual revelation. Mention of *the king's business* implies that Daniel had been transported only in vision to Susa and was about his work in Babylon as usual, but *appalled by the vision*. The verb *šāmēm,* 'appalled', is the word for 'makes desolate' in 8 : 13; 9 : 27 and 12 : 11. The ultimate horror is transgression of God's law, and it is the man of God who by revelation becomes sensitive to the suffering such transgression entails.

Summary

Chapter 8 completes the symbolic presentations of the future contained in the book. The dream image of chapter 2 and the four wild beasts of chapter 7 are parallel. Both span the time from the Babylonian kingdom to the establishment of God's kingdom, symbolized by the stone that became a great mountain and filled the whole earth (2 : 35) and the presentation of kingship to one like a son of man (7 : 13, 14). Chapter 8 presents only two animals, this time from the flock. The Babylonian empire is disregarded and no mention is made of the kingdom of God. Instead, interest is centred in the fate of one who deliberately took his atheism to its logical conclusion; the vision is parallel to the other two chapters, but covers only parts two and three, expanding particularly part three in detail. A diagram may help to make the structure clear.

Chapter 2	Chapter 7	Chapter 8	Interpretation
Gold	Lion		Babylon (2 : 38)
Silver	Bear	Ram	Medo-Persia (8 : 20)
Bronze	Leopard	He-goat	Greece (8 : 21)
Iron/clay	Indescribable beast		(Rome)
Supernatural stone	Heavenly court		God's kingdom

In chapter 11 the writer will return to the Greek period, and in particular to the eastern part of the Greek empire in the third and second centuries BC, though he uses enigmatic language. The book ends with a warning of intense suffering, deliverance for the faithful, resurrection for 'many' and a call to endurance, which is relevant for all time (Mt. 24 : 13; Rev. 2 : 10). The author does not name the fourth kingdom. Historically it was, of course, the Roman empire which superseded the Greek.

Such an understanding of the last two periods demands that the little horn of 8 : 9, which grew out of one of the four horns of the he-goat, be distinguished from the little horn of 7 : 8, which came up among the ten horns of the indescribable beast. Though they have a superficial similarity, there are many differences between them[1] and they do not belong to the same era. This fact is an indication that we are being introduced to a recurring historical phenomenon : the clever but ruthless world dictator, who stops at nothing in order to achieve his ambitions. The book proclaims that such rulers cannot ultimately succeed. Though they talk and act big, and though they cause great suffering to many, their end is sure.

IV. DANIEL'S PRAYER AND THE VISION OF THE SEVENTY 'WEEKS' (9:1–27)

For the first time in the book Daniel's initiative occasions a revelation. He is aware of the prophecy of Jeremiah that there would be an interval of seventy years before the restoration of the sanctuary, and calculated that this period of time had almost passed. He therefore undertook to prepare himself by fasting for a period of specific prayer on behalf of all Israel, scattered as they were in many different lands. This state of affairs he accepted as divine judgment on God's people, justly inflicted on them for their failure to keep covenant, and therefore, after recalling the faithfulness of God, he confessed on behalf of the nation the sins of unfaithfulness which had brought disaster on them. Yet they were the Lord's covenant people, whom He had brought out of Egypt, and Jerusalem was called by His name. On these grounds Daniel asked for mercy in accordance with the known character of the Lord.

---

[1] E. J. Young (*The Prophecy of Daniel,* pp. 276f.) tabulates the distinctive features of each. The most decisive difference between chapters 7 and 8 is that in chapter 7 the persecuted saints receive the kingdom, whereas in chapter 8, though the power of the little horn is broken, nothing is said about God's kingdom.

The message through Gabriel took for granted the rebuilding of the sanctuary and reinterpreted the seventy years to make them applicable to the later period of which chapter 8 had already spoken and, according to some interpreters, to the present day. Others see here an error on the part of the author, who mixed up his divine revelation with 'wrong-headed arithmetical calculations' in his effort to show his contemporaries that God is available in every crisis in history.[1] The last four verses present the most difficult text in the book, as commentators agree, but they most certainly do not agree as to the right way to understand the figures given. Where others have failed it would be presumptuous to assume that one more commentator will succeed. All one can do is to continue to apply agreed criteria as consistently as possible, weigh carefully the conclusions of others, and make suggestions as to the most likely solution to a difficult problem.

a. Jerusalem still desolate (9:1–3)

1. *In the first year of Darius,* the king already named in 5:31 and chapter 6, is distinguished here from Darius Hystaspes, who came to the throne in 522 BC and is referred to in Ezra 4:24ff., Haggai and Zechariah. *Son of Ahasuerus,* or Xerxes in its Greek form, is a name which occurs in Ezra 4:6 and in the book of Esther, but belongs to a fifth-century king (486–465/4). To some commentators these facts have seemed to prove conclusively that the writer had confused his history, but their judgment may be premature, for 'it is . . . now recognized that Xerxes (Ahasuerus) may be an ancient Achaemenid royal "title" '.[2] W. F. Albright has argued that the name Darius may be an old Iranian title,[3] and while this remains a theory it is in keeping with known history for a monarch to have more than one name, as, *e.g.,* in the case of Tiglath-Pileser who is also called Pul (2 Ki. 15:19, 29; 1 Ch. 5:26). Whatever the identity of Darius,[4] the writer has in mind the

---

[1] Porteous, p. 134.
[2] D. J. Wiseman, *Notes on Some Problems in the Book of Daniel,* p. 15, based on R. N. Frye, *The Heritage of Persia* (1962), p. 97, *cf.* p. 95.
[3] W. F. Albright, 'The Date and Personality of the Chronicler', *JBL,* 40, 1921, p. 112n. and quoted by J. C. Whitcomb, *Darius the Mede,* p. 27.
[4] *Cf.* the Introduction, above, pp. 23–28.

first year of the Persian empire, 539 BC, and referred to in Ezra 1 : 1 as the first year of Cyrus king of Persia.

Of the seed of the Medes (AV, RV). What the writer is saying, if the identity of Darius and Cyrus as one and the same person be accepted, is that this ruler was able to claim descent from both Median and Persian ancestors. The two nations were closely related, and such an ancestry would commend him to both countries.

2. Emphasis on *the first year of his reign* (*cf.* verse 1) may indicate a throne-name, adopted for the first year only. Mention of *the books* (or 'the Scriptures', NIV) indicates that prophetic books were considered canonical at the time of writing. Though this is the first occurrence of the idea of 'Scriptures', there are earlier examples of appeal to precedent (*e.g.* Je. 26 : 18, 19). Now that the subject is the future of the Promised Land and may be echoing Jeremiah, the covenant-name Yahweh, LORD, replaces the more distant names for God, usual in chapters 1–8. *Seventy years* (*cf.* Je. 25 : 11; 29 : 10) were to pass *before the end of the desolations.* The writer implies that the years of desolation were fulfilling some role, and had to take their course before any new building could take place. Seventy years was the fixed term of divine indignation (Zc. 1-: 12),[1] described in 2 Chronicles 36 : 21 as 'the days . . . it kept sabbath, to fulfil seventy years'. This ritual understanding of the term takes it beyond the merely numerical into the theological and ethical realm. There are various ways of reckoning the years of exile, none of which comes exactly to seventy years;[2] but theologically the important point was that restoration marked acceptance with the Lord, who, by restoring His people to their land, demonstrated that He had forgiven and reinstated them (Is. 40 : 1ff.). It is possible to be so preoccupied with numbers as to miss the essential truth which those numbers declare.

---

[1] There is some evidence that 70 years was the accepted period during which the gods decreed ruin upon a city which had incurred divine displeasure. E. Lipinski ('Recherches sur le Livre de Zacharie', *VT*, XX, 1970, pp. 38f.) quotes an inscription of Esarhaddon, in which Marduk had decreed seventy years as the time of Babylon's ruin.

[2] *E.g.* 605 BC, the date of Je. 25:11, to 539, the restoration under Cyrus; or 587, the destruction of Jerusalem, to 516, when the Temple restoration was completed. The period of Jerusalem's abandonment, when no worship was offered there, was much less than 70 years (587–538).

3. Divine decree or no, the Scriptures never support the idea that God's purpose will be accomplished irrespective of the prayers of His people. Daniel, by taking God at His word and expecting Him to honour it, was rewarded not only by an assurance that his prayer was heard (23), but also by a further revelation (24–27). The ritual use of *fasting* at this period is illustrated by Zechariah 7 : 1–7; *sackcloth* denoted mourning and together with *ashes* symbolized the penitence with which Daniel came to represent his people before the Lord.

b. Daniel's prayer (9:4–19) [1]
There is no indication that Daniel was officially qualified to take upon himself this ministry of intercession. He did not belong to a priestly family, nor was he in the ordinary sense a prophet. Solomon, whose great prayer in 1 Kings 8 is often compared with that of Daniel, could claim as king to speak on behalf of Israel, but it is one of the glories of Scripture that no special permission is required for intercession on behalf of others (*cf.* Ne. 1 : 5ff.). Thanks to the study of 'the books' and the habit of prayer three times a day (6 : 10), the instructed Jew was not at a loss when he came to put his prayer into words.

4. The ascription '*O Lord, the great and terrible God . . .*' is almost word for word the same as that of Nehemiah 1 : 5, reflecting perhaps a common liturgical prayer of confession. The faithfulness and *steadfast love* (*ḥeseḏ*) of the Lord show up by contrast human fickleness and disloyalty, and appropriately introduce a prayer that depends for its appeal on the reliability of the word of God.

5, 6. The first four verbs are not mere synonyms but between them bring out different aspects of Israel's wrongheadedness: it is an offence against God and man (*ḥāṭṭā'*), perversion (*'āwôn*), rebellion (*māraḏ*), and involves guilt (*rāsa'*); it was rebellion (*māraḏ*) against God's known will, His *commandments*, the great principles of the law, and the *ordinances*, which are the application of those principles to particular circumstances. *My servants the prophets* is a phrase of Jeremiah (26 : 5; *cf.* 25 : 3, 4, the chapter in which the seventy-year servitude of Babylon is predicted) and taken up by other post-exilic writers (Ezr. 9 : 11; Zc. 1 : 6). They spoke

[1] On the question of the authenticity of the prayer, see Porteous, pp. 135ff.

to all strata of society (Je. 44:17, 21), for all were responsible people; and since they did not listen, all, including Daniel, bear their guilt.

7, 8. *To thee . . . to us. . . .* The contrast in the opening theme is sustained throughout the prayer. The Lord is *righteous*; He has right on His side in all His dealings with Israel (*cf.* verse 14); and their *confusion of face* is also right. They have been humiliated for the wrong they have done. 'They' includes not only the people of Judah but *all Israel* also, that is, the northern tribes who had been deported by the Assyrians.

9, 10. The prayer is so worded that the deadlock created by Israel's rebellion may be broken. Only if the Lord's *mercy and forgiveness* prevail can the relationship be restored between Him and His people, *because we have rebelled against him.* The thought is that Israel is in no position to mend the relationship and her only possible plea is the character of God. The lengths to which God would go to make reconciliation possible (Rom. 3:21–26) were not yet revealed.

11–14. Here the prayer enlarges on the conviction that the exiles had no grounds for complaint against their Lord. The consequences of disobedience had been made plain beforehand (at length, in, *e.g.*, Lv. 26:14–45 and Dt. 28:15–68) in the *law (tôrâ) of Moses*, meaning instruction in all its aspects. *As it is written* (13) implies that the experience of judgment had confirmed the authority of the Mosaic writings because their words had come to pass. The destruction of Jerusalem was in a category apart from the destruction of any other city, because in no other had the Lord deigned to dwell (verse 19; *cf.* Ps. 9:11), yet despite this there had been no decisive move on His people's part to seek His forgiveness. Such apathy was in itself blameworthy.

Numerous quotations in these verses from Deuteronomy and Jeremiah may be traced with the help of a reference Bible. The prayer in 1 Baruch 2 seems to have been modelled on this prayer.

15. *And now* marks Daniel's next theme, an appeal to the Lord to act in accordance with the deliverance He achieved for Israel from Egypt, which had gained Him renown (*cf.* Je. 32:20). The way is being prepared for the appeal to the Lord's reputation, in verses 16–19.

16. There is more than a side-glance at the nations, *all who* *are round about us,* because the captivity of Judah and the non-existence of the Jerusalem sanctuary were interpreted by the nations to mean that Judah's God was either powerless or a delusion. The fact that God's name has been dishonoured by the disciplinary measures His people have forced Him to take makes the appeal to Him to vindicate His righteousness a powerful plea.

17-19. Using phrases familiar from many parts of the Old Testament, Daniel asserts his expectation that his prayer will be heard, that God will cause both the city and Temple at Jerusalem to be rebuilt, and that He will do so now without further delay. *Thy sanctuary, thy name, thy city and thy people* are at stake; action will be *for thy own sake.* Total lack of self-interest and deep concern for God's name, kingdom and will characterize this prayer, which Montgomery calls 'a liturgical gem in form and expression'.[1] His comment, 'The saint prays as the Church prays', draws attention to the importance of public prayer in shaping private devotion, and the great prayers of the Bible, including this one, provide principles which we do well to incorporate in both public and private prayer today. Above all we need to recapture the assurance that God answers prayer.

c. Reassurance and further understanding (9:20-27)

20-23. The divine message is not given direct, but comes through a messenger described as *the man Gabriel, whom I had seen in the vision at the first* (8:16). Unity of authorship is thus implied with the previous chapter, which is itself similarly linked with chapter 7 (see 8:1). *The time of the evening sacrifice* was mid-afternoon. Mention of this does not prove that sacrifices were again being offered, but only that the regular times were remembered in exile (*cf.* 6:10; Ps. 141:2). There is strong emphasis here on the instantaneous answer to Daniel's prayer, while he was still offering it. Indeed *at the beginning* of his supplications *a word went forth*; this word (*dābār*) is a divine decree or oracle, entrusted to Daniel because he is *greatly beloved*. But it requires study. 'One of the most important contributions of the book Daniel is its new insistence on the link between faith and intelligence.'[2] *Wisdom* and *understanding* were a gift (22), but he was still told to

[1] *ICC,* p. 361.
[2] Lacocque, p. 141.

consider the word and understand the vision (23). In the light of what follows *vision* may seem a strange word to use, for in this context the Hebrew *mar'eh*, like *ḥāzôn* in verse 21, refers to what is heard rather than what is seen : it has acquired the general meaning 'revelation' (Ob. 1 : 1; Na. 1 : 1). If his prayer was heard, then the period of exile would come to an end and God's house and city would be rebuilt. The oracle, however, looks even further ahead.

24. If Daniel is truly concerned about the accomplishment of God's purposes, he must think in terms of *seventy weeks of years*. Seventy years had a symbolic significance (see note on 9 : 2) and so the new term may be expected to have an element of symbolism, to be taken into account in any attempt at interpretation. More important than Babylonian background for our understanding of the numbers is the legislation of Leviticus 25 : 8, with its calculation of seven weeks of years, forty-nine years; seventy weeks are therefore 490 years. 'Seven' occurs in the following chapter in connection with punishment for spurning God's commandments : 'I will chastise you again sevenfold for your sins' (Lv. 26 : 18; *cf.* verse 21). Exile is the punishment envisaged for persistent impenitence, and 'then the land shall enjoy its sabbaths' (verse 34; *cf.* 2 Ch. 36 : 21), to fulfil seventy years. At the end of this time six goals will have been accomplished, the explanation of which is of major importance for an understanding of the application of the oracle. These are the ends to which God is working; stages in achieving them are outlined in verses 25–27.

The six verbs divide into two sets of three; the first three are concerned with the problem which exercised Daniel in his prayer, namely the grounds on which God could forgive human sin, and the second three with the positive fulfilment of God's right purposes. *To finish the transgression* (*peša'*), a word which did not occur in verse 5 but which, combining as it does the idea of rebellion and self-assertion, stands for sin in general and in its many forms. If this is to be *finished*,[1] we are being told about the final triumph of God's kingdom and the end of human history. *To put an end to sin*. Again there is a query about the verb. The Hebrew text has 'to seal' (*cf.* RV, NEB mg.), the verb used later in the verse, and to which it is very similar. Most scholars take the reading in the margin of

---

[1] The weight of scholarly opinion favours this translation, but there is a similar verb, meaning 'restrain', noted in the margin of most EVV.

the Hebrew text and support the standard translations. *Sin* (*ḥāṭṭāʾ*) is the first of the list in verse 5 and is used as a general term for all wrong. If there is progression and not repetition in these parallel clauses, the last marks the climax : *to atone* (or 'make reconciliation') *for iniquity*. The verb is regularly used in the Old Testament for making atonement, especially by the blood sacrifices. If God is regarded as the subject, it is announcing that God has found a way of forgiving sin without being untrue to His own righteousness. This assurance was what the prayer had been feeling after; it was the great longing expressed in the Old Testament as a whole.

With sin done away, God promises *to bring in everlasting righteousness*. Daniel had perceived (verses 7, 14, 16) that righteousness was the attribute of God alone (*cf.* Je. 23 :6), and so it is a short step to justification by faith (Rom. 3 :25, 26), a truth grasped also by Zechariah (Zc. 3 :4). *To seal* (*ḥāṭam*) *both vision and prophet* : that is, to set seal to all that God has revealed by accomplishing all that has been promised by Jeremiah. To seal a document may involve closing it, but in law the meaning is rather to authenticate it with one's seal and signature. That is the meaning here. *To anoint a most holy place* (lit. 'a most holy'; the object is not specified; *cf.* RSV mg.). The ambiguity may best be explained by the context. In 539 BC concern was centred on the holy place in Jerusalem, and the rededication of the Temple was not excluded, but the Lord's anointed was ultimately to be a man (Mt. 12 :6, 'a greater thing than the temple is here', RV mg.) who was the subject of 'vision and prophet'.

If we may tentatively interpret the verse, it is speaking of the accomplishment of God's purpose for all history. If we look at this from our vantage-point it was accomplished partly in the coming of Christ, but it still has to be consummated (Eph. 1 :10; 1 Cor. 15 :28). If the historical work of Christ and His second coming are telescoped this is not unusual, even in the New Testament (*e.g.* in the discourse of Mt. 24).

25. In other chapters of the book the starting-point for revelation has been the historical setting indicated by the date or, in chapter 8, by the geographical details, which indicated a new capital city. On the face of it the same is true here. The starting-point of the interpretation is the command to rebuild the Temple, given by Cyrus in 539 BC (Ezr. 1 :1–4), unless a distinction is made between the Temple and the city, in which case the time of Nehemiah would be the starting-point (Ne. 2 : 5, 445 BC). No other alternative seems possible.[1] The assurance that rebuilding was about to be ordered (before the edict of Cyrus had been made) would have been most important to Daniel. *The coming of an anointed one, a prince* is open to more than one interpretation, because the terms are vaguer than the English reader might suspect. Though the Hebrew word for 'an anointed' is *māšiaḥ*, the term was applied to the Persian, Cyrus (Is. 45 : 1) and did not yet have the technical meaning of Messiah. 'The Lord's anointed' is used frequently in the Old Testament for the Davidic king, but priests were also anointed (Lv. 4 : 3, 5) and so Zechariah can call both prince and priest 'sons of oil', *i.e.* anointed ones (Zc. 4 : 14). The term for *prince* (*nāgîḏ*) means basically 'leader' and is not more specific; it is used in Daniel 11 : 22 where it could be either king or high priest. Accordingly no identification can be made at this point.

The time-gap between the command to rebuild and the coming 'anointed one' is literally 'seven sevens and sixty-two sevens' (so AV, RV mg.), the punctuation not being part of the original text; *it shall be built* will then begin a new sentence. In Leviticus 25 : 8–24 seven sabbaths of years had been specified in order to calculate the year of jubilee, during which every man was to return to his inherited land and liberty was proclaimed to prisoners. It is this that would come to a mind reared on the law of Moses, and told to understand 'seven sevens'. Though the command to build was given in 539, it was not until the time of Nehemiah that Jerusalem as a city was completed *with squares and moat*. As the second of the two words comes only here in the Old Testament, its meaning is not certain, but 'the word has now turned up in Hebrew with the meaning "conduit" in the Dead Sea Copper Scroll, a welcome confirmation of the accuracy of the Massoretic Text here'.[2]

26. The seven sevens had marked the answer to prayer

---

[1] *E.g.* 587 BC; so Porteous, p. 141 and F. F. Bruce, *Biblical Exegesis in the Qumran Texts* (Tyndale Press, 1960), p. 69. This date is arrived at by associating 9:2 with Je. 30:18; 31:38f., which is taken to be the 'word that went forth' just before 587 and the destruction of the city. The question is whether it was a command to rebuild. This word to restore and rebuild was clear in the decree of Cyrus, who was unwittingly fulfilling God's purpose (Is. 45:1).

[2] Porteous, p. 142.

concerning the city, but sixty-two more sevens were to take their course before the next significant event : *an anointed one shall be cut off*. The numbers are symbolic and not arithmetical; by the time sixty-nine sevens have passed, God's allotted seventy is almost complete, and *an anointed one* is evidently significant in accomplishing the purposes outlined in verse 24. He *shall be cut off* : this verb (*kārat*) is used of 'cutting a covenant', a ritual which involved the death of the sacrificial victim (Gn. 15 :10, 18); it was also frequently used of death generally. *And shall have nothing* : the exact meaning is far from clear : 'with no one to take his part', NEB; 'without trial', Porteous; 'unjustly', TEV. The last two translations depend on Theodotion's Greek version.

The people of the prince who is to come is a vague reference to enemies who are to destroy Jerusalem and the Temple for a second time, as happened in AD 70 under the Roman general Titus, but the mention of war *to the end* implies continuing conflict between a powerful enemy and God's cause till the end of the seventy weeks. Commentators who argue that Antiochus Epiphanes fulfilled this prophecy are at a loss to account for the fact that he destroyed neither the Temple nor the city of Jerusalem, though undoubtedly much damage was done (1 Macc. 1 :31, 38). *Desolations are decreed* takes up the prayer of verse 18. In the long term no promise can be made that Jerusalem will be spared suffering; rather the truth is that suffering is inevitable.

27. The last 'seven' sees the completion of God's purpose. If *he* refers to the last-named person, 'the prince who is to come', the subject is the enemy of God's cause. The unusual verb used in *make a strong covenant* (*gābar*) bears this out, for it has the implication of forcing an agreement by means of superior strength. By causing *sacrifice and offering to cease* he evidently was successful in his opposition to God's people (*cf*. Zc. 14 :2). *For half of the week* will mean for half the period intended by the 'seven'; God's people will not have to experience such intense suffering throughout the whole of the last period of time. *The wing of abominations* is an obscure phrase. Young points out that the 'pinnacle' of the Temple (Mt. 4 :5) is literally 'little wing' (Gk. *pterugion*)[1] and argues

---

[1] E. J. Young, *The Prophecy of Daniel*, p. 218. So also Montgomery (*ICC*, p. 387), who takes it to mean a wing of the building, perhaps a portico.

that 'wing' is the summit of the Temple. *Abominations*. The word is used frequently of idolatry and implies something filthy and loathsome of which people should be ashamed (Ho. 9 : 10; Na. 3 : 6). Whatever the exact meaning (NEB 'in the train of these abominations' is as near as possible), some coming leader is going to cause desolation, and the context suggests that this will be directed to God's people and God's cause. But as in the case of the cruel Assyrian invader (Is. 10 : 23), an end has been decreed for him, and will be *poured out*, as God's wrath had been on His people (verse 11).

Additional Note: Some interpretations of the seventy sevens

For the sake of clarity no attempt has been made in the commentary on 9 : 24–27 to draw attention to any of the multitude of other interpretations which have been given to the seventy sevens by commentators through the centuries.[1] It is important for the sake of perspective and as a corrective to over-confidence in any one theory to know how these verses have been interpreted by the church, and an attempt will be made briefly to survey representative views.

1. The historical interpretation

According to this view the second-century BC writer was convinced that the conflict which the Jewish people of his day were enduring was a prelude to the fulfilment of God's promises, *e.g.* in Isaiah 40–55. God was about to act, and would want His people to be encouraged to bear the suffering inflicted on them by knowing that it was for a limited time. One way of proclaiming this message was to make use of Jeremiah's prophecy of seventy years by multiplying it into seventy times seven, of which sixty-nine sevens had already run their course. The division into seven sevens is variously interpreted, but covers the Babylonian period, the 'anointed one, a prince' being reckoned as Cyrus by some and as Jeshua (Ezr. 3 : 2; Hg. 1 : 1; Zc. 3 : 1) by others. The sixty-two sevens

---

[1] An admirable summary is given by Montgomery (*ICC*, pp. 390–401).

cover the period to 171 BC, when the legitimate high priest Onias was murdered, and the last seven represents the short time before the end comes and God vindicates His own. The restoration of the Temple in 164 was the symbol of that victory.

It is taken for granted that the weeks, or sevens, are meant to represent years and that the numbers were intended literally. The fact that they do not work out exactly is due to the vague historical knowledge of the writer. The end, of course, did not come then, but the writer was not mistaken in teaching that God is present in every crisis with His people. The numbers are merely the 'clothing' of the writer's thoughts and are of no significance now.

This is the point of view of such writers as J. A. Montgomery, E. W. Heaton, N. W. Porteous and many others, including F. F. Bruce.[1] It has the great merit of starting where the writer was (as they think), and of relating the prophecy with known history. In this way it is earthed, and saved from the danger of fanciful theory, but it is also deprived of any right to be called a prophecy, because it is regarded as an account of the history after the event. Though written as if it referred to the future, it was 'known history cast in the form of prophecy, and it may very well be that the more instructed readers of the book were quite aware of this'.[2] According to this view, to regard the book as prophecy is naively to misunderstand it.

The author of 1 Maccabees, writing at the end of the second century BC, described the desecration of the altar of the Temple by Antiochus in 167 in terms of 'an abomination of desolation' (1 Macc. 1:54; cf. Dn. 9:27). The failure of the hope of immediate deliverance did not prevent the writer from seeing a fulfilment of Daniel's words in that event, but that does not mean that he necessarily dismissed the ultimate hope of victory which the book of Daniel proclaimed.

The historical interpretation is surely correct in seeing a primary fulfilment of Daniel's prophecy in the second century BC, but to confine its meaning to that period is to close one's eyes to the witness of Jesus and of the New Testament writers in general that it also had a future significance.

[1] F. F. Bruce, *Biblical Exegesis in the Qumran Texts,* pp. 67–74. He explains the mathematical disparity in terms of schematic numbers.
[2] Porteous, p. 144.

ADDITIONAL NOTE: THE SEVENTY SEVENS

2. Interpretation at Qumran

There is so far no commentary on Daniel from Qumran, but there is in the Damascus Rule 1:5–11[1] a use of numbers for a similar purpose :

'And in the age of wrath, three hundred and ninety years after He had given them into the hand of king Nebuchadnezzar of Babylon, He visited them, and He caused a plant root to spring up from Israel and Aaron to inherit His Land and to prosper on the good things of His earth. And they perceived their iniquity and recognized that they were guilty men, yet for twenty years they were like blind men groping for the way.

'And God observed their deeds, that they sought Him with a whole heart, and He raised for them a Teacher of righteousness. . . .'

The number 390 is evidently inspired by Ezekiel 4:4f., where it stands for the years during which Israel must bear her guilt. Neither F. F. Bruce nor A. Mertens[2] takes the number historically but rather schematically, and Bruce goes so far as to show how, by adding twenty years of waiting, forty for the life of the Teacher and forty that were to elapse after his death, the 390 years of Ezekiel may have been incorporated into Daniel's 490 years, so interpreting to their own time the promised end of evil-doers. If Bruce is right, the earliest interpreters of the text to whose work we have access saw the numbers schematically and not arithmetically. They were convinced of the canonical status of Daniel[3] and believed the seventy sevens applied to their own time and that the end was near.

3. Interpretation in the New Testament

In the Gospels Jesus makes reference to the seventy weeks only in terms of 'the abomination of desolation' (Mt. 24:15; Mk. 13:14, AV, RV; 'the desolating sacrilege', RSV), which is to be the sign of the coming destruction of Jerusalem, fulfilled in AD 70. For Him the significance of the phrase was not exhausted by its applicability to the outrages of Antiochus Epiphanes. The book of the Revelation takes up the symbolism of 'half

---

[1] G. Vermes, *The Dead Sea Scrolls in English* (Penguin, 1962), p. 97.
[2] F. F. Bruce, 'The Book of Daniel and the Qumran Community', in *Neotestamentica et Semitica*, p. 232; A. Mertens, *Das Buch Daniel im Lichte der Texte vom Toten Meer*, p. 85.
[3] F. F. Bruce, *op. cit.*, p. 235, footnote.

of the week', expressed in 11 : 2 as forty-two months, during which the holy city is trampled under foot, and in 13 : 5 the beast has authority for the same period. If this book was written, as most scholars claim it was, after the fall of Jerusalem, it makes a further application of our passage to an end-time yet to be. Thus the New Testament positively encourages the view that, while there are interim events which bear out the truth of the imagery, it points forward to a culmination at the end of history.

More generally the New Testament writers were convinced that the ministry of Jesus marked the beginning of the fulfilment of the coming kingdom announced in the book of Daniel (*cf.* Mk. 1 : 15) and of the end of the age (1 Cor. 10 : 11; Heb. 1 : 2; 9 : 26; 1 Pet. 1 : 5).

4. Jewish and early Christian interpretation

Josephus, writing his account of the destruction of Jerusalem, made allusion to a double application of Daniel 9 : 27. Having pointed out that Daniel wrote of the nation's sufferings under Antiochus Epiphanes, he went on : 'In the very same manner Daniel also wrote concerning the Roman government, and that our country should be made desolate by them.'[1] His interpretation of the fall of Jerusalem as the ending of the seventy sevens of Daniel became standard Jewish teaching, and passed into Christian exegesis.[2] Only at the end of the second century did Christian scholars begin to compute the seventy sevens so as to make them terminate in the coming of Christ. There were many variations in detail; three and a half sevens most commonly marked either the end of Jewish ritual or the death of Christ. The remaining three and a half sevens was often vaguely related to the period of the Antichrist. The influence of Jerome's translation of 'an anointed one, a prince' (9 : 25), 'ad Christum ducem', continues in the margin of JB, 'or Prince Messiah'. This Messianic interpretation is still popular and is represented by the commentaries of Pusey, C. H. H. Wright and E. J. Young. It is adopted in a modified form in this commentary.

[1] *Jewish Antiquities* x. 276.
[2] *ICC*, p. 397. Among further details Montgomery refers to Jerome's information that 'the Jews admitted a reference to Jesus Christ in the death of the Aointed One, but cleverly interpreted the $w^{e'}ên\ lô$ by "but the kingdom of the Jews will not be his" '.

5. Present-day interpretations

We have already outlined the 'historical interpretation', which is still widely held, and have indicated that it makes an important point, but the fact that Jesus took up and interpreted chapters 7 and 12 must be considered of prime importance. He not only adopted for Himself the title 'Son of man' (7 : 13), but He also assigned to those who stood with Him in His trials a share in the royal banquet, and thrones from which to judge the twelve tribes of Israel (Lk. 22 : 28–30). 'The "thrones" figure in Dan. vii.9, and the twelve as the nucleus of the new people of God, represent the "saints" to whom judgment is given' (Dn. 7 : 22).[1] With reference to the 'seventy years', Daniel 9 : 24 has been expounded in detail to refer to the first advent of our Lord,[2] all six items in that verse being shown to have been accomplished in His life, death and resurrection.

Some writers would go further and claim that the sixty-nine sevens of Daniel 9 : 25, 26 predict the exact time of the crucifixion.[3] The calculation is reckoned from the decree of Artaxerxes I (Ne. 2 : 1) in 445 BC, using 360 days to the year and adding extra days for leap years. Two difficulties arise : in view of the fact that other numbers, such as the number 70, have symbolic significance, to take one particular number and apply it literally is to take the best of both worlds, and calls in question one's methodology; the second difficulty is that Artaxerxes did not make any decree about the rebuilding of Jerusalem, whereas Cyrus did (Ezr. 1 : 2, 539 BC). On these grounds it is better to be consistent and to keep to a symbolic interpretation of all the numbers.

We noted that chapter 9 accounted for sixty-nine and a half weeks of the seventy, but that three and a half 'days' remained without explanation. If we accept that the work of Christ concluded the sixty-ninth week, what of the seventieth? Many would see a prophetic 'gap' here,[4] during which the age in which we live would be placed. Dispensationalists see this as the 'Church age', which forms a 'parenthesis' between the first coming of Christ and the revived Roman empire

---

[1] C. H. Dodd, *According to the Scriptures* (Fontana, 1967), p. 68.
[2] E. J. Young, *The Prophecy of Daniel,* pp. 195–201.
[3] Most recently Bruce K. Waltke, 'The Date of the Book of Daniel', *Bibliotheca Sacra,* 133, 1976, p. 329.
[4] *E.g.* J. C. Whitcomb, *NBD,* art. 'Daniel'.

whose prince will be the Antichrist. According to this view Daniel 9 :24 is a programme for the future, not a summary of what took place in the work of Christ. Since the rebuilding of the Temple and the restoration of Jewish worship is envisaged according to this view, the official establishment of the state of Israel in 1948 has been greeted as heralding the events of the final week.[1] Against that, Jesus looked for a replacement of the Temple centred on Himself. 'He transferred the activities of the temple from Jerusalem to another entity. This entity was Jesus himself and the group around him as Messiah . . . A new fellowship with God would be set up through his death and resurrection; in effect he himself would become the replacement for the temple.'[2] As the Epistle to the Hebrews so clearly demonstrates, Christ's death accomplished all that the old sacrifices had foreshadowed, and there can be no way of salvation apart from the way which He opened for Jew and Gentile. The growth of the kingdom in every part of the world is part and parcel of the purpose of God as seen in Daniel 2 :44 and in the teaching of Jesus, and therefore cannot be relegated to a 'parenthesis'.

How then is the last week of the seventy to be thought of in relation to the present time? From the point of view of the author's own perspective the first coming of Christ is the focal point of the forward look, though the second coming in judgment is also envisaged. To him the seventy years covered the whole of future time, and the coming of the kingdom looked from his vantage-point like one event. It is in the light of the New Testament that we have learnt to separate the first and second comings of Christ, and with the help of His teaching to realize that there is a recognizable pattern in history which His followers do well to note and expect to see worked out in the events of their own lifetime. The reinterpretation of Daniel's visions given by Jesus in Matthew 24 and 25 does not underestimate the suffering which can be expected by His followers; 'desolations are decreed' (Dn. 9 :26), though 'the end is not yet' (Mt. 24 :6–8). Even before the final intense

---

[1] For an assessment of the teaching of Jesus on this subject see R. T. France, 'Old Testament Prophecy and the Future of Israel', *Tyndale Bulletin,* 26, 1975, pp. 53–78.
[2] B. Gärtner, *The Temple and the Community in Qumran and the New Testament* (CUP, 1965), p. 114, quoted by R. T. France, *art. cit.,* p. 71.

opposition (Mt. 24 : 15) the believer can expect opposition such as the Master knew (Jn. 15 :20), and so can the church as a whole. Daniel's vision ended with the persecutor meeting his deserved judgment. Jesus took the message a stage further and focused hope on His coming in glory (Mt. 24 :30), described in terms already coined in Daniel 7 : 13. The fuller picture was yet to be given in the book of the Revelation.

V. VISION OF THE HEAVENLY MESSENGER AND HIS FINAL REVELATION (10:1 – 12:13)

The total overthrow of opposition had been pronounced by Gabriel in chapter 9, but that could hardly be the final message. Some more positive assurance for God's people was to be expected, and this is given in the longest and most detailed oracle in the book. Like the previous revelation, it is prefaced by self-discipline and fasting on Daniel's part, but the one who appears to him, though he is described as 'a man', is more radiant than Gabriel and greater than Michael, and has power to strengthen Daniel (11 : 1).

Far from being elated by the vision, Daniel is drained of all strength, deprived of speech and even of consciousness. Three times he needs the touch of his heavenly visitor before he is capable of receiving the revelation intended for him. Such a reaction is not confined to apocalyptic contexts (Dt. 5 :26; Acts 9 :8; 22 :11) and is a salutary reminder of the majesty of our God and of the amazing condescension of the incarnation.

Like chapter 8, to which it is parallel, chapter 11 presents only two empires, the Persian (verse 2) and the Greek, represented by its founder Alexander the Great (3, 4). Two subdivisions of his kingdom and the relationship between them are the subject of the next section (5–20), and then the villainous ruler takes the stage, gains sweeping victories, meets some opposition, vents his wrath in the holy temple and city and generally does as he pleases (21–39). Opinions differ as to the setting of the rest of the chapter, introduced by the words 'At the time of the end' (40); it all depends on whether the reference is to that particular tyrant or whether he comes to represent oppressors of all time, culminating in the final Antichrist.

The episode ends with a warning of unprecedented suffering, compensated by the promise of resurrection (12:1-4), and with a concluding exhortation to Daniel.

a. Vision of the heavenly messenger (10:1 – 11:1)

1. What appears to be an editorial note in the third person prefaces the narrative and gives the date. *The third year of Cyrus king of Persia* was 537 BC; the first group of exiles had returned to Jerusalem, but Daniel and many others remained behind. Mention of the name *Belteshazzar* is a reminder of the occasion, nearly seventy years before, when the name had been given to him by Nebuchadrezzar, and a reminder also perhaps of 1:21, where Cyrus was first mentioned; the author/ editor was presenting the book as a unity.

The truth of the *word* is emphasized, but *it was a great conflict*; this cryptic expression refers to the struggle involved in understanding it. It cost toil and suffering (*cf.* Is. 40:2, 'warfare'); 'the time appointed was long' (AV) arose from a rabbinic interpretation.[1] Such personal cost to the seer may be compared with the 'burden' of Zechariah 9:1; 12:1 (AV, RV). Whereas earlier Daniel expressly said he did not understand the vision (8:27), in the light of this revelation he comes to understand both the word spoken and the vision; but the vision in this chapter (verses 5, 6) hardly needs understanding in the same sense as previous ones. Evidently Daniel assumed that all the visions had a bearing on the same subject.

2, 3. The first month of the year (4), when Passover took place on the fourteenth day and the Feast of Unleavened Bread from the fifteenth to twenty-first, was traditionally a time for remembering the deliverance from Egypt and for feasting in preparation for an expected word from the Lord. Apparently the vegetable diet (1:12, 16) to which he restricted himself in the beginning had not applied to the whole of his time at court. *Nor did I anoint myself*, for that was a sign of rejoicing (Ps. 45:7).

4. *The twenty-fourth day of the . . . month* may have had some special significance after the exile (*cf.* Hg. 1:15; 2:10, 18; Zc. 1:7), but what it was we do not know. *The great river* is usually the Euphrates (*e.g.* Jos. 1:4); there seems to be no special significance in this mention of the Tigris. No doubt the

---

[1] *CB*, p. 152. Driver understands 'it was a great conflict' as applying to the coming time of severe hardship, but this is a less likely meaning.

absence of 'great rivers' in Palestine made the many rivers and canals of the Babylonian plains especially remarkable to the captives.

5. *I lifted up my eyes* . . . (*cf.* 8 :3); as we might say, 'I just looked up and there was . . . *a man*', literally 'a certain man'. The narrative lays stress throughout on the humanity of the messenger (verses 16, 18; 12 : 6, 7), despite his glory. *A man clothed in linen*; *cf.* the angelic figure of Ezekiel 9:2, *etc. Linen,* of which the priestly garments were made (Lv. 16 :4), was ordinarily bleached white and, though coloured threads and bands were sometimes incorporated, we are justified in assuming that these linen garments were white. The girdle of *gold of Uphaz* should probably be translated 'finest gold'. Uphaz is unknown as a place-name. NEB has Ophir (*cf.* RV mg.) with some MSS. The location of Ophir is uncertain, but the region of Somaliland extending to S. Arabia is most likely.

6. The translucent precious stone, the flash of lightning, the brilliance of flames and the gleam of polished metal all convey impressions of the one who appears to Daniel but who is beyond description. His words, confused like the murmuring of a crowd, required careful attention on Daniel's part if he was to tune in to their message. The description bears resemblances to Ezekiel 1 :26–28 and to Revelation 1 :12–16, both of which portray the glory of the Lord. Here no such identification is made, and most commentators speak of an angel, for he was sent as a messenger (verse 11).

7–9. The terrified departure of Daniel's companions left him without human help in an experience of severe weakness. 'I became a sorry figure of a man' (NEB) captures the sense of *my radiant appearance was fearfully changed.* To judge by the description, the trance experience was not one to envy.

10–12. The hand that touched Daniel mediated strength and enabled him to move out of his prostrate position, as did the word of command to stand upright. God's commands are His enablings, but to be named as the recipient of a special divine message was a costly privilege. The striking expression *man greatly beloved* (*cf.* 9 :23; 10 :19) means 'one in whom God takes delight'. Few are so described in Scripture : Abraham was called 'friend of God' (2 Ch. 20 :7; Is. 41 :8; Jas. 2 :23) but not, so far as we know, in his lifetime; Mary was greeted as having found favour with God (Lk. 1 :28, 30);

above all, the Lord's Servant was the one in whom He delighted (Is. 42 : 1; Mt. 3 : 17). For each of these people suffering was inescapable.

The efficacy of prayer is underlined (though not specifically mentioned, it is implied in verse 2), and in particular the prayer which takes seriously God's revelation and acknowledges, as Daniel's prayer had done (9 : 5–14), utter unworthiness before Him. *I have come because of your words* implies that this visitation would not have occurred apart from Daniel's specific prayer.

13, 14. Why had there been delay for three weeks if his prayer had been heard at the beginning? *The prince of the kingdom of Persia* was to blame. A representative of Persia in the heavenlies is intended; Greece also has an angelic counterpart (20), and Michael, *one of the chief princes*, belongs to Israel. Evidently the hierarchy in the heavenlies is not a replica of that on earth, where little Israel had no prestige and Persia was the great dominating power. If God's messenger was so delayed, the inference is that there is a measure of contingency in human history, even though the final outcome is certain. The imagery of warfare also implies this (*cf*. Eph. 6 : 12; Rev. 12 : 7), and yet any foretelling of the future would be impossible apart from a thoroughgoing belief in the sovereignty of God. *The latter days*, a phrase already used in 2 : 28, has been shown to mean 'in the future';[1] usually (Gn. 49 : 1; Nu. 24 : 14; Is. 2 : 2; Je. 23 : 20) it refers to the events of history as opposed to God's supernatural intervention at the end of time, but not, of course, to history after the event. When the end of an age is meant the writer uses the expression 'the time of the end' (8 : 17; 11 : 35, 40; 12 : 4, 9). In the Qumran texts 'the latter days' has an eschatological reference, probably due to the influence of LXX 'the end of days', and is used whether or not the context requires it.[2] Commentators who argue for a second-century date tend to think that there is eschatological significance in this verse. *The vision* is the revelation of chapter 11.

15–17. Despite the healing touch of verse 10, Daniel was again prostrate, and in addition *dumb* (*cf*. Ps. 39 : 9). He was literally deprived of the power of speech until he received a second supernatural touch, this time on his lips, and was given

[1] E. Lipinski, *VT*, XX, 1970, pp. 445–450. See also note on 2 : 28.
[2] Delcor, p. 213.

power of speech once again. *Pains*, usually the word used of travail in birth, but also metaphorically (Is. 21 :3), imply at least some 'new thing' as a result of the suffering.

18, 19. The seer was strengthened both by the third touch of the messenger and by the words he spoke : *he said, '. . . be strong . . .' I was strengthened*. At last he had the capacity to receive the vision.

20, 21. The heavenly warfare is to be directed against first Persia and then Greece, because each of these in turn will have power over God's people. Though apparently defenceless, they have on their side the divine Messenger, who is assisted by Michael. The conflict will be such as to cause doubt as to whether God's people can survive, and the vision is intended to give unshakeable assurance that, desperate as the situation will be, God is so fully in control as to be able to disclose the sequence of events before they happen. Indeed they are already inscribed in His *book of truth*, which, though figurative, aptly conveys God's control and knowledge of past, present and future (Ps. 139 :16; Mal. 3 :16), for they are officially entered in His records.

11:1. *The first year of Darius* was that in which orders were given to the captives to return to Jerusalem.[1] Though this had appeared to be the free decision of a polytheistic ruler, Michael had been strengthened, his people had been set free to return to their land, all because God's favour was once again towards them. Spiritual factors prove to be all-important in human history.

In the events which the messenger goes on to foretell, the glorious land, the Temple and the wise among the people are at the centre of the writer's concern. Two hundred years of Persian rule are passed over in a verse (2) because they are not relevant to his theme; the Greek empire, and the struggles between two eastern areas, have more attention (3–20), because armies were to march through Judea and put increasing pressure on God's people. All this, however, is merely leading into the main theme, the time of oppression which is to overthrow all that the loyal believer holds dear. Whereas the exile

---

[1] Montgomery's judgment that verse 1a should be treated as a gloss and omitted has been followed by subsequent commentators, but the date was not intended as a new chapter-heading. It is rather a glimpse back to a recent event in order to show the heavenly action behind it.

had been explained by the prophets and accepted in the end by the people as a judgment well deserved, this coming terror is not presented in those terms. It is rather the brutal attack of a megalomaniac against 'the holy covenant' (28). He will have such massive international support that opposition is ineffective and his armies will cause the death of many before he comes 'to his end' (45). That is the signal for unprecedented trouble, deliverance of the faithful and resurrection for judgment (12:1–4).

Though all this is presented as if it were future, the considered opinion of most scholars is that the writer was using an accepted literary form, which would have deceived no-one. The intention would be to show that the course of history was under God's direction, and so achieving His purposes. The standpoint of the writer is betrayed by the increasing detail of the account from verse 21 to verse 35, and also by the alleged error in his portrayal of the downfall of the tyrant (40–45). When the history becomes prophecy the transition can be detected, because events proved him wrong. Given that the ruler in question is Antiochus Epiphanes, and on this there is no disagreement, it is possible to arrive at the time when the chapter, and maybe the book, was written, namely between 165 and 164 BC.[1] No other part of the Old Testament, or even of the New Testament, has ever been dated so confidently. It has to be asked whether that confidence is soundly based.[2] Supposing for the moment that it is, we are then faced with a fairly sophisticated fictional element in the book.

Given that this dating is correct, the so-called revelation was in fact nothing of the sort. Even if the original readers were able to take in their stride the fiction regarding the events of chapter 11, it follows that the preparation for the vision in chapter 10 was also a fiction put in as local colour for the sake of effect. What it says about the efficacy of prayer or about heavenly warfare between representatives of the nations reflects only the subjective ideas of the writer. Admittedly spiritual truth may be conveyed in parable form, but there is no indication that we are dealing here with a parable. If the author proved to be wrong in his prediction of the way Antio-

---

[1] *E.g.* Porteous, p. 170, 'The critic . . . is grateful for this only in part fulfilled prophecy of Antiochus's death, inasmuch as it has made possible the accurate dating of the Book of Daniel.'

[2] *Cf.* the Introduction, above, pp. 35ff.

chus would meet his end, there was no reason to suppose he would be any more reliable in his understanding of spiritual issues.

The interpreter who would maintain a sixth/fifth-century date is not exempt from difficulties. If he accepts as axiomatic the fact of foretelling in the Bible as a whole and therefore in this book, nowhere else is prediction as specific and detailed as here. Even when it is centred round the coming king, references are spasmodic and elusive. The Gospels bear witness to the mistaken ideas entertained not only by Jesus' enemies but even by His friends and disciples. Why, then, should unprecedented attention be focused on an evil ruler such as Antiochus Epiphanes, so that his life-history is revealed in advance? What would be gained by such prediction?

It seems best to approach the chapter with this diversity of opinion in mind and to return to the point having studied its contents. Any reader who is not a student of ancient history finds the many allusions baffling. Even when the details have been spelt out, one has the lurking feeling that the commentator could have pulled the wool over one's eyes. For this reason it is good to have at hand a secular history of the period to give a perspective wider than that of the chapter in question. It is, for example, instructive to find that the relevant part of *The Cambridge Ancient History*, volume VIII, is entitled *Rome and the Mediterranean 218–133 BC*. Already before the end of the third century the shadow of Rome was falling over the eastern Mediterranean, and no supernatural prophet was needed in the middle of the second century to forecast the rise of a new world empire. It is therefore naïve to suggest that the writer thought the end of all things was imminent in the time of Antiochus Epiphanes. His brief was to give divine warning that suffering was not always in the nature of divine punishment, as the Exile had been. Rulers of the nations, in so far as they ignore God and are a law to themselves, become beasts who oppress others. At their hands the godly are to suffer, and the chapter shows how one such tyrant comes to behave as he does, building on the example of his predecessors and working their strategies through to their logical conclusion.

With regard to prophecy as foretelling, the church has lost its nerve. An earthbound, rationalistic humanism has so invaded Christian thinking as to tinge with faint ridicule all claims to see in the Bible anything more than the vaguest references to future events. Human thought, enthroned, has judged a chapter such as Daniel 11 to be history written after the event, whereas God enthroned, the one who was present at the beginning of time and will be present when time is no more, may surely claim with justification to 'announce from of old the things to come' (Is. 44 :7). An attempt will therefore be made to treat this chapter as a prophecy.

b. The Persian empire (11:2)

The standpoint of the writer, according to 10 :1, was the reign of Cyrus. The Persian empire had already overrun the world and the first exilic group had found its highway prepared across the desert to Zion (Ezr. 1 :1–4; *cf.* Is. 40 :3), though that event is not referred to in the vision, which is for a time to come.

Roughly two hundred years were to elapse before the end of Persian world-rule. Four kings after Cyrus were too few to span so long a period and historically there were nine, excluding the usurpers between Cambyses and Darius I. The fourth, *richer than all of them*, is usually taken to be Xerxes (486–465), who, like his father, engaged in wholesale war against *Greece*; but there is no 'against' in the text, and, as Montgomery points out, other Persian kings were wealthy enough to arouse envy. If we are dealing with history, the mention of only four kings is taken by most interpreters to indicate that the writer was weak on his history of the period, and mentioned only those Persian kings who are named in the Old Testament, that is, Cyrus, Darius, Xerxes (Ahasuerus) and Artaxerxes, but that does not make Xerxes the fourth. E. J. Young, who interprets the chapter as prophecy, suggests that four epochs are intended, but he does not elaborate. The difficulty in identifying the details in this verse supports the prophetic viewpoint, for prophecy usually highlights only certain significant features, and passes over much that the historian would feel obliged to include. The use of *three . . . and a fourth* is a familiar Hebraism (Pr. 30 :15, 18, 21, 29; Am. 1 :3, 6, *etc.*); may the same idiom not be employed here in Daniel? The author would be deliberately vague in that case about the number of Persian kings to be expected, but the point is made that Persian wealth will eventually invite attack from all, even the kingdom of Greece.

c. The Greek conqueror (11:3, 4)

Though the writer does not name the next king, or rather the founder of the next empire, Greece has already been referred to in the previous verse and was named as the successor to Persia in 8:21. Little is said of this *mighty king*, whom we know as Alexander the Great; he *shall rule with great dominion*, or, more likely because more closely in line with the idiom, 'he shall rule a great realm' (*cf.* NEB, 'He will rule a vast kingdom'), and *do according to his will*, a phrase which at one and the same time implies personal success and culpable self-centredness. Therefore, no sooner has he established his empire than it will be split into four (*cf.* 7:6; 8:8) and ruled, not by his sons, but by others. Instead of *the four winds of heaven*, English idiom uses the four points of the compass, two of which, north and south, feature in the subsequent account. Between the two lay the holy land. The style of rule exercised by the successors of the Greek conqueror would differ from his, necessarily, because in a divided empire one leader would vie with another.

d. South versus north (11:5-9)

At first it is *the king of the south* (*negeḇ*) who dominates the scene. Our interpretation of 'south' and 'north' must be governed by the setting of the chapter, and not go beyond the boundaries of the world empires of the time. Egypt was the southernmost limit of the Persian, Greek and Roman empires, and would be readily identified with the south (*cf.* verse 8). Unlike the Roman empire, the Persian and Greek extended eastwards to the borders of India, but northward there was little incentive to conquest. This was the direction from which dreaded invasions of uncivilized hordes had traditionally come (Je. 1:14; 4:6; 6:1, *etc.*); the Armenian and Caucasus mountains formed a natural barrier, and Syria was 'north' so far as the Asian empire was concerned.

5. Though the king of Egypt is at first in control, *one of his princes* (or 'generals', for *šar* can mean either) is to gain power. 'His' means Alexander's generals, and the verse indicates that Egypt's king will face a rival whose empire will outstrip his own. The comings and goings between Egypt and Syria would necessarily harass the holy land and threaten its security.

6. An arranged marriage, intended to gain political objectives for the Egyptian king, is to fail. His daughter is a pawn in the international contest and, according to RSV, *her child,* a potential heir to both kingdoms, would inherit nothing, but be *given up,* betrayed, together with his mother and her entourage. The passing of time is indicated by the introductory phrase *after some years.* So the translator has interpreted a difficult text, for the Hebrew consonantal text will bear two meanings, according to the vowel-pointing which the reader supplied : *cf.* RV 'his arm' instead of 'his offspring'. (RSV follows three of the ancient versions in their plausible reading.) Instead of 'he and his offspring shall not endure' we should then read 'he and his forces . . .', meaning her husband, and instead of 'her child', literally 'he that begat her', namely her Egyptian king and father. Either way the plan ends in a fiasco. Montgomery outlines 'the sequence which tallies best with history' in expounding the second part of the verse, thus admitting that the prophecy was not patently obvious in meaning.

7-9. *In those times* is a connecting-link inserted here by the RSV translators from the end of verse 6 (Heb.). The Egyptian queen is to be avenged by *a branch (nēṣēr) from her roots,* the idiom used in Isaiah 11:1; as the inheritor of his father's kingdom he is her close relative, born of the same stock. The general sense of the sequel is plain : an attack on the northern fortress-capital is successful and enables the Egyptian army to return home with great spoils. An unsuccessful attempt at a reprisal raid takes place after a long delay.

e. North versus south (11:10-20)

Initiative now passes into the northern kingdom. Emphasis is on the size of the northern armies which would sweep through the holy land on their way to Egypt.

10-12. *His fortress* is now that of the king of Egypt, who will retaliate with massive forces and apparently win the war. The phrase *overflow and pass through* is exactly that of Isaiah 8:8, where the prophet speaks of the advance of the Assyrian army. *His heart shall be exalted* prepares the reader for an expected downfall.

13. This reversal is to be secured by means of a superior army and supplies, 'when the years come round' (NEB).

14. For the first time reference is made to the reaction of Jews, in whose land much of this military activity must necessarily take place. Some among them will side with the invader against the Egyptians, under whose control they would have been living. They are *the men of violence* (lit. 'sons of violence', 'revolutionaries') with an ideology, *vision* (*ḥāzôn*); whether or not this vision is inspired by a prophet of the Lord, their method of achieving it certainly is not, and their efforts will fail.

15, 16. The offensive of the northern king is now decisive. What a few Jewish revolutionaries could not achieve will be accomplished because *there shall be no strength to stand*. The heavenly messenger speaks from the position of control at the source of all strength; behind the passive verb lies God's active will, putting down one and setting up another (Ps. 75:3–7). The southern king will undoubtedly think that his superior strategy and preparation has won him the victory, but that is only because in doing *according to his own will* he will be in line with the purposes of God at that point in his career. Judea, *the glorious land* (*cf.* verses 41, 45 and 8:9), favoured to be the place of the Lord's honour and beauty (Is. 4:2), has now been brought by the change of allegiance entirely into *his power*. Different vowel-pointing of the Hebrew gives a variant meaning, *cf.* 'he will have power to destroy it' (NIV). God does not plan a political Utopia, even for His people.

17. *He shall set his face,* with the determination of a mind made up (*cf.* Je. 42:15; 44:12), to consolidate his victory over Egypt. First, he will bring *terms of peace*. The reading is that of the Greek versions; Hebrew 'righteous ones' suggests 'fair terms' (NEB). Secondly, he will also use the stratagem of providing a wife for the Egyptian king, with a view to bringing Egypt under his control. The *daughter of women*, like 'son of man', suggests 'woman *par excellence*'; one of his own daughters would be intended. *It shall not stand* again draws attention to the ineffectiveness of human intrigue.

18, 19. Ambition carries the northern king in search of further conquests. *The coastlands* were traditionally those of the Mediterranean including the Greek islands of the Aegean Sea. In the course of extending his empire he will meet his match, a sure sign that another empire is to follow the Greek. *He* (the opposing commander) *shall turn his insolence back upon him,* that is, give him as good as he gave. His ignominious retreat and sudden disappearance from the scene underlines

the stupidity of setting store by human rulers. Suddenly they
are nowhere to be found.

20. His successor is to be faced with financial problems,
which he will try to meet by taxing the remains of the empire;
he shall send an exactor of tribute through is reminiscent of
Zechariah 9:8, 'no exactor shall pass through'. Is the Zechariah reference connected in some way with this verse in
Daniel? *Within a few days* implies a short reign. *He shall be
broken*, again the passive, indicating that a higher than he has
power over him; *nor in battle*, which was a glorious death.
'Not with his boots on' (Montgomery).

A review of the chapter to this point will conveniently mark
a dividing-point and provide a pause for reflection.

The writer has been overworking certain verbs throughout
this prediction of future events: they are 'arise', 'be strong',
'shall not stand'. The first and third are different translations
of the same Hebrew root, *'āmaḏ*, a common verb meaning
'stand up', 'confirm', used figuratively in this chapter to convey
the idea of ruling with authority and power. Yet, despite the
fact that rulers become strong, suddenly they stand no longer;
their kingdoms are broken, they retreat, they fall. This pattern
recurs in the remainder of the chapter and emphasizes the
fleeting glory achieved by conquest.

Another point to observe is the general nature of the
allusions. Given the 'world map' of the period and the memory
of Israel's traditional enemies, there was nothing mysterious
about a divided empire north and south, with rival kings and
their attempts to dominate. When it comes to demonstrating
how the course of history bore out (or suggested, according to
the point of view taken) the prophecy, while the main turning-
points are agreed, there are different opinions as to detail.
From the death of Alexander in 323 BC (verse 4) to the death
of the 'exactor of tribute' (verse 20), universally identified with
Seleucus IV in 175, a century and a half has passed. Within
that period there is jostling for power on the part of Alexander's generals which resulted in the establishment of Seleucus
in 312 over Syria and, by 250, of his successor over the whole
Greek empire except Palestine and Egypt, which remained in
the hands of the Ptolemy (5). It was at that time (250 BC) that
the ill-fated marriage-alliance between the two states occurred,
which, far from strengthening the bonds between them,

resulted in a bitter, protracted war which lasted from early in the reign of Ptolemy III (246–221) until the Battle of Panium in 198, when the Syrian king, Antiochus the Great, emerged as victor (verses 7–16).

History then repeats itself. Antiochus attempts to use marriage as a means of giving him power in Egypt, but, as in the scheming of Ptolemy, no such advantage was gained. This time the lady, Cleopatra the first, sided with her Egyptian husband against her father. Militarily he fared better until in 191 he was defeated at Thermopylae and in 190 at Magnesia by the Romans under the command of Lucius Cornelius Scipio. Thus his greatness, like that of Alexander whom he was emulating, was short-lived. His successor, Seleucus IV, was left with debts he could not pay, and was murdered as the result of a conspiracy headed by his prime minister, Heliodorus (2 Macc. 3).

These events tie up with the prophecy according to most commentators, but this still leaves open the question whether the chapter is prophecy or history. As Montgomery says, 'The writer gives the historian no new data until he reaches his own age, and even then his history is so veiled that all possible secular help is required for its interpretation.'[1] Such help is found in Polybius, the Greek historian of the second-century BC, whose history extends to 145/4 BC. Other secular historians are later, though they may embody older material; they include Appian, Livy, Josephus and Porphyry. The last-named has had a lasting influence on the interpretation of Daniel through the commentary of Jerome, whom he instructed. When a secular history of the period has to be written the other contemporary sources are the book of Daniel itself and 1 Maccabees. Other books of the Apocrypha and Pseudepigrapha are of doubtful date.[2] Curiously, then, our chapter stands as a primary source of the history of the period, though it is itself in need of interpretation. At one moment it is a worthy historical document, and at another (*e.g.* in its summary of the Persian period, verse 2) it is suspect.[3]

Differences of opinion as to the people and events referred

---

[1] *ICC,* p. 421.

[2] *The Cambridge Ancient History,* VIII, pp. 720ff. and especially p. 778.

[3] *E.g.* Porteous, p. 159: 'It may be suspected that the writer was dependent on unreliable traditions.'

to in the chapter may be cited. Regarding the fourth king of Persia (verse 2) we owe his identification with Xerxes to Jerome, but, as Montgomery points out, other kings who succeeded him were equally rich, and he quotes C. C. Torrey's view that the king intended is Darius Codomannus,[1] the last before Alexander conquered Persia. A similar difference concerns the interpretation of verse 15, where the defeat of Ptolemy may have been either at Gaza in 201 or in 198 at Panium, near the source of the Jordan (Josephus xii. 3, 3), or both. The writer is concerned with the final outcome. The last clause of verse 16 is also enigmatic, both because the ancient versions translate it with different senses and because the historical allusion is not known. In short, the course of events is veiled. The use of the passive voice, of abstract rather than concrete concepts, and the recurring emphasis on the downfall of human pride and ambitious conquests are in keeping with a supernatural survey of human politics, whether past or future. The one ruler to whom all that has gone before is paving the way is introduced in the next verse.

f. A contemptible person (11:21–45)

The ultimate in despicable rulers is a usurper who wields great power by means of bribery. His dedicated pursuit of personal ambition will bring him into conflict with one stronger than himself, and in the fury roused by his humiliation he will vent his indignation on God's people.

There is universal agreement that Antiochus Epiphanes (175–163) fulfilled the description given here, but we may well wonder why so much space should be given in Scripture to an obscure (to us) upstart of the second century BC. Why should he be the subject of a special revelation, and why should the Christian reader concern himself with him?

The exile of both northern and southern kingdoms had been the subject of prophetic warning; there was no excuse for accusing God of injustice when the great world empires proceeded to engulf first the northern and then the southern kingdom. The history of the period becomes sufficiently familiar for the Christian reader to follow the story as it affected God's people. The exile was God's doing, designed to punish, but with restoration in mind. Now that that restoration has taken place there is another learning situation to be

[1] *ICC*, p. 424.

faced in God's school of discipleship. World-rulers of Assyrian and Babylonian empires had not been paragons of virtue. They invaded the holy land and carried off God's people to the ends of the earth, and Nebuchadrezzar went so far as to destroy the Temple and sanctuary in Jerusalem. What distinguishes Antiochus is that he attempts to unify his kingdom by imposing a particular ideology. Nebuchadrezzar had attempted this on one occasion (chapter 3); a ruler was coming who would make religion his main tool in imposing his will, and so would precipitate a conflict between commitment to the one God, revealed to His people, and the worldly-wise, unscrupulous way of life advocated by diplomacy. In the unequal struggle God's faithful servants would go through intense suffering. The era of the persecution of 'the church' had begun.

Consequently the chapter speaks to generations of believers and is not confined in its scope to the second century BC. Rulers will commit themselves wholly to fulfil their ambitions, regardless of what is right. Antiochus is the prototype of many who will come after him, hence the interest shown here in his methods and progress.

21–24. Whatever else may be true of this usurper *to whom royal majesty has not been given,* his methods will achieve success, at least initially. People will rally round him, taken in by his inducements and plausible assurances : *flatteries* trans-lates a word meaning 'smooth methods', 'slippery ways' (Pss. 35 :6; 73 :18). *The prince of the covenant* should be indefinite, 'a prince' or 'a covenant prince', and could refer to a secular king with whom Antiochus is in alliance, or to a high priest appointed within the terms of God's covenant. In the light of history the latter is usually preferred; the high priest is taken to be Onias III, deposed in 175 and assassinated as the result of intrigues against him in 171 BC. The date marks the inter-ference of the secular state in things spiritual. A precedent had been set which Roman emperors would not be slow to follow and which has become a commonplace in twentieth-century politics. To remove from office and subject to persecution and death those who are legitimately set over God's people is to attack the originator of the covenant, God Himself.

This king, Antiochus IV, will make covenants without the slightest intention of inconveniencing himself to keep them, motivated by desire for his own aggrandizement. Though his collaborators were *a small people*, he would succeed in pene-trating the sources of wealth and use the *plunder, spoil, and goods* to lavish on those who would then support his cause. Plans to take further lucrative cities would be made, *but only for a time*. The living God whom he had defied would intervene.

25-28. In the meantime ambition will demand that the king of Egypt be defeated and his kingdom incorporated in the one great empire of the northern king. The opposition is intense, but the Egyptian king is to be betrayed by those *who eat his rich food* (*cf.* 1 :13, 15), *even* by them, for to accept hospitality, especially as the king's counsellors, as seems implied here, was to acknowledge an obligation of utmost allegiance. Moreover *the two kings* will *speak lies at the same table*. What may appear to be a cynical observation on round-table con-ferences is no more than a statement of fact; lies beget lies, *to no avail*. Only truth endures and *the end* of lies *is yet to be at the time appointed*. Though evil is rampant, the Lord has the timing of its defeat in His hand. *And he shall return to his land* indicates the virtual defeat of the northern king, even though he has *great substance*, for he will want the kingdom of Egypt. On the rebound he will set his heart *against the holy covenant*; animosity against the Jews will break out again, but by using this phraseology 'holy covenant' more than that is implied, for it took two to make a covenant and God's initia-tion of it made any opponent anti-God. Assyrians and Baby-lonians had invaded and taken captive God's people, but in so doing they had fulfilled God's purpose of judgment. In the new situation the enemy will be taking on God Himself. *He shall work* (the Heb. idiom has no object), but knowing the sort of character he was, the reader finds the silence ominous.

The vague references of the prediction are clearly applicable in general to the career of Antiochus IV as it is known from 1 Maccabees and Polybius. He seized the throne to which his nephew Demetrius was heir and was therefore one 'to whom royal majesty has not been given' (*cf.* 1 Ch. 29 :25). Having begun without any right to the throne he used his own con-siderable intelligence, personal magnetism and generosity to advance his cause, and was not slow to silence all opposition, even to deposing and executing the legitimate high priest Onias III, as we have seen. Historians differ as to the exact events referred to in verse 23 and verse 24 is equally difficult to apply exactly. What we are given is a swift character-study of an unscrupulous diplomat, raiding in one place and bargaining with the loot in another. The general meaning is clear but, as is characteristic of prophecy, the detail is not.

That the same applies to the next section (verses 25–28) is admitted by Porteous when he says, 'In vv. 24ff. our author makes his own important contribution to the tangled history of Antiochus's campaigns in Egypt and of his dealings with the Jews.' Yet the Bible account is cryptically brief, laying stress only upon the relative strength of the two armies in the war of 170–169 BC, and the effective use of intrigue which put the young Egyptian, Ptolemy VI Philometor, at a disadvantage. These are the details not known from other sources. Another account is in 1 Maccabees 1 : 16–19, where no mention is made of any negotiation between Antiochus and the Ptolemy, such as we have in verse 27. 1 Maccabees is independent of the Daniel passage, and is much more interested in the opposition to Antiochus than in his doings. It is hard to believe that after the events described in 1 Maccabees 1 : 20–28 the writer of Daniel would have been content to pass so briefly over them as he does in verse 28. Not only had the Temple been profaned and plundered, but believers had been massacred.

29, 30. Worse yet was to come. Antiochus's second campaign to Egypt two years later (1 Macc. 1 : 29) is well known from the account of Livy, who derives his information from Polybius.[1] For the Roman historian the event marked a turning-point in his country's history; the great Antiochus was reduced to size and from this point on had to bow to the superior might of Rome. In chapter 11 it also marks a turning-point. This time the contemptible person will not get away with anything, but will be humiliated by *ships of Kittim. Kittim* is an ancient name for Cyprus (Is. 23 : 1), later used generally for the islands and coastlands to the west of Palestine. Here the writer is referring back to the ancient prophecy of Balaam (Nu. 24 : 24), but the power intended is Rome.[2] The Roman fleet brought to Egypt the consul Gaius Popilius Laenas, who faced Antiochus with an ultimatum by drawing round him a circle and ordering him to respond before stepping out of it.

[1] Livy xlv.11ff.; Polybius xxix.1.
[2] Among the Dead Sea Scrolls 1Qp Hab. 2.12, 14; 3.4, 9 uses the term, and so does the War Scroll 1QM 1.2, 4ff. Opinions differ as to the nation intended in these passages. F. F. Bruce (*Biblical Exegesis in the Qumran Texts*, p. 71) takes the Kittim to be the Romans.

So much for the fulfilment. Humiliation arouses anger and will result in punitive action against a *holy covenant*, aided by *those who forsake* it. A wedge will be driven between the true and the false among the people of God, between those who remain loyal and those who opt for foreign ways.

31. The extremity of sacrilege is now about to be committed. The army of the northern king will profane *the temple and fortress*, one building, fortified now to resist invaders. They will do away with *the continual burnt offering*, for the fortifications will fail to keep out the enemy. *The continual hattāmîd* is the daily morning and evening sacrifice, which had been laid down as a requirement in Numbers 28 : 2–8. The intention was to impose by force worship of another god, described as *the abomination that makes desolate*, which is the literal translation of the Hebrew circumlocution used by the writer to express his disgust, and avoid all mention of the despicable name. Just as (Abed)nego defaced the name of the deity Nebo (1 : 7), so it has been suggested that we have here an international parody of the name *Baʿal-shᵉmaim*, 'lord of heaven', the common title of Baʿal among both Aramaeans and Canaanites. Philo of Byblos identifies Baʿal with Zeus Olympios of the Greeks.[1] The transliterated Hebrew, *šiqqûṣ mᵉšômēm*, may at first sight bear little resemblance to the suggested original, but Baʿal was commonly replaced by *šiqqûṣ* (*e.g.* 1 Ki. 11 : 5, 7), and *šômēm* (*cf.* on 9 : 27) has the same basic consonants as the word for 'heaven'. It means 'causing horror' because of the impending judgment expected.

The history of the event, as recorded in 1 Maccabees 1 : 54 taken together with verse 59, tells of an altar built on the altar of burnt-offering, not of any statue such as the Daniel reference would suggest.[2]

32, 33. Polarization between those who are seduced by flattery and those who *know their God* is the theme of the next verses. Persecution eliminates the waverers. Either they *violate the covenant* by their alliance with the prevailing

---

[1] W. D. McHardy, commenting on 'A Letter from Saqqarah' in *DOTT*, p. 253. The document belongs to the early period of Nebuchadrezzar's reign. See also *ICC*, p. 388.

[2] Driver (*CB*, p. 188) refers in a footnote to the Mishna (*Taanith* iv. 6), which in Danby's translation reads '. . . an idol was set up in the sanctuary'. According to Danby's note the reference is to the siege by the Romans; *cf.* the mention of 'the god of Olympus' by Eusebius and of 'Jove Olympius' by Jerome.

regime or they *stand firm and take action* (lit. 'do', as in verse 30). The resistance movement is made up of *people who are wise* (*maśkîlîm*); commentators have favoured the suggestion that a religious group known as the Wise is intended. In support reference is made to history (1 Macc. 2:42), for Ḥasidim or 'pious ones', ancestors of the Pharisees, played an important part in opposing the imposition of Greek ways, but the term can best be defined by its use in this book. The wise are the people who know their God (verse 32), who turn many to righteousness (12:3), who have understanding (12:10). It is the word 'skilful' in 1:4, and in 1:17 the God-given ability to apply learning. Though this gift is displayed as providing a solution in times of crisis, as the early chapters of the book illustrated, in this instance success is at the price of suffering. In Jeremiah's day those who professed to be wise belied the fact (Je. 8:8, 9); Isaiah drew a contrast between the counsel of the Lord and that of Judah's wise men (Is. 29:14) in words which served Paul well in his treatment of the same theme (1 Cor. 1:19). The wisdom which rallied men and women to give their lives in the cause of righteousness was more likely to be dubbed foolishness by all except those who were thoroughly committed to their God. When have these ever coincided with a sect or group or party? There is no barrier of race or sex or education to the wisdom of total commitment to God's cause, but in the event not many who are wise by human standards are included (1 Cor. 1:26).

Daniel and his friends had been delivered by unusual divine interventions from death, but the warning here is that this will not always be the case. *Sword and flame, captivity and plunder* sum up the sufferings of faithful men and women to this day.

34, 35. *A little help* is a disparaging way to refer to the support that men will attempt to give. As Porteous comments, 'the writer is more impressed by the action of the martyrs who proved their loyalty in the fires of persecution and contributed to the purifying of the community.'[1] This would be an extraordinary viewpoint for an author in the years 165/164 to take, when the struggle against the Greeks was going in the favour of the Maccabean resistance, and the Temple was about to be rededicated (December 165 or 164 BC) unless, perhaps, he

[1] Porteous, p. 168.

disapproved of the violent methods employed. The fervour of support which this movement aroused permeates the account in 1 Maccabees, especially 4 :36–61. The fact that some who rallied did so from insincere motives and that their resistance movement is superfluous to the divine plan is not mentioned by the historian. To the writer of Daniel, as he records the words of the heavenly messenger, the persecution has its purpose in God's plan to refine and He will bring it to an end at the time He has appointed. The Maccabean resistance movement did not come to any decisive end because it struggled on after political independence, and when this was for a brief spell achieved under John Hyrcanus and his successors, any advantage was frittered away by internal dissatisfactions and intrigue connected with problems of succession.

36. Attention returns to *the king*, whose character and deeds are the main subject of the chapter; here the constant stress is on his presumptuous claims to be god. Genesis 3 :5 shows this to be at the root of all human sin, and therefore not the monstrous claim only of certain rulers of this world. Nevertheless the ruler is in a better position than most to work out to the logical conclusion his egotistic pretensions. He has the power to *do according to his will* (*cf.* 8 :4 and 11 :3, referring to Alexander, and 11 :16, referring to Antiochus the Great); this is the key to the anti-God campaign described in the remainder of the sentence (verse 36). So thoroughgoing is his egotism that he has no option but to be an atheist. Before expanding on this key theme the writer makes sure the reader knows that apparent prosperity is permitted only until *the indignation is accomplished* or 'the time of wrath is completed' (NIV). God's *indignation* (*zā'am*), threatening destruction but delaying it until the last possible moment, is a familiar theme of the prophets (*e.g.* Is. 13 :5; 26 :20, 21; 30 :27; 66 :14; Je. 10 :10, *etc.* and *cf.* Dn. 8 :19). There is an echo of Isaiah 10 :23, 'a full end, as decreed', in the Hebrew of *what is determined*: God will be God whatever pretensions men may adopt.

37–39. Enlarging now on the king's atheism, the author remarks on his disregard of family traditions in worship, and of *the one beloved by women,* most probably Tammuz (Ezk. 8 :14), whose legendary death was mourned annually in Canaanite rituals. In Syria and Egypt a similar ritual was associated with Adonis and Osiris respectively. The motive appears to be that the king must be more popular than the most popular of gods, though illogically he too will honour *the god of fortresses.* The contradiction is intentional. This man 'turned god' will put all his wealth and energies into the war-machine, accept help of *a foreign god*[1] if it suits him, and bestow his favours in the form of subregencies over conquered lands.

Commentators vary their assessment of verses 36–39 as a history of the career of Antiochus Epiphanes. Whereas Montgomery says, 'This obscure passage throws novel side-lights upon Antiochus' religious history',[2] Porteous sees them as clearly applicable to him.[3] Certainly Antiochus was obsessed with his own importance, as his coins prove conclusively. Bearing early in his reign his own portrait and the inscription 'King Antiochus', they become increasingly pretentious, with the addition of such symbols as a star above the king's head, and the words 'God Manifest' (Epiphanes) attached to a portrait with the features of Apollo or, later, Zeus, crowned with laurels or with the sun's rays.[4] Polybius makes reference to popular reaction to his self-adopted title : 'Antiochus surnamed Epiphanes gained the name of Epimanes [madman] by his conduct' (Book 26). Evidence which does not fit in so well (though maybe verse 38 is relevant) is the information given by Livy (xli.20) that he made munificent gifts to cities and temples so that, at least among the Greeks, he gained a reputation for piety. He apparently honoured first Apollo and later Zeus. If the 'god of fortresses' was the name of a god, it is otherwise unknown. In short, while it is true that Antiochus IV fulfils in a general way the description given in these verses, there are discrepancies when it comes to detail regarding his religious practice.

There are also references to campaigns which are obscure, as Montgomery admits of verse 39a.[5] Consequently he adopts revocalization, which has the effect of changing the sense to 'And he shall make for defenders of fortresses a-people-of [reading *'am*, 'people', for *'im*, 'with'] a foreign god', and implying a reference to the heathen garrison, the Akra, set up

---

[1] According to O. Plöger, *Daniel (Kommentar zum Alten Testament,* 1965), this represents Antiochus himself.

[2] *ICC*, p. 460.

[3] Porteous, p. 169.

[4] Sample coins, illustrating the gradual assumption of deity, can be seen in *CB*, pp. 191f.

[5] *ICC*, p. 463: 'The allusions are totally obscure.'

by Antiochus to spy on the Temple and to provide military support (1 Macc. 1:33, 34).[1] The interpretation is adopted not because the text requires it but out of a desire to make the account in Daniel 11 approximate more exactly to the known history of Antiochus' reign.

At this point we do well to consider the time-honoured question whether in this chapter reference is being made only to Antiochus IV, or whether there is a secondary reference also to some later ruler or rulers of whom he is a prototype. Jerome thought that the chapter took a new turn at verse 21, and from that point on he saw what he took to be references to Anti-Christ. Hippolytus and Theodotion made verse 36 the turning-point, while Chrysostom applied the whole chapter to Anti-Christ.[2] Jerome's method has been most influential. Though he judged that from verse 21 the text was more than historical, he continued to give historical references and 'Western scholarship has been delivered from the vagaries of apocalyptic exegesis through the mediation of Jerome'.[3] This is indeed a providence for which to be thankful. The fact that Jerome was persuaded of the historical outworking of the general theme in the Greek period by the interpretation of the unbelieving Porphyry adds another to the many proofs of God's sovereignty adduced in the book of Daniel.

The very introduction of the term Anti-Christ to a text given before the Christ had even come raises the question of *a-priori* reasoning. It raises acutely the matter of exegetical method, and it is preferable to avoid a term which occurs first in the Epistles of John (1 Jn. 2:18, 22f.; 4:3; 2 Jn. 7). Nevertheless there are reasons for thinking that, although the chapter finds its first fulfilment in the character and reign of Antiochus IV, the matter does not stop there. Notice that (i) there are details which do not apply to Antiochus if our information about him from other sources is accurate. (ii) The

---

[1] The revocalization was first proposed by Jephet Ibn 'Ali, *Commentary on Daniel*, edited by D. S. Margoliouth, in *Anecdota Oxoniensia*, 1889. Though Driver is unenthusiastic (*CB*, p. 195), many commentators since that time have adopted the emendation, *e.g.* Charles, Heaton and Porteous.

[2] For more detail see the excellent summary by Montgomery in *ICC*, pp. 468–470.

[3] *Ibid.*, p. 469.

emphasis throughout is less on the king's deeds than on his character which prompts his deeds. (iii) The account keeps returning to the persecution which will be directed against the godly people and the covenant. (iv) Throughout the book the proud are manifestly brought low or suddenly cut out of the picture by death. God's sovereign way of bringing this about is a marked emphasis in the case of Nebuchadrezzar, Belshazzar, Alexander and his successors. (v) These rulers become progressively more anti-God as the book draws to its conclusion. (vi) The chapter takes up the point made in 8 : 17, where that vision was 'for the time of the end'. At the height of his vindictive cruelty Antiochus will be serving God's purpose to refine and cleanse His people 'for the time of the end' (*cf.* verse 40).

The book envisages, as we have shown above, the rise of the power that turned Antiochus out of Egypt, namely Rome (*cf.* the Kittim of Nu. 24 : 24, who carry out a reprisal on Asshur), and therefore it is not valid to claim, as many commentators do, that the author pictured the final end of the present order of things as coinciding with the close of Antiochus' reign.[1] A contemporary historian writes, 'From the day when Popillius Laenas drew with his stick the circle in the sand round the feet of Antiochus Epiphanes, there was no doubt who ruled the Mediterranean. . . . A Seleucid king, and that king Antiochus, stepped out of the circle to go home as he was told.'[2] If, as the majority of commentators claim, the chapter was written within three years or so of that event, Antiochus was already virtually finished, and our author would have been short-sighted if he did not make provision for the coming Roman empire. The comparison of chapters 2, 7 and 8[3] shows that there is ground for thinking that he did so. 'The end' in the Old Testament is 'not merely and only the historical last moment in a series of historical moments; it is also and primarily the *meaning* of the whole series of moments'.[4] Thus the end of which Amos preached (Am. 8 : 2) came in 722 BC; that of Ezekiel (Ezk. 7 : 2) in 587; that predicted of Belshazzar

---

[1] So Driver (*CB*, p. 193), with a reference to verse 40.
[2] T. R. Glover, in *Cambridge Ancient History,* vol. VIII, pp. 14, 15.
[3] See above, p. 161.
[4] G. A. F. Knight, *A Christian Theology of the Old Testament* (SCM Press, 1964), p. 285.

(Dn. 5 :26) in the very same night in 539. That the author of Daniel did indeed envisage the end of history as we know it is clear from the interpretation of the stone which filled the earth (2 :44), and from the vision of the coming kingdom in 7 :14ff.; he probably would have had a foreshortened view of the end times, but it does not follow that he expected it to follow immediately upon the reign of Antiochus. Antiochus' end will indeed come, but he is only the prototype; the fourth kingdom will be even worse. Whereas the leopard (Dn. 7 :6) had four heads, the terrible beast will have ten horns and great iron teeth and will devour the whole earth (7 :7, 23).

If this way of reading the chapter is followed through, it will be seen that the writer is never speaking only about one era of history, even though the prediction was to be applied to Antiochus as the first of many oppressors. There is within the chapter, as in the rest of the book, an insistence on the audacity of human pride, which is not confined to any one era. A man sets himself up as his own final authority, acts ruthlessly in pursuit of his own policies (the more so if he is frustrated, as was Antiochus), finds a scapegoat on whom to vent his bitterness, and sets in motion all the weapons of war, psychological as well as material, against the people of God. The cycle is familiar in history, including that of the twentieth century. What the book suggests and later prophecy confirms (*cf*. Mk. 13 :14ff. and the parallelism of the book of Revelation) is that the escalation of opposition will culminate in a final onslaught in which evil will appear to triumph, and only the intervention of God will prove the contrary. This will be the occasion of final judgment and the setting up of God's kingdom.

40–45. At this point most commentators are persuaded that the author ceases to write history and looks ahead to describe how the tyrant will meet his end. In evidence it is noted that there is no mention of events recorded in the history (1 Macc. 3; 4), which took place in the later part of 166 BC, and the events that *are* mentioned, such as the conquest of Egypt and the battle between the sea and the glorious holy mountain (45), never took place. Antiochus died, not in Palestine but in Syria, as Polybius bears witness.[1] Just so. If one takes the view that

---

[1] 31.9: 'In Syria King Antiochus, wishing to provide himself with money, decided to make an expedition against the sanctuary of Artemis in Elymais. On reaching the spot he was foiled in his hopes, as the barbarian tribes who dwelt in the neighbourhood would not permit

what we have here is history, then this account is mistaken; but if the book is allowed to provide the genre, and what we have here is prophecy, there is no problem. Biblical prophecy regularly exhibits this characteristic of telescoping the future, so that the more distant event appears to merge with the nearer so as to become indistinguishable from it. The best-known passage in which this telescoping features is the discourse of Jesus in Matthew 24 and Mark 13, where He speaks both of the fall of Jerusalem and of the end of this age. Only after the latter event had taken place did it become possible to distinguish which passages applied to the events of AD 70, and which were predictions of the more distant future. The common factors in judgment, whenever it takes place, and the similarity between the methods of one tyrant and another, account for the apparent homogeneity of the chapter. 'It seems . . . that neither an exclusively historical nor an exclusively eschatological interpretation is satisfactory, and that we must allow for a double reference, for a mingling of historical and eschatological.'[1] The historical is still future at the time of writing, but relates to a recognizable situation identifiable when the event takes place. Other parts of the discourse look to the second coming and the end of the age. So it is with Daniel 11:40–45.

40. *At the time of the end* is an expression which has already been introduced (verse 35; *cf.* 27), and applies to the end of the reign of Antiochus, though it carries the secondary idea of the end of all things, implied in 2:35 and 7:26, 27. The offensive is taken by the southern power, to which the northern king responds with overwhelming numbers of men and supporting military equipment. The allusive language is highly evocative : *like a whirlwind* (*cf.* Is. 21:1; Je. 4:13; Hab. 3:14; Zc. 9:14) bringing sudden destruction; *overflow and pass through* is an expression of Isaiah 8:8, already used in Daniel 11:10, and comparing the inescapable devastation caused by enemy armies to that of a flood.

41–43. *He shall come into the glorious land,* the land of the ancient promises, and therefore its invasion raises questions

---

the outrage, and on his retreat he died at Tabae in Persia, smitten with madness, as some say, owing to certain manifestations of divine displeasure when he was attempting this outrage on the above sanctuary' (Loeb Edition).

[1] C. E. B. Cranfield, *The Gospel according to St. Mark* (CUP, 1963), p. 402, with reference to Mark 13:14–20.

of principle, especially since *Edom and Moab and the main part of the Ammonites* are to escape (contrast Is. 11:14 and Mal. 1:2–5). In the second century BC, as in the sixth, they co-operated with the enemy and so were allied with the persecutor. *The main part* (*r'ēšît*, 'beginning', 'chief', 'first-fruits') implies the best of the nation of Ammon. The expression occurs in poetry for the flower of a people or nation (Gn. 49:3; Nu. 24:20; Pss. 78:51; 105:36), whose destiny is being determined, and may be a hint that in the context these nations stand for typical enemies of God's cause.[1] Temporarily they escape by throwing in their lot with the victorious leader, who takes possession of all the lands and their riches, including those of Egypt. Lybia to the west and Ethiopia (Cush) to the south of Egypt will be in his train.

44. At the height of his success this conqueror will suddenly be recalled, like Sennacherib before him (Is. 37:7f.), by bad news from the opposite side of his empire. Like a trapped animal he rages against all he meets, exterminating them.

45. The royal encampment is so situated as to threaten the mountain of Jerusalem. The word for *sea* is plural, as in the poetry of Deuteronomy 33:19 and Judges 5:17, but the meaning is the Mediterranean. *Palatial* translates a Persian word, *apadana*. The prediction is silent as to the battle, but its outcome is certain. The oppressor will find himself without allies and will meet his end. That is what the believer needs to keep in mind above all, come what may.

g. Death and resurrection (12:1–4)

1. The chapter division should not be allowed to obscure the continuity of the text with what has gone before. *At that time* applies to the interval between the beginning and the end of the conflict mentioned in the previous verse. The positive assurance of help has first place before the announcement of unparalleled trouble (*cf.* Mk. 13:19). Michael, already referred to in 10:13, 21, is now *the great prince who has charge of your people*; essentially a fighter (*cf.* Rev. 12:7), his charge is to protect God's suffering people. Though he is great, he does not prevent them from enduring the suffering; rather he delivers them in the midst of it (*cf.* chapters 3 and 6). *The book* in this context is the book of the living, as in Psalm

---

[1] So Lacocque, p. 172.

69 :28; that is, there will be survivors, despite heavy loss of life.

2. In the fighting both godly and ungodly will be killed and so *sleep in the dust of the earth* (Gn. 3 :19; Ps. 22 :29). The reason for using 'sleep' here as a metaphor for 'die' is that sleep is a temporary state from which we normally awake, and so the reader is prepared for the thought of resurrection. *Many of those who sleep* appears to imply a limited resurrection, and this is the view taken by those interpreters who think in terms of a setting in the Maccabean period. According to them it was essential that justice should be seen to be done, because in the general massacre good and bad alike perished. The resurrection is in that case 'a flash of inspired insight', as Porteous calls it, a way of making possible God's vindication of the martyrs and His judgment on the opposition. But the use of the word 'many' in Hebrew is not quite parallel with its use in English. Hebrew *rabbîm*, 'many', tends to mean 'all', as in Deuteronomy 7 :1; Isaiah 2 :2, where 'all nations' becomes 'many peoples' in the parallel verse 3; and in Isaiah 52 :14, 15; 53 :11, 12, where this key-word occurs no less than five times, with an inclusive significance.[1] As Jeremias points out, the Hebrew word *kol*, 'all', means either 'totality' or 'sum'; there is no word for 'all' as a plural. For this *rabbîm* does duty, and so comes to mean 'the great multitude', 'all'; *cf*. 'Multitudes who sleep in the dust of the earth . . .' (NIV). The emphasis is not upon many as opposed to all, but rather on the numbers involved.

In the light of this usage our author can be seen to be thinking of a general resurrection prior to judgment. Jesus almost certainly has this verse in mind in Matthew 25 :46 and John 5 :28, 29. As in chapters 2 and 7, the world as we know it has come to an end and an entirely new order has come, because the everlasting God has broken into time. He is the source of everlasting righteousness (9 :24) and of *everlasting life,* wording first coined[2] here in the Old Testament, though

[1] See J. Jeremias, *TDNT,* VI, pp. 536ff.; F. Graber, *DNTT,* I, pp. 95–97.

[2] M. Dahood, *Psalms,* I (*Anchor Bible,* 1965) argues on the basis of Ugaritic parallels that the Psalms are full of expressions of hope for immortality and resurrection (p. 106) and that these are very ancient indeed. He finds in Ps. 16:11 reference to life eternal, *hayyîm,* as in Daniel 12 :2, and in Ps. 17:15b he translates 'when I awake' as 'At the resurrection'. This verse he links with Is. 26:19 and Dn. 12:2, as

other writers express the conviction that the warmth of fellow-ship with the Lord that they enjoyed on earth could not be ended merely by death (Pss. 16:11; 17:15; 73:23, 24; Is. 26:19). Mention of the tree of life and the possibility of living for ever (Gn. 3:22) must have kept the thought before the Israelite believer from early times. The phrase *the dust of the earth* is reminiscent also of Genesis 3, and suggests that that chapter was in mind, but it was the beginning of rebellion and therefore of condemnation, from which few had found the way of deliverance. For all but those few remained *shame and everlasting contempt,* or 'abhorrence', a word used elsewhere only in Isaiah 66:24.

3. *Those who are wise* (*maśkilîm* : see note on 11:32, 33). There is no reason to restrict this term to leaders such as the heroes of the Maccabean wars. It is the root of the verb 'understand' in 9:25; the same verb in 9:13 is 'give attention to' the truth. The understanding is God-given (9:22) and intended to be passed on to others (11:33) to strengthen them in suffering. As the servant succeeds through obedience and suffering (Is. 52:13ff.), so will those of whom our author writes (11:35), and believers of every epoch are to exemplify the same characteristics, especially thoughtful attention to the word of God, for this wisdom is the wisdom of God.[1] Similarly their transfiguration bears marks of the one whom Ezekiel saw in his vision (Ezk. 8:2) : they *shall shine like the brightness* (shining) *of the firmament,* clear and transparent (*cf.* Ex. 24:10; Mt. 13:43).

Those who turn many to righteousness are also the 'wise'. Once again there is an echo of the Servant of the Lord who will 'make many to be accounted righteous' (Is. 53:11). How this is to be achieved is not spelt out, but there is only one source of righteousness (Dn. 9:7, 14) and one aspect of that righteousness is 'mercy and forgiveness' (9:9). The early

does D. Kidner, *Psalms 1–72* (*TOTC*, 1973), p. 90. See also Elmer B. Smick in *NPOT*, p. 115: 'A distorted concept of immortality ante-dates the Bible in written records of the Egyptians and Babylonians, and some notion of resurrection from the dead was a part of Sumerian mythology.' In the light of the evidence from ancient sources it would be strange if there were not similar longings, and even assurances of life eternal, expressed in the Old Testament. The relevant passages have for years been interpreted very cautiously, probably too cautiously, though it remains true that only after the resurrection of Jesus did eternal life become an established tenet of biblical faith.

[1] See Henri Blocher, *Songs of the Servant* (IVP, 1975), p. 78.

chapters of the book show how Daniel and his friends sought to introduce rulers to this righteous God, and how two responded (4 :34; 6 :26). Each expressed the conviction that he had met with the living God, who had been seen to be at work in specific situations, and to whom he was beginning to reach out in faith and fear. Those who lead others to righteousness, then, are those who demonstrate their faith and encourage others to faith, and this the humblest believer can do.

The idea behind the simile *like the stars* is that these faithful believers radiate light and thus help others to see (*cf.* Mt. 13 :43), not that they should be in any way spectacular.

4. *Shut up the words* implies keeping them safely until the time when they will be needed, much as a present is kept a treasured secret until the day for presentation arrives. *Seal the book* has the double sense of authenticating and of preserving intact (*cf.* Is. 8 :16; Je. 32 :11, 14). The Jeremiah reference is especially helpful, for it shows that the tablet on which the deed of purchase was written was enclosed in a sealed 'envelope' of clay, on which was summarized the contents. This summary was open and so could be tampered with; if it should be questioned, then the clay covering could be broken to verify the facts.[1] If we think in terms of a papyrus roll, then two copies were prepared, one open and the other sealed. A further implication of sealing a document is that it was kept from general knowledge, just as Isaiah kept his teaching within the confines of his own circle of disciples (Is. 8 :16). The reason why Daniel was to keep his last two visions sealed was that they were not yet relevant (8 :26; 12 :9), at least not in all their detail. According to those who date the book in Maccabean times, this is part of the fiction that it had been written in the sixth century, when in fact it was a contemporary second-century document. There is, however, the metaphorical meaning of the word, as it is used in Isaiah 29 :9–12, where the trouble is spiritual stupor : seeing they do not see. For this reason Jesus taught in parables (Mt. 13 :14, 15); much that was of value was hidden except to those who wanted it sufficiently to give all in exchange for it (Mt. 13 :44, 45). Ultimately the seals would be removed (Rev. 22 :10), but by then repentance would be impossible.

We are not intended to take this sealing of the book too

[1] *ANEP*, p. 75.

literally. There is no indication that any part of the prophecy of Isaiah was kept secret in the sense that no-one was permitted to read it, nor that the last four chapters of Daniel were treated differently from the rest of the book. God had revealed the purpose of history, but it was not placarded for all to see. Indeed men would look for it everywhere but in the word of God (Am. 8:12) and therefore would not find it, though *knowledge shall increase*. But those who look in the right place and go steadily on believing and enduring will understand, or perhaps better, 'many will go here and there to increase knowledge' (NIV; *cf.* Montgomery, *ICC*). LXX reads 'evil shall increase' and is followed in this by the Vulgate, hence JB: 'wickedness will go on increasing', but there is no reason to prefer these to the MT.

Thus ends the long revelation given by the heavenly messenger. A question session concludes the whole book.

h. Epilogue (12:5-13)

5. The river, which had been the setting at the beginning of the last great revelation (10:4), again sets the scene. Two other heavenly messengers appear, one on either side of the river, and one of them raises the first crucial question.

6. *I said* is the reading of LXX; 'he said' is the MT, translated 'one of them' (TEV, NIV), 'one said' (JB). The question is not as we might expect, 'When will all this happen?' (as in Mt. 24:3), but *How long shall it be till the end?* (*Cf.* 8:13 for both angelic dialogue and the question, 'How long?') The vivid reality of the revelation creates the impression that all is about to be implemented and the final curtain fall on human history. Though it might at first sight seem likely that Daniel would be the one to ask the question, little purpose is served by mentioning the two other heavenly messengers unless they play some part in the drama. *Wonders*, or 'astonishing things' (NIV), are the sufferings and deliverances in 11:31 – 12:3.

7. The majestic figure in the centre of the stage and poised above the river enters into the most solemn oath in pronouncing his answer. Whereas it was usual to lift one's hand (singular) in taking an oath (Gn. 14:22; Ex. 6:8; Ezk. 20:5), here the heavenly messenger raised both *his right hand and his left hand toward heaven*, 'as the more complete guarantee of the truth of what is about to be affirmed'.[1] *Him who lives*

[1] *CB*, p. 204.

for ever (*cf*. Dn. 4 : 34) is reminiscent of Deuteronomy 32 : 40, the one place where the Lord so speaks of Himself. He alone qualifies to be guarantor of the prediction about to be made. This took the form of a repetition of the mysterious *time, two times, and half a time* of 7 : 25, to which is added the statement that the end is bound up with *the shattering of the power of the holy people* (*cf*. 12 : 1). Now the historical Antiochus did not succeed in breaking their power, *i.e.* reducing them to helplessness (Driver). Not only were the efforts of the Maccabeans surprisingly successful, but he had already been shown the door by the Romans (*cf*. note on 11 : 30). The implication is that there are yet to be other Antiochus-like oppressors, that time will apparently roll on uneventfully as if belying the truth of the prophecy (*cf*. Ezk. 12 : 22), but that suddenly and surely, at the appropriate moment, divine intervention will interrupt history's course. The visible sign of that moment, of interest only to those enduring suffering, is the utter helplessness of believers in the face of their persecutors; thus, paradoxically, when they are enduring the greatest agony of unjust trial and torture they are to look expectantly for the promised intervention of God's deliverance (*cf*. Lk. 21 : 28).

8, 9. In his bewilderment Daniel formulates a slightly different question. He wants to know *what is to be the outcome* (JB, NIV); but the full significance of the revelation is hidden even from Daniel, *shut up and sealed* (*cf*. verse 4), though he has heard the very words from the mouth of the heavenly messenger. The text thus confirms that the word 'sealed' is meant to be taken metaphorically; he hears the word but it signifies nothing to him. Only after the event can a prophetic word be seen to have been fulfilled. It does not supply information from which a programme can be constructed, for that is not its purpose.

10. The purpose is clearly shown to be to keep in the faith those who will be severely tempted to give up in the face of opposition. The suffering is neither accidental nor meaningless, but serves the positive goal of purifying, cleansing and refining God's people (*cf*. 11 : 35). The reflexive, *shall purify themselves*, represents a form equally well translated by 'shall show themselves to be pure', that is, 'be purified' (NIV, TEV); similarly 'be made spotless and refined'. The refining process which improves the quality of gold and silver at the same time separates out the dross, that is *the wicked*. No longer are the two indistinguishable, but only by fire can the separation be made, and the metal's purity be assured. For the modern world the refining of steel provides a more telling symbol. If impurities remain in the metal the fracture of a girder under stress results in total collapse, and all because the refining fire has not been allowed to complete its work. The idea of dependability as the outcome of testing is often implicit in the metaphor, especially when the word of the Lord is in question (Pss. 12 :6; 18 :30; 119 :140; Pr. 30 :5). Here the thought is rather that suffering will prepare a people for the immediate presence of their Lord (*cf.* Mal. 3 :2, 3).

The wicked shall do wickedly, because they are unwittingly providing the test and are not themselves subject to it; so they go on in their usual routine, untroubled but unblessed, unaware that the last opportunity for repentance has sadly passed.

11, 12. The heavenly messenger now turns to the original question of verse 6, 'How long will it be until these amazing events come to an end?' (TEV). The answer is given in the number symbolism typical of the book, but it is an enigmatic answer, as the many different ways of understanding it prove.

On the one hand, many commentators have taken these numbers literally, in the belief that the original writer was thinking in terms of the period between the removal of the continual burnt-offering by Antiochus Epiphanes and either the rededication of the Temple or the death of Antiochus. S. R. Driver, for example, takes the end of the 1,290 days as synchronizing with the latter event, though 'the exact date of it is not known'.[1] H. Gunkel noted the mention of 1,150 days in 8 :14, and put forward the suggestion that the 1,290 and 1,335 days are successive corrections, made when the end did not come at the time originally expected.[2] He was followed by Montgomery, Bentzen, Delcor and Lacocque, but Porteous confesses to difficulty in seeing how urgent corrections could have been added to a book that had just been issued, even though in a limited number of copies.[3] The numbers did not fit, and it is difficult to make them fit any scheme.

Furthermore, the 'correction' theory breaks down when the context of 8 :14 is examined, for in that chapter the third

[1] *CB*, p. 205.
[2] H. Gunkel, *Schöpfung und Chaos,* p. 269; referred to by Montgomery (*ICC,* p. 477).
[3] Porteous, p. 172.

empire is in question, whereas in 7 :25 and 12 :7 we have argued that the period is the fourth empire. The verses are parallel but do not refer to the identical occasion. In 8 :11–14 Antiochus' attack on the Temple is indicated, but in 12 :7 the fulfilment of the book's prophecies as a whole is envisaged. True, verse 11 picks up the language of 8 :11–14 and the 'desolations' of 9 :2. The Temple was first left desolate in the 'seventy years' of exile; it was again to be made desolate for a short while when Antiochus profaned it; but these were no more than preliminary anticipations of the onslaught to be expected.

On the other hand, all attempts to find an exact application of the literal numbers break down. We turn next to the symbolic interpretation, keeping in mind that there have already been indications of symbolic numbers in the book, notably the seventy sevens of years in 9 :24–27. These were divided into $7 + 62 + \frac{1}{2}$, thus leaving the total short of seventy, and implying 'the end is not yet'. The addition of 1,290 days, or just over three and a half years,[1] would complete the seventy sevens of years, so bringing persecution to an end. Even so there is need to persevere a little longer, till 1,335 days, another month and a half, have passed.

Thus, as in the teaching of Jesus, the emphasis is on endurance to the end (Mk. 13 :13). A particular blessing awaits the one who goes on expectantly even after the time for the fulfilment of the prophecy is apparently passed, as in the parable of Jesus there is a special blessing for the servant who continues to be faithful even when his master does not come home at the stated time (Mt. 24 :45–51).

13. The last word is addressed to Daniel. He too must go on, though he is already an old man. *You shall rest* implies 'in the grave', as in Isaiah 57 :2, but he is reckoned among the 'wise' (12 :2) who will rise from the dead to enter into an allotted inheritance. He was not given to expect that the end of time would come before the end of his own lifetime, but he would experience resurrection life (*cf.* Mt. 28 :20), and in that hope he could be content.

[1] The Hebrew calendar was based on lunar months and no precise details are known of the method used to keep it in harmony with the solar year. It is presumed that an intercalary month would have been inserted, perhaps every three years, which could account for the apparent discrepancy between 1,290 days and $3\frac{1}{2}$ years.